How
MUNICIPAL
BONDS
WORK

Robert Zipf

NEW YORK INSTITUTE OF FINANCE
NEW YORK • TORONTO • SYDNEY • TOKYO • SINGAPORE

10 9 8 7 6 5 4 3 2 1

This publication is designed to provide accurate and authoritative information in regard
to the subject matter covered. It is sold with the understanding that the publisher is
not engaged in rendering legal, accounting, or other professional service. If legal advice
or other expert assistance is required, the services of a competent professional person
should be sought.

*—From a Declaration of Principles jointly adopted by a Committee of the
American Bar Association and a Committee of Publishers and Associations.*

Library of Congress Cataloging-in-Publication Data

Zipf, Robert.
    How municipal bonds work / Robert Zipf.
       p. cm.
    Includes index.
    ISBN 0-13-122656-8
    1. Municipal bonds—United States. I. Title.
HG4726.Z56 1995
332.63'233—dc20

94-36766
CIP

ISBN: 0-13-122656-8

NEW YORK INSTITUTE OF FINANCE
Englewood Cliffs, NJ 07632

Simon & Schuster, A Paramount Communications Company

Printed in the United States of America

Contents

Preface *xi*

Chapter **1**

Understanding the Bond Contract 1

Zero Coupon Bonds *2*
How to Learn the Terms of Your Bond Contract *3*
What the Indenture Contains *3*
How to Read a Bond *4*

    Bond 1—New York State *5*
    Bond 2—Allegheny County Industrial Development
        Authority *13*
    Security 3—California Housing Finance Agency *19*

Chapter **2**

How Bonds Can Differ in Physical Form 27

Bearer Bonds *28*
Registered Bonds *29*
Book Entry Bonds *31*

    Certificated Book Entry *31*
    Pure Book Entry *31*

Chapter **3**

Making Contractual Changes to the Bond's Cash Flow 33

How the Funds Flow Can Change *34*

The Call Feature *34*
The Put Option *34*
Variable-Rate Bonds *34*
Defeasance *34*
Default *35*

How to Use Call Features *35*

The Optional Redemption *35*
The Mandatory Sinking Fund *36*
The Extraordinary Call *38*

How a Bond Is Called *39*
How the Investor Should Manage Call Features *40*
How to Use Put Options *43*
How Variable-Rate Bonds Work *44*
How Defeasance Works *44*

Why an Issuer Will Defease Bonds *45*
How Call Features of Defeased Bonds Are Handled *45*
What Escrowed to Maturity (ETM) Means *46*

What Default Means *47*

Chapter **4**

How Recent Bond Market Changes Will Affect Your Investment *49*

Evaluating the Rise and Decline of Interest Rates *49*
What Increased Volatility Means to You *50*
Training More and Better Informed Investors *51*
Evaluating the Results of These Market Changes *52*

Resulting New Issue Volume Increase *55*

How the Market Has Responded to These Changes *55*

Contractual Responses to the Changes *55*
Put Bonds *56*
Variable Rate Bonds *56*
Bonds Having a Shorter Term to Maturity *57*

Behavioral Responses to the Changes *58*

Disintermediation *58*
Trading Increase *60*
Registered and Book Entry Forms *61*

Chapter **5**
*Other Municipal Security Contracts
and Related Features 63*

Notes *64*
Certificates of Participation *65*
Tax-Exempt Commercial Paper *66*
Variable-Rate Bonds *66*
Municipal Derivatives *68*

Floaters and Inverse Floaters *69*
How to Evaluate an Inverse Floater *71*

Detatched Call Options *72*
Interest Rate Swaps *72*

Tax-Exemption of Municipal Securities *73*
Understanding Original Issue Discount and Market Discount *75*
CUSIP (Committee for Uniform Securities Identification Procedure)
Numbers and Their Use *77*

Chapter **6**
*Understanding the Importance of United States
Treasury Obligations 79*

How Treasury Obligations Can Influence Trading Strategies *81*
Examining the Public Debt of the United States *82*
United States Treasury Bills *82*
United States Treasury Notes *86*
United States Treasury Bonds *88*
Treasury STRIPS *89*
Non-Marketable Treasury Securities *90*

United States Savings Bonds *90*
State and Local Government Series *91*
The Remaining Nonmarketable Debt *92*

Chapter 7

Applying the Mathematics of Finance to
Bond Investments 93

Compound Interest *94*

   The Equation for Compound Interest *97*

Calculating Present Values *98*

   The Equation for Present Value of a Future Payment *99*

Calculating an Annuity Certain *100*

   The Equation for the Annuity Certain *101*

How to Use Compound Interest and Annuity Tables *101*
How to Calculate a Municipal Bond Price *115*

   Examples of Bond Price Calculation *116*

How to Accrue (or Accrete) Discount *118*
How to Amortize a Premium *120*

   The Straight-Line Method *122*
   Tax Consequences *123*

Understanding the Municipal Securities Rulemaking Board Price
   Calculation Formula (Rule G-33) *123*
Some General Rules for Prices and Yields *125*
How to Understand a Bond Basis Book *126*
A Final Word *131*

Chapter 8

The Municipal Bond Marketplace 133

Who Issues Municipal Bonds? *133*

   Authorities and Other Governmental Agencies *135*
   Know Your Issuer *138*

Who Buys Municipal Bonds? *139*

   How Individuals Can Buy Municipal Bonds *139*
   How Banks Buy Municipal Bonds *141*

How Property and Casualty Insurance Companies Buy
   Municipal Bonds *141*

How Municipal Dealers, Dealer Banks, and Brokers Function *142*
Who Works in the Municipal Bond Industry? *143*

What Traders Do *143*
What Underwriters Do *144*
What Investment Bankers Do *144*
What Institutional Sales Representatives Do *145*
What Marketing Personnel Do *146*
What Municipal Research People Do *146*
How the Retail Broker Works in Municipal Bonds *146*
How a Municipal Bond Department Is Organized *147*

Regulating Municipal Bonds *149*
How Municipal Research Is Done *151*
Understanding Municipal Bond Ratings and Rating Agencies *152*

Why Ratings Are Important *156*

How Bond Municipal Investment Trusts and Mutual Funds Work *157*

Historical Background *158*
Municipal Investment Trusts (Unit Investment Trusts) *158*
Municipal Bond Mutual Funds *160*
Comparing Municipal Investment Trusts and Municipal Bond
   Mutual Funds *161*

How Municipal Bond Insurance Works *162*

The Bond Insurance Contract *162*
Understanding the Benefits of Municipal Bond Insurance *163*
   How Bond Insurers Provide Additional Security *163*
   How Bond Insurers Provide a Higher Rating *165*
   How Bond Insurance Provides Improved Bond Salability *165*

Understanding the Place of Bond Insurance in the Municipal
   Bond Market *166*
Regulating Bond Insurance Companies *166*
How Bonds Can Be Insured *167*
How Municipal Bond Reinsurance Works *168*

Who Insures Municipal Bonds? *168*
Insuring a New Bond Issue *169*

How Retail Investors Buy and Sell Municipal Bonds *170*
Understanding Bond Swapping *173*

Reasons for Swapping Bonds *173*
Change in Market Levels *173*
Change in Investor Requirements *174*
Change in Bond Characteristics *175*
Portfolio Improvement *177*

Finding Information in the Municipal Marketplace *178*

Organizations Providing Municipal Information Services *178*

Hedging and Speculating Using Municipal Bonds *182*
Short Selling of Municipal Bonds *184*
How Municipal Bond Industry Trends Will Affect You *186*

How Issuers Have Changed *186*
How Bond Buyers Have Changed *188*
How Municipal Regulation Has Changed *188*
How These Changes Affect You, the Municipal Investor *189*
What Individual Investors Can Do *191*

Chapter **9**

Understanding the New Issue Process
for Municipal Bonds 193

Why the New-Issue Process Is Important *193*
How an Issuer Comes to Market *194*

The Role of the Financial Advisor *196*
Comparing Competitive and Negotiated Bids *198*

Understanding Competitive Bids and Sales *198*
Understanding a Negotiated New-Issue Underwriting *201*
Understanding New-Issue Bidding Scales *202*
Computing Net Interest Cost *205*
Understanding True Interest Cost *206*
Reporting Competitive Sales *208*

Reporting Negotiated Deals *211*
Understanding New-Issue Spreads *213*
Understanding Bidding Restrictions *215*
How the Alternative Minimum Tax Can Affect Investors *217*
How Bank-Qualified Bonds Work *217*
Selling New Issues and Priority Business *218*

   Group Business *218*
   Designated Sales *218*

Swapping *219*
The New Issue Selling Process *219*
How a Lead Manager Meets His or Her Responsibilities *221*
Regulating the New Issue Process *222*

   How Underwritings Are Assessed by the MSRB (Rule A-13) *222*
   Regulating Sales of New Issue Municipal Securities During the
      Underwriting Period (Rule G-11) *223*
   Official Statements, or Disclosure in Connection with New
      Issues (Rule G-32) *223*
   How Calculations Are Done (Rule G-33) *224*

How Legal Work on New Issues Is Done *224*
Understanding Closing and Settlement of New Issues *226*
Understanding When-Issued and Final Confirmations *227*

Glossary *231*

Index *255*

Preface

In 1993, over 250 billion dollars of new issue municipal bonds were sold by over ten thousand different issuers. These bonds financed an enormous number of different projects, ranging from the New York City water supply system to the purchase of fire trucks and construction of school buildings, roads, and public office buildings.

These bonds also met the needs of millions of investors—mostly individual investors—who wanted a high-quality fixed-income investment that sheltered them from federal income taxes, and in many cases from state and local income taxes as well.

If you are one of those investors, or are considering becoming one of them by buying even one municipal bond or one share in a municipal bond mutual fund or investment trust, this book is for you. It provides in handy, readable form information you will need to manage intelligently in the municipal bond market. You will learn what questions to ask, the sources of municipal bond information, and which documents you should insist upon receiving. You will gain a general idea of how the municipal bond market works.

New entrants into the municipal bond business or related activities should also find this book useful. Indeed, the book is based on a successful series of seminars I presented at the brokerage firm of Merrill Lynch in New York to computer people who were very competent at computers but wanted to learn more about municipal bonds. This book provides such new entrants with a quick introduction to the municipal bond business.

Throughout the book I have paid special attention to the needs of the individual investor to show the importance of particular topics and how they relate to his or her municipal security investments. I hope that the investor will find this information of special value in managing his or her municipal investments.

CHAPTER 1

Understanding the Bond Contract

Suppose you lend money to a friend or co-worker, perhaps five dollars to buy lunch. You would probably be satisfied with his statement, "I'll pay it back to you on payday." If he forgets to repay you, you might also forget about it yourself.

But suppose you were asked to lend a much larger amount, this time $10,000 or more. You would probably insist on a written contract, with security and other guarantees of payment. More than likely, you would insist on receiving interest to compensate you for the use of your money. And you probably wouldn't forget about it.

This chapter discusses a special case of this kind of arrangement, called the *bond contract*. In the chapter, we show three examples of bonds; you should study these examples.

Figure 1.1 shows the first of these examples, a bond issued by the State of New York. A bond contract is an agreement between a borrower of money, the *issuer,* and a lender of money, the *buyer.* A bond is a loan. In this example, the State of New York has borrowed $5,000, and the owner of the bond has lent $5,000 to the State of New York.

A bond is not ownership in a business, a piece of property, or anything else, although some bonds (corporate bonds) may be converted into these; these are called *convertible bonds.* For example, if you buy the bond issued by New York State, you have lent money to New York State and expect to get your money back with interest; you do not own a share in the State Capitol Building in Albany.

The buyer of the bond has lent money to the issuer. In exchange, he expects to receive back both the money he lent, called *principal,* and additional payment for the use of the money, called *interest.*

Usually, the interest is paid periodically during the time the bond is outstanding, the *life of the bond,* with a final payment due on the day the principal is returned, the *maturity date.* These payments are called *coupon payments,* or coupons. Municipal bond interest is almost always paid semiannually.

Zero Coupon Bonds

Sometimes no interest is paid until the maturity date, when all the interest is paid at once. These bonds are called *zero coupon bonds,* because no interest is paid during the life of the bond and no coupons exist. The most common zero coupon bond is a United States Savings Bond, which pays no interest until it matures or is redeemed before maturity by the owner.

Some bonds pay no interest for a period of time, then pay interest after that time until final maturity. For example, a bond issued on March 1, 1994, might pay no interest until March 1, 2004, at which time it starts to pay interest at 6 percent per year. The first payment on a $10,000 par amount would be $300.00, paid on September 1, 2004.

HOW TO LEARN THE TERMS OF YOUR BOND CONTRACT

The bond certificate contains a summary of the terms of the contract. Many bond issues also have a separate document called an *indenture,* which contains the complete agreement between the issuer and the bondholders. The bondholders do not receive a copy of the indenture, although they have the right to examine it. The indenture will name an agent to act on behalf of the bondholders; this agent is called the *trustee.* For example, Chemical Bank was trustee for some of the Washington Public Power Supply System (WPPSS) bonds. When WPPSS defaulted on these issues in 1983, Chemical Bank brought suit against WPPSS on behalf of the bondholders in an effort to recover some of the money for the bondholders.

Many recently issued bonds don't have certificates. In this case, you should get a copy of the official statement, which is distributed at the time the bonds were first issued. The official statement contains the terms of the contract.

WHAT THE INDENTURE CONTAINS

The indenture might require the borrower to make other payments as well as interest and principal, and the trustee would have the responsibility for making sure that the borrower makes the required payments.

The borrower might be required to make payments into a sinking fund. A sinking fund is a series of payments set up to repay all or part of the issue before the final maturity. The issuer might be required to make payments into other special funds. In a related example, most home mortgages require the homeowner to make payments into an escrow fund for real estate taxes. The real estate taxes are paid out of this escrow fund by the firm servicing the mortgage, rather than directly by the homeowner.

Let's say that the borrower is a local bridge authority (LBA) borrowing to build and operate a bridge. Good bridge maintenance might require that the bridge be painted every two years. If the cost of painting the bridge was $240,000, the LBA might be required to pay $10,000 into a special bridge painting fund account each month. After 24 months, the amount needed for painting the bridge would be on deposit in the bridge painting fund and the bridge could be painted. The trustee named in the indenture would be required to make sure that the LBA actually made the payments, and to take appropriate action if the LBA did not do so. This action might range from a simple letter reminding LBA of its obligation to make the payments to a lawsuit forcing LBA to make the required payments. The indenture would also define the events of default. If the LBA failed to make a payment into the bridge painting fund, this might be an act of default under the terms of the indenture.

The borrower also promises to do certain things to maintain the value of the bonds. Many towns, villages, and cities obtain some or all of their revenues from taxes on real estate located in the town, village, or city. They issue bonds which are based on taxes levied on real estate. The borrower promises to levy sufficient taxes to pay the bonds. In this case, the applicable phrase is "unlimited *ad valorem* taxes," taxes on the value of the property, without limit as to rate or amount.

Some bonds are secured by earnings from a governmental enterprise. These are called *revenue bonds*, because they depend on the revenues from these governmental enterprises for their interest and principal payments. For example, the Port Authority of New York and New Jersey promises to levy sufficient tolls and fees at the New York City airports, the George Washington Bridge, and their other facilities to ensure that the bonds issued by the Port Authority will be paid. This arrangement also requires that the borrower take responsibility for maintaining the property which earns those revenues.

HOW TO READ A BOND

We show three different municipal securities. Two of them, the Allegheny County Industrial Development Authority bond, shown in Figure 1.2, and the California Housing Finance Agency note, shown in Figure 1.3, are specimens of real securities. They are printed certificates, but have not been actually signed. They are additional copies of the genuine securities. One of these is a bond and the other is a note. The third security, shown in Figure 1.1, is a genuine bond issued by New York State. The reader might wish to refer to these pictures as needed during the next few chapters.

Some of the terms used are defined more fully later on in the book. Don't let that stop you from looking at the securities now.

Bond 1 - New York State (Figure 1.1)

Issuer (borrower): State of New York (not the United States of America)

Face amount, or par value: The face amount of this bond is $5,000. The State of New York promises to pay this amount to the bondholder when the bond matures on June 1, 2000.

Maturity date: June 1, 2000. The face amount of the bond ($5,000) will be repaid on this date.

Interest rate: 3.40 percent per year. This is $170 per year on the par amount of $5,000. It is paid semiannually, with payments of $85 on June 1 and December 1 of each year until maturity. The last interest payment is June 1, 2000. This interest rate was agreed to when the bond was issued in 1962.

Dated date: June 1, 1962. Interest started to accrue on this date.

Payable to: The bond is payable to the bearer. This is a bearer, or coupon, bond. The person with the bond in his or her possession is presumed to be the owner or the owner's agent.

Next coupon: The next coupon due is payable on December 1, 1994. The interest payment of $85 is six months interest on $5,000 par (principal) amount at 3.40 percent per year ($5,000 × .034 × 1/2 = $85.00). The owner of the bond should cut off (clip) this coupon just before December 1, 1994, and present it for payment, either to the Chase Manhattan Bank or his own bank for collection.

Paying agent: The paying agent for this bond is the Chase Manhattan Bank. The owner of the bond should present this coupon

Figure 1.1

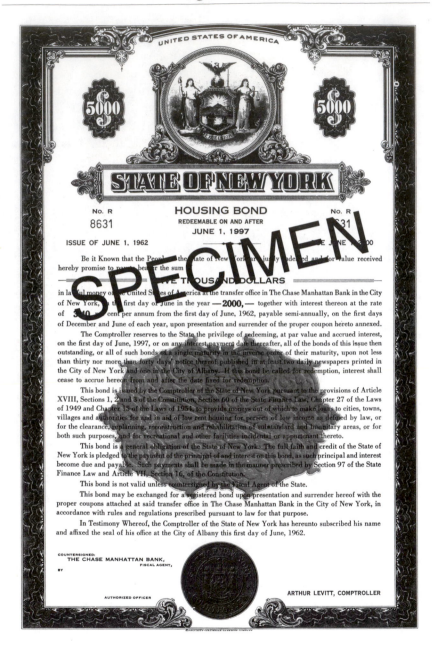

6

Figure 1.1 (continued)

Be it Known that the People of the State of New York are justly indebted and for value received hereby promise to pay to bearer the sum of

FIVE THOUSAND DOLLARS

in lawful money of the United States of America at the transfer office in The Chase Manhattan Bank in the City of New York, on the first day of June in the year —**2000,**— together with interest thereon at the rate of **3.40** per cent per annum from the first day of June, 1962, payable semi-annually, on the first days of December and June of each year, upon presentation and surrender of the proper coupon hereto annexed.

The Comptroller reserves to the State the privilege of redeeming, at par value and accrued interest, on the first day of June, 1997, or on any interest payment date thereafter, all of the bonds of this issue then outstanding, or all of such bonds of a single maturity in the inverse order of their maturity, upon not less than thirty nor more than forty days' notice thereof published in at least two daily newspapers printed in the City of New York and one in the City of Albany. If this bond be called for redemption, interest shall cease to accrue hereon from and after the date fixed for redemption.

This bond is issued by the Comptroller of the State of New York pursuant to the provisions of Article XVIII, Sections 1, 2 and 3 of the Constitution, Section 60 of the State Finance Law, Chapter 27 of the Laws of 1949 and Chapter 15 of the Laws of 1954, to provide moneys out of which to make loans to cities, towns, villages and authorities for and in aid of low rent housing for persons of low income as defined by law, or for the clearance, replanning, reconstruction and rehabilitation of substandard and insanitary areas, or for both such purposes, and for recreational and other facilities incidental or appurtenant thereto.

This bond is a general obligation of the State of New York. The full faith and credit of the State of New York is pledged to the payment of the principal of and interest on this bond, as such principal and interest become due and payable. Such payments shall be made in the manner prescribed by Section 97 of the State Finance Law and Article VII, Section 16, of the Constitution.

This bond is not valid unless countersigned by the Fiscal Agent of the State.

This bond may be exchanged for a registered bond upon presentation and surrender hereof with the proper coupons attached at said transfer office in The Chase Manhattan Bank in the City of New York, in accordance with rules and regulations prescribed pursuant to law for that purpose.

In Testimony Whereof, the Comptroller of the State of New York has hereunto subscribed his name and affixed the seal of his office at the City of Albany this first day of June, 1962.

Figure 1.1 (continued)

Figure 1.1 (continued)

Figure 1.1 (continued)

(SEAL of the)
(STATE)
(of)
(NEW YORK)

State of New York
Department of Law
Albany

Louis J. Lefkowitz
Attorney General
Paxton Blair
Solicitor General

June 12, 1962

Hon. Arthur Levitt
State Comptroller
Department of Audit and Control
State Office Building
Albany, New York

Dear Sir:

You have requested my opinion regarding the validity of $57,330,000.00 Housing Bonds of the State of New York, which were sold by you on May 23, 1962.

These bonds are being issued pursuant to Article XVIII, Sections 1, 2 and 3 of the Constitution, Section 60 of the State Finance Law, Chapter 27 of the Laws of 1949 and Chapter 15 of the Laws of 1954. The bonds will be dated June 1, 1962 and will mature at $1,170,000.00 annually on June 1 in each of the years 1964-2012 both inclusive. Interest being payable semiannually on December 1 and June 1 upon the respective maturities at the following rates of interest:

MATURITIES	RATE OF INTEREST
1964-1983 (both inclusive)	4.00
1984-1988 (both inclusive)	3.50
1989-1992 (both inclusive)	3.25
1993-1999 (both inclusive)	3.30
2000-2007 (both inclusive)	3.40
2008-2012 (both inclusive)	2.00

Provision is also made for the redemption of outstanding bonds on June 1, 1997 or on any interest payment date thereafter.

Figure 1.1 (continued)

Hon. Arthur Levitt   2.

Any or all of such bonds will be issued in coupon form in the denomination of $5,000.00 or in registered form in the denominations of $1,000.00, $5,000.00, $10,000.00 and $50,000.00 and multiples of $50,000.00 at the option of the purchaser.

I have examined the Constitution and Statutes of the State of New York as well as the transcript of the proceedings and the form of the bonds and it is my opinion that upon the execution and delivery of said bonds and the receipt of the purchase price or balance thereof from the successful bidder said bonds will constitute valid and legally binding obligations of the State of New York to which its full faith and credit will be pledged.

I am of the further opinion that interest on such bonds is exempt under existing statutes and court decisions from federal income taxes and by statute from New York State income tax.

The transcript of proceedings is returned herewith.

                              Very truly yours,

                              LOUIS J. LEFKOWITZ
                              Attorney General

                              BY: /s/ Paxton Blair

                              PAXTON BLAIR
                              Solicitor General

A TRUE COPY OF A PHOTO OFF–SET REPRODUCTION OF THE ORIGINAL OPINION

to the Chase Manhattan Bank for payment of interest. The bank will issue him a check for the interest. The Chase Manhattan Bank will also redeem the bond upon maturity or when the bond is called, if it is called. If the owner presents the bond coupons to his own bank, his own bank will send it to the Chase Manhattan Bank for payment.

Trustee: This bond has no trustee. It is a general obligation bond of the State of New York.

Call feature: New York State may redeem this bond ahead of time on June 1, 1997, or any interest payment date thereafter until maturity, at 100 percent of par value. This act is called *calling the bond*. The bond may not be called on any date except an interest payment date. If the entire outstanding bond issue is not called, the bonds must be called in inverse order of maturity; that is, the bonds with the longest maturity date will be redeemed first. A call notice must be published in two daily newspapers published in New York City and one published in Albany. The legal opinion, which is also displayed and is printed separately for this bond, states the coupon rates on all the bonds of this issue. If the bonds are called in inverse order of maturity, the bonds with a 2.00 percent coupon will be called before the bonds with a 3.40 percent coupon because they mature later. This coupon arrangement is called a high-low arrangement by municipal bond underwriters.

Legal opinion: This legal opinion is issued by the Attorney General of the State of New York, at that time Louis J. Lefkowitz. The legal opinion states that the bonds have been legally issued and constitute full and valid binding obligations on the State of New York and that they are exempt from federal income taxes, in the opinion of Mr. Lefkowitz, and that they are by statute exempt from New York State income tax. This legal opinion is on a separate paper; at that time, legal opinions were not printed on the bond as they are now. Municipal bonds cannot be sold without a legal opinion; see a later chapter for a fuller discussion of the legal opinion.

This is a general obligation bond. The full faith and credit of the State of New York guarantees payment of interest and principal of this bond. In other words, New York State promises to levy enough taxes to pay the principal and interest on the bond.

This bond has a certificate serial number printed on it, because it is a genuine bond. The other two bonds shown are sample bonds or specimens, and therefore do not have serial numbers printed on them. They are, however, specimens of real securities.

Bond 2 - Allegheny County Industrial Development Authority (Figure 1.2)

Issuer (borrower): Allegheny County Industrial Development Authority (McDonald's Corporation Warrendale, Pennsylvania Project). The issuer is not the United States of America, nor the Commonwealth of Pennsylvania, nor Allegheny County, nor McDonald's Corporation, although McDonald's Corporation is responsible for payment. This is called an *industrial revenue bond.* The issuer, Allegheny County Industrial Development Authority, is an agency of the Commonwealth of Pennsylvania, and acts as a conduit to borrow funds and make them available to firms for industrial development purposes. Each such firm (in this case, McDonald's Corporation) is responsible for its payments, usually under either a lease arrangement or an installment purchase agreement. The actual issuer (Allegheny County Industrial Development Authority, in this case) only acts as a conduit, and will not make any of its own funds available in case the business which leases or purchases the facilities (McDonald's Corporation) defaults. In this case, the funds to pay the bonds come from McDonald's Corporation, to pay for purchase, on the installment plan, of some property (perhaps some hamburger stands) in Allegheny County. This property was bought or built with the proceeds of the sale of the bonds.

Face amount: The face amount of this bond is $5,000.

Maturity date: December 15, 1991. On this date, the issuer will repay $5,000, the principal (par) amount of the bond.

Interest rate: 11.75 percent per year. This rate was agreed to at the time of issue. It looks high now (early 1994), but in 1981 it was a quite reasonable rate for industrial revenue bonds.

Dated date: December 15, 1981. Interest started to accrue on this date.

Figure 1.2

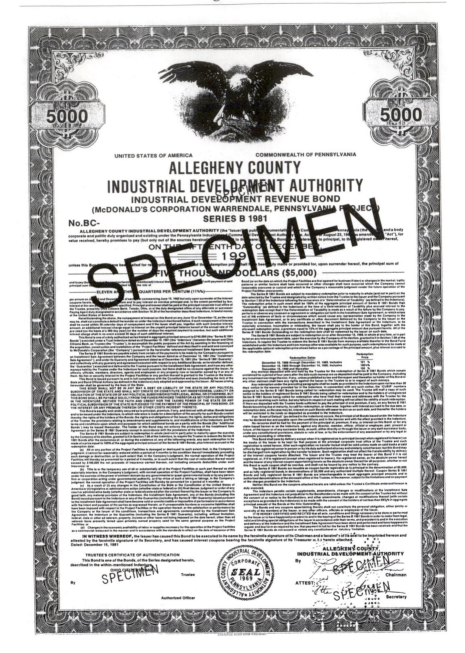

14

Figure 1.2 (continued)

—————————ELEVEN AND THREE-QUARTERS PER CENTUM (11¾%)—————————

per annum on June 15 and December 15 of each year commencing June 15, 1982 but only upon surrender of the interest coupons hereto attached as they mature and to pay interest on overdue principal and, to the extent permitted by law, interest at the rate per annum above specified. Principal and interest shall be paid at the principal corporate trust office of the Trustee, presently Ohio Citizens Bank, Toledo, Ohio, or at the duly designated office of any alternate or successor Paying Agent duly designated in accordance with Section 10.20 of the hereinafter described Indenture, in lawful money of the United States of America.

Notwithstanding the above, the nonpayment of interest on this Bond on any June 15 or December 15, as the case may be, shall not constitute a default hereunder or under the Indenture mentioned below, if such nonpayment of interest shall be cured within 30 calendar days of nonpayment and if the Issuer shall pay, together with such overdue interest amount, an additional interest charge equal to interest on the unpaid principal balance hereof at the annual rate of 1% pro rated (on the basis of a 360 day year) for the number of days the required payment is overdue, but such additional interest charge shall in no event exceed 30 days of such additional interest.

This Bond is one of a duly authorized series limited in aggregate principal amount to $740,000 (the "Series B 1981 Bonds") executed under a Trust Indenture dated as of December 15, 1981 (the "Indenture") between the Issuer and Ohio Citizens Bank, as Trustee (the "Trustee"), to accomplish the public purposes of the Act by assisting in the financing of the acquisition, construction and installation of the "Project Facilities" defined and described in and sold and conveyed to McDonald's Corporation (the "Company") pursuant to the hereinafter referenced Installment Sale Agreement.

The Series B 1981 Bonds are payable solely from certain of the payments to be made by the Company pursuant to an Installment Sale Agreement between the Company and the Issuer dated as of December 15, 1981 (the "Installment Sale Agreement"), and under its Guaranty and Agreement dated as of December 15, 1981 (the "Series B 1981 Guaranty", and collectively with any guaranty and agreement executed with respect to any Additional Bonds, as hereinafter defined, the "Guaranties") executed and delivered to the Trustee pursuant to the Installment Sale Agreement, and from any other moneys held by the Trustee under the Indenture for such purpose, but there shall be no recourse against the Issuer, its officers, officials, members, directors, agents and employees or any property now or hereafter owned by it or any of them. No lien or security interest in the Project Facilities or any portion thereof is granted to the Trustee or the Issuer.

This Bond is issued pursuant to and in full compliance with the Constitution and laws (including the Act) of the State and Bond Official Actions (as defined in the Indenture) duly adopted and approved by the Issuer. All issues arising hereunder shall be governed by the laws of the State.

THIS BOND SHALL NOT BE IN ANY WAY A DEBT OR LIABILITY OF THE STATE OR ANY POLITICAL SUBDIVISION OF THE STATE AND SHALL NOT CREATE OR CONSTITUTE ANY INDEBTEDNESS, LIABILITY OR OBLIGATION OF THE STATE OR OF ANY POLITICAL SUBDIVISION EITHER LEGAL, MORAL OR OTHERWISE. BUT THIS BOND SHALL BE PAYABLE SOLELY FROM THE FUNDS PROVIDED THEREFOR AS SET FORTH HEREIN AND IN THE INDENTURE. NEITHER THE FAITH AND CREDIT NOR THE TAXING POWER OF THE STATE OR ANY POLITICAL SUBDIVISION OF THE STATE IS PLEDGED TO THE PAYMENT OF THE PRINCIPAL OF THIS BOND, OR THE INTEREST OR ANY PREMIUM THEREON OR OTHER COSTS INCIDENT THERETO.

This Bond is equally and ratably secured as to principal, premium, if any, and interest with all other Bonds issued and to be issued under the Indenture, to which reference is made for a description of the security for such Bonds created thereby; the rights of the holders of the Bonds; the rights and obligations of the Issuer; the rights, duties and obligations of the Trustee; the provisions relating to amendments and supplements to, and modifications of the Indenture; and the terms and conditions upon which and purposes for which additional bonds on a parity with the Bonds (the "Additional Bonds") may be issued thereunder. The holder of this Bond may not enforce the provisions of the Installment Sale Agreement or the Series B 1981 Guaranty except in accordance with the provisions of the Indenture.

The Series B 1981 Bonds are subject to redemption in whole (and not in part) prior to maturity upon the exercise by the Company of its election, granted to it in Section 7.06 of the Indenture, to require the Trustee to redeem the Series B 1981 Bonds after the occurrence of, or during the existence of, any of the following events, any such redemption to be made at a price equal to 100% of the aggregate principal amount of the Series B 1981 Bonds, plus interest accrued to the redemption date:

(a)   All or any portion of the Project Facilities is damaged or destroyed to such extent that, in the Company's judgment, it cannot be reasonably restored within a period of 4 months to the condition thereof immediately preceding such damage or destruction, or to such extent that, in the Company's judgment, the normal operation of the Project Facilities will thereby be prevented for a period of 4 months, or to such extent that the cost of restoration thereof would exceed by $100,000 the net proceeds of insurance carried thereon, not including amounts deductible under such insurance; or

(b)   Title to or the temporary use of all or substantially all of the Project Facilities or such part thereof as shall materially interfere, in the Company's judgment, with normal operation of the Project Facilities, shall have been taken under the exercise of the power of eminent domain by any governmental or quasi-governmental body or by any person, firm or corporation acting under governmental authority, or if by virtue of such a taking or takings, in the Company's judgment, the normal operation of the Project Facilities will thereby be prevented for a period of 4 months; or

(c)   As a result of (i) any changes in the Constitution of the State or the Constitution of the United States of America or (ii) legislative or administrative action (whether state or federal) or (iii) final decree, judgment or order of any court or administrative body (whether state or federal) entered after the contest thereof by the Issuer or the Company in good faith, any material provision of the Indenture, the Installment Sale Agreement, any of the Bonds (including this Bond) issued pursuant to the Indenture or any of the Guaranties (including the Series B 1981 Guaranty) issued pursuant to the Installment Sale Agreement shall have become void or unenforceable or impossible of performance in accordance with the intent and purpose of the parties as expressed therein, or if unreasonable burdens or excessive liabilities shall have been imposed with respect to the Project Facilities or the operation thereof, or the satisfaction or performance by the Company or the Issuer of the conditions, transactions and agreements contemplated by the Installment Sale Agreement, the Indenture or the Guaranties (including the Series B 1981 Guaranty), including, without limitation, federal, state or other ad valorem, property, income or other taxes not being imposed on the date hereof, other than ad valorem taxes presently levied upon privately owned property used for the same general purpose as the Project Facilities; or

(d)   Changes in the economic availability of labor or supplies necessary for the operation of the Project Facilities as a commercial restaurant in the manner and in accordance with the standards in effect on the date of issuance of this

15

Figure 1.2 (continued)

Bond (or on the date on which the Project Facilities are first opened for business if later) or changes in the market, traffic patterns or similar factors shall have occurred or other changes shall have occurred which the Company cannot reasonably overcome or control and which in the Company's reasonable judgment render the future operation of the Project Facilities uneconomic.

The Series B 1981 Bonds are subject to mandatory redemption prior to maturity in whole (and not in part) on the date selected by the Trustee and designated by written notice from the Trustee to the Issuer and the Company pursuant to Section 7.05 of the Indenture following the occurrence of a "Determination of Taxability" (as defined in the Indenture). The redemption price in such event shall be 100% of the aggregate principal amount of Series B 1981 Bonds then "Outstanding" (as defined in the Indenture) at the time of a Determination of Taxability plus accrued interest to the redemption date except that if the Determination of Taxability is made as a result of the failure by the Company to pay, perform or observe any covenant or agreement or obligation set forth in the Installment Sale Agreement, or which arises out of the existence of facts or circumstances which would cause any representation made by the Company in the Installment Sale Agreement, or in any certificate or other document delivered by the Company to the Issuer or the Trustee in connection with the transactions described in the Installment Sale Agreement or the Indenture, to be materially erroneous, incomplete or misleading, the Issuer shall pay to the holder of this Bond, together with the aforesaid redemption price, a premium equal to 12% of the aggregate principal amount due pursuant hereto. All of the Series B 1981 Bonds Outstanding on the redemption date shall be redeemed by the Issuer on such date.

The Series B 1981 Bonds are subject to redemption on or after December 15, 1988, in whole at any time, or in part by lot on any interest payment date, upon the exercise by the Company of its election, granted to it in Section 7.06 of the Indenture, to require the Trustee to redeem the Series B 1981 Bonds from moneys available therefor in the Bond Fund established under the Indenture and from moneys otherwise available for such purpose, such redemptions to be made at the applicable optional redemption price shown below as a percentage of the principal amount, plus interest accrued to the redemption date:

Redemption Dates	Redemption Price
December 15, 1988 through December 14, 1989, inclusive	101 %
December 15, 1989 through December 14, 1990, inclusive	100½%
December 15, 1990 and thereafter	100 %

Any moneys deposited with and held by the Trustee for the redemption of Series B 1981 Bonds which remain unclaimed for a period of four years after the date such moneys are so deposited shall be paid to the Company, including any investment earnings thereon, if any, unless prohibited by law and thereupon and thereafter no holder of this Bond or any other claimant shall have any rights against the Issuer or the Trustee to or in respect of such moneys.

Any redemption under the preceding paragraphs shall be made as provided in the Indenture upon not less than 30 days' notice in the manner provided for in the Indenture. In connection with any such notice, the "CUSIP" numbers assigned to the Series B 1981 Bonds being called for redemption may be used. The Trustee will mail a copy of such notice to the holders of registered Series B 1981 Bonds being called for redemption and to the holders of unregistered Series B 1981 Bonds being called for redemption who have filed their names and addresses with the Trustee for the purpose of receiving such notice, but any failure in respect of such mailing will not affect the validity of such redemption. If there are deposited with the Trustee funds sufficient to pay the principal of and premium, if any, on any Series B 1981 Bonds becoming due at maturity, by call for redemption, or otherwise, together with interest accrued to the due date, or redemption date, as the case may be, interest on such Bonds will cease to accrue on such date, and thereafter the holders will be restricted to the funds so deposited as provided in the Indenture.

If an "Event of Default" (as defined in the Indenture) occurs, the principal of all Bonds issued under the Indenture may be declared due and payable upon the conditions and in the manner and with the effect provided in the Indenture.

No recourse shall be had for the payment of the principal of, premium, if any, or interest on this Bond, or for any claim based hereon or on the Indenture, against any director, member, officer, official or employee, past, present or future, of the Issuer or of any successor body, as such, either directly or through the Issuer or any such successor body, under any constitutional provisions, statute or rule of law, or by the enforcement of any assessment or by any legal or equitable proceeding or otherwise.

This Bond shall pass by delivery except when it is registered as to principal (except when registered to bearer) on the books of the Issuer to be kept for that purpose at the principal corporate trust office of the Trustee and such registration is noted hereon. After such registration no transfer hereof shall be valid unless made on said books at said office by the registered owner in person or by his duly authorized attorney and similarly noted hereon; but this Bond may be discharged from registration by like transfer to bearer. Such registration shall not affect the transferability by delivery of the interest coupons hereto attached. The Issuer and the Trustee may treat the bearer of this Bond if it is not registered, or, if it is registered (except when registered to bearer), the registered owner, as the absolute owner hereof and the bearer of any interest coupon appertaining hereto as the absolute owner thereof for all purposes, whether or not this Bond or such coupon shall be overdue, and shall not be bound by any notice to the contrary.

The Series B 1981 Bonds are issuable as coupon bonds registrable as to principal in the denomination of $5,000, and as fully registered bonds in denominations of $5,000 and any authorized multiple thereof. Coupon Series B 1981 Bonds and fully registered Series B 1981 Bonds are interchangeable in equal aggregate principal amounts and in authorized denominations at the aforesaid office of the Trustee, in the manner, subject to the limitations and on payment of the charges provided in the Indenture.

Neither this Bond nor the coupons attached hereto are valid unless the Trustee's Certificate endorsed hereon is duly executed.

The Indenture permits certain supplements, amendments, changes or modifications of the Installment Sale Agreement and the Indenture not prejudicial to the Bondholders to be made with the consent of the Trustee but without the consent of or notice to the Bondholders, and other amendments, changes or modifications thereof (with certain exceptions as provided in the Indenture) to be made with the consent of the holders of not less than 66⅔% in aggregate principal amount of the Bonds at the time Outstanding.

The Bonds and any coupons appertaining thereto shall not constitute the personal obligation, either jointly or severally of the members of the Issuer, or any other officers, officials or employees of the Issuer.

IT IS HEREBY CERTIFIED AND RECITED that all acts, conditions and things necessary to be done or performed by the Issuer or to have happened precedent to and in the issuing of the Series B 1981 Bonds in order to make them legal, valid and binding special obligations of the Issuer in accordance with their terms, and precedent to and in the execution and delivery of the Indenture and the Installment Sale Agreement have been done and performed and have happened in regular and due form as required by law; that payment in full for the Series B 1981 Bonds has been received; and that the Series B 1981 Bonds do not exceed or violate any constitutional or statutory limitation.

16

Figure 1.2 (continued)

Figure 1.2 (continued)

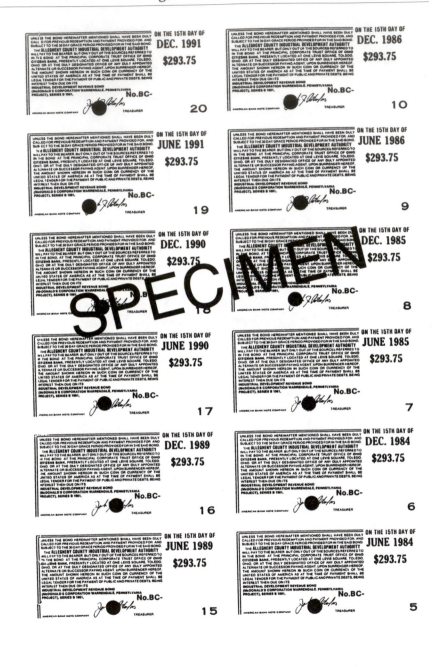

Payable to: Bearer. This is a bearer (coupon) bond. It is similar in that respect to Figure 1.1, the New York State bond.

Next coupon due: June 15, 1982. This coupon is payable at the offices of the Ohio Citizens Bank in Toledo, Ohio. The total amount of the coupon is $293.75 ($5,000 × .1175 × .5 = $293.75).

Paying agent: The Ohio Citizens Bank, at One Levis Square, in Toledo, Ohio. If the bearer presented the coupons at this bank, they would issue him a check. If the bearer presented the coupons to his own bank, they would send them to the Ohio Citizens Bank for payment, and would credit the bearer's account.

Trustee: The Ohio Citizens Bank. If the Ohio Citizens Bank was taken over by another bank during the time this bond was outstanding, presumably the new bank would continue as trustee for this issue. The indenture would state how a successor trustee would be chosen.

Call feature: The bonds may be called on any date, not just any interest payment date, as follows:

December 15, 1988 through December 14, 1989 at 101 percent of par

December 15, 1989 through December 14, 1990 at 100.5 percent of par

December 15, 1990 and thereafter at 100 percent of par

Legal opinion: This legal opinion came from Ballard, Spahr, Andrews & Ingersoll, a law firm located in Philadelphia, with offices in other cities. In their opinion, the bonds are legally issued, are exempt from federal income taxes, and are exempt from Pennsylvania personal property taxes, income taxes, and capital gains taxes. The bonds do not pledge the credit of the Commonwealth of Pennsylvania or any political subdivision of the Commonwealth of Pennsylvania, in the opinion of Ballard, Spahr, Andrews & Ingersoll.

Security 3 - California Housing Finance Agency (Figure 1.3)

This security is a note, not a bond. It is issued under a different set of laws.

Figure 1.3

Figure 1.3 (continued)

In lawful money of the United States of America; and to pay interest thereon in like money from the interest payment date next preceding the date of authentication of this Note (unless this Note is authenticated on an interest payment date, in which event it shall bear interest from such date of authentication, or unless this Note is authenticated prior to September 1, 1982, in which event it shall bear interest from March 1, 1982) until payment of such principal sum shall have been discharged as provided in the Indenture hereinafter mentioned, at the rate of

———————————————nine and one-eighth percent (9⅛%)———————————————

per annum, payable on September 1, 1982, and semiannually thereafter on March 1 and September 1 in each year. Both the principal hereof and interest hereon are payable at the principal office in Sacramento, California, of the Treasurer of the State of California.

This Note is one of the duly authorized notes of the Agency designated as the "California Housing Finance Agency Construction Loan Revenue Notes, 1982 Series A" (herein called the "Notes"), issued or to be issued pursuant to the Zenovich-Moscone-Chacon Housing and Home Finance Act, constituting Division 31 of the Health and Safety Code of the State of California, as amended (herein called the "Act"), and pursuant to an Indenture dated as of March 1, 1982, by and between the Agency and the Treasurer of the State of California, as trustee (herein called the "Trustee"), (herein called the "Indenture"), originally delivered with an Issue Date (as defined in the Indenture) of March 1, 1982, and limited to an aggregate principal amount of $35,000,000. Reference is hereby made to the Act and to the Indenture, a copy of which is on file at the principal office of the Trustee, and all Indentures supplemental thereto for a description of the rights thereunder of the registered owners of the Notes, of the nature and extent of the security, of the rights, duties and immunities of the Trustee and of the rights and obligations of the Agency thereunder, to all the provisions of which Indenture the registered owner of this Note, by acceptance hereof, assents and agrees. The Notes are special obligations of the Agency payable from the Revenues (as defined by the Indenture) and the other moneys and assets pledged to the payment thereof pursuant to the Indenture.

The Indenture contains provisions permitting the Agency and the Trustee, with the consent of the holders of not less than sixty percent (60%) in aggregate principal amount of the Notes at the time outstanding, evidenced as in the Indenture provided, and in certain instances without such consent, to execute supplemental indentures adding any provisions to, or changing in any manner, or eliminating any of the provisions of, the Indenture; provided, however, that no such supplemental indenture shall (1) permit a change in the terms of maturity of the principal of this Note or of any installment of interest hereon or reduce the principal amount hereof or the rate of interest hereon without the consent of the holder of this Note, or (2) reduce the aforesaid percentage of Notes the consent of the holders of which is required to effect any such modification or amendment or permit the creation of any lien on the Pledged Property (as defined in the Indenture) prior to or on a parity with the lien created by the Indenture, or deprive the holders of the Notes of the lien of the Indenture (except as expressly provided in the Indenture), without the consent of the holders of all the Notes then outstanding, all as more fully set forth in the Indenture.

The Notes are subject to mandatory redemption, in whole, or in part by lot, on March 1, 1984, and September 1, 1984, from unexpended proceeds of the sale of the Notes, without premium. The Notes are also subject to redemption at the option of the Agency, in whole, or in part by lot, on March 1, 1984, and September 1, 1984, from any source of available funds, without premium.

If less than all of the Notes are to be redeemed, the particular notes to be redeemed shall be selected by lot as provided in the Indenture. As provided in the Indenture, notice of redemption shall be given by publication at least once in one or more newspapers or journals, printed in the English language, customarily published on each business day and one of which is of general circulation in San Francisco,

Figure 1.3 (continued)

California, and one of which is a financial newspaper circulated in the Borough of Manhattan, New York, New York, such publication to be not less than thirty (30) nor more than sixty (60) days before the redemption date.

Notice of redemption hereof shall also be mailed, not less than twenty (20) days prior to the redemption date, to the registered owner of this Note, but neither failure to mail such notice nor any defect in the notice so mailed shall affect the sufficiency of the proceedings for redemption.

If this Note is called for redemption and payment is duly provided therefor as specified in the Indenture, interest shall cease to accrue hereon from and after the date fixed for redemption.

If an Event of Default, as defined in the Indenture, shall occur, the principal of all Notes may be declared due and payable upon the conditions, in the manner and with the effect provided in the Indenture. The Indenture provides that in certain events such declaration and its consequences may be rescinded by the holders of at least twenty-five percent (25%) in aggregate principal amount of the Notes then outstanding.

The Notes are issuable as fully registered Notes without coupons in denominations of $5,000 and any authorized multiple thereof. Subject to the limitations and conditions and upon payment of the charges, if any, as provided in the Indenture, fully registered Notes may be exchanged at the principal office of the Trustee for a like aggregate principal amount of fully registered Notes of the same maturity of other authorized denominations.

This Note is transferable by the registered owner hereof, in person or by his, her or its attorney duly authorized in writing, at said office of the Trustee, but only in the manner, subject to the limitations and upon payment of the charges provided in the Indenture, and upon surrender and cancellation of this Note. Upon such transfer a new fully registered Note or Notes without coupons, of the same maturity and of authorized denomination or denominations, for the same aggregate principal amount will be issued to the transferee in exchange herefor.

The Agency and the Trustee may treat the registered owner hereof as the absolute owner hereof for all purposes, and the Agency and the Trustee shall not be affected by any notice to the contrary.

This Note shall not be deemed to constitute a debt or liability of the State of California or of any political subdivision thereof, other than the Agency, or a pledge of the faith and credit of the State of California or of any such political subdivision, other than the Agency to the extent herein provided, but shall be payable solely from funds provided therefor pursuant to the Indenture. Neither the faith and credit nor the taxing power of the State of California is pledged to the payment of the principal of or interest on this Note.

Neither the members of the Board of Directors of the Agency nor any officer or employee of the Agency nor any person executing this Note shall be subject to any personal liability or accountability by reason of the issuance hereof.

This Note shall not be entitled to any benefit under the Indenture, or become valid or obligatory for any purpose, until the certificate of authentication and registration hereon endorsed shall have been signed by the Trustee.

It is hereby certified and recited that all conditions, acts and things required by the Constitution and statutes of the State of California or by the Act or the Indenture to exist, to have happened or to have been performed precedent to or in the issuance of the Notes exist, have happened and have been performed and that the issue of the Notes, together with all other indebtedness of the Agency, is within every debt and other limit prescribed by said Constitution, statutes, or Indenture.

IN WITNESS WHEREOF, California Housing Finance Agency has caused this Note to be executed on its behalf by its Executive Director, and its corporate seal to be reproduced hereon and attested by the Secretary of its Board of Directors, all as of March 1, 1982.

Figure 1.3 (continued)

CERTIFICATE AS TO LEGAL OPINION

The undersigned, Executive Director of the California Housing Finance Agency, certifies that the following is a full, true and correct copy of the original legal opinion of The Honorable George Deukmejian, Attorney General of the State of California, and Orrick, Herrington & Sutcliffe, A Professional Corporation, of San Francisco, California, Bond Counsel, as to the validity and security of the issue of notes of which the within note is one, dated as of the date of delivery of said notes and delivered as of said date.

CALIFORNIA HOUSING FINANCE AGENCY

Executive Director

GEORGE DEUKMEJIAN
ATTORNEY GENERAL
STATE OF CALIFORNIA
555 CAPITOL MALL, SUITE 350
SACRAMENTO, CALIFORNIA 95814

ORRICK, HERRINGTON & SUTCLIFFE
A PROFESSIONAL CORPORATION
600 MONTGOMERY STREET
SAN FRANCISCO, CALIFORNIA 94111

Re: California Housing Finance Agency
Construction Loan Revenue Notes, 1982 Series A
(Final Opinion)

We have examined a record of proceedings relating to the issuance of $35,000,000 Construction Loan Revenue Notes, 1982 Series A (herein called the "Notes"), of the California Housing Finance Agency (herein called the "Agency"). The Agency was created by the Zenovich-Moscone-Chacon Housing and Home Finance Act, constituting Division 31 of the Health and Safety Code of the State of California (herein called the "Act").

The Notes are authorized to be issued pursuant to the Act and an Indenture, dated as of March 1, 1982 (herein called the "Indenture"), by and between the Agency and the Treasurer of the State of California, as trustee (herein called the "Trustee"). The Notes are authorized to be issued for the purpose of providing funds for financing construction loans for multi-unit rental housing developments intended for occupancy primarily by persons or families of low or moderate income. In accordance with the Indenture, each construction loan financed with the proceeds of the sale of the Notes will be the subject of a commitment by the Government National Mortgage Association ("GNMA") to an approved GNMA seller for purchase of the construction loan following completion of construction and final endorsement for insurance by the Federal Housing Administration.

The Notes are authorized to be issued only in fully registered form without coupons in denominations of $5,000 or any authorized multiple thereof. The Notes are dated March 1, 1982, mature on March 1, 1985, and bear interest at the rate of nine and one-eighth percent (9⅛%) per annum, payable on September 1, 1982, and semiannually thereafter on March 1, and September 1, in each year.

The Notes are subject to redemption prior to their stated maturity, in whole, or in part by lot, from any source of available funds, on March 1, 1984, and September 1, 1984, under the circumstances prescribed in the Indenture, at the principal amount of the Notes to be redeemed and accrued interest thereon to the date fixed for redemption, without premium.

No additional Construction Loan Revenue Notes are authorized to be issued under the Indenture.

The Indenture and the rights and obligations of the Agency and the holders of the Notes may be modified in the manner and subject to the limitations set forth in the Indenture.

We are of the opinion that:

1. The Agency has been duly created and validly exists with good right and lawful authority to perform its obligations in accordance with law and the terms and provisions of the Indenture.

2. The Indenture has been duly and legally authorized, executed and delivered and constitutes a valid, legal and binding obligation of the Agency.

3. The Notes have been duly authorized by and constitute valid and binding special obligations of the Agency payable solely from the sources referred to in the Indenture, and, to the payment of which, in accordance with their terms, the Agency has pledged the Pledged Property, as defined in the Indenture, subject to the provisions of the Indenture permitting the use and application thereof for or to the purposes and on the terms and conditions set forth in the Indenture.

4. The Notes do not constitute a debt or liability of the State of California or any political subdivision thereof, other than the Agency, or a pledge of the faith and credit of the State of California or any such political subdivision, other than the Agency to the extent provided in the Indenture. Neither the faith and credit nor the taxing power of the State of California is pledged to the payment of the principal of or interest on the Notes.

5. Interest on the Notes is exempt under existing statutes, regulations, administrative interpretations, and court decisions from State of California personal income taxes and Federal income taxes, except that no opinion is expressed as to the exemption from Federal income taxes of interest on any Note for any period during which such Note is held by a person who, within the meaning of Section 103(b)(10) of the Internal Revenue Code of 1954, as amended, is a substantial user of facilities with respect to which the proceeds of the Notes were used or is a related person.

Very truly yours,
GEORGE DEUKMEJIAN
Attorney General

By

Deputy Attorney General

ORRICK, HERRINGTON & SUTCLIFFE
A Professional Corporation

per

ENDORSEMENT

Notice: No writing below except by the Trustee.

This Note represents Note(s) of this issue, series, interest rate and maturity, assigned identification numbers by the Trustee of _____

each number representing $5,000 in principal amount of Notes.

Issuer (borrower): California Housing Finance Agency (not the State of California)

Face amount: The face amount is not shown, because this is a specimen, not a real security. This note is in registered form. The face amount of an actual certificate delivered to the bond buyer would be printed in the space provided for it.

Maturity date: March 1, 1985

Interest rate: 9 1/8 percent (9.125 percent) per year

Dated date: March 1, 1982. Interest started to accrue on this date.

Payable to: The name and address of the registered owner of the bonds will be printed in this space. This note is in registered form, so no name and address appears in this specimen.

Coupon due: This note has no coupons, because it is in registered form. Interest payments will be sent directly to the owner of the note as recorded on the books of the transfer agent. The transfer agent keeps a record of ownership of the notes. The owner of the bond does not have to clip coupons and present them for payment; he or she will get the interest checks in the mail.

Paying agent: The Treasurer of the State of California, at his principal office in Sacramento, California

Trustee: The Treasurer of the State of California is the trustee.

Call feature: These notes have two call features. They may be called on March 1, 1984, and September 1, 1984, at par (100 percent of face value) from any available source of funds; this is an optional call.

They must be called on March 1, 1984 and September 1, 1984, at par, in whole or in part, by lot, from any unexpended proceeds of the sale of the notes; this is an extraordinary call. This means that any part of the proceeds from the sale of the notes that was not used to buy mortgages will be used to call notes at par. *By lot* means that the individual certificates called will be chosen at random, usually done by a lottery.

Legal opinion: This legal opinion was given jointly by the Attorney General of the State of California, at that time George

Deukmejian, and Orrick, Herrington & Sutcliffe, a law firm. In their opinion, the notes have been legally issued, are not an obligation of the State of California (they are revenue notes), and are exempt from Federal and California income taxes, except that no opinion is given on tax exemption if the holder of the notes is a substantial user of the facilities with respect to which the proceeds of the notes were used, or a related person.

CHAPTER 2

How Bonds Can Differ in Physical Form

If you lent your friend five dollars for lunch, you might ask for some document that confirms that he owes you the five dollars. He might give you a simple IOU with his signature. You could then transfer the IOU by giving it to someone else. This is comparable to the bearer form for bonds.

Your friend might put your name on the form: "IO Joe" (your name). You are identified on the IOU as the owner. If you wanted to transfer ownership to another person, you would have to state this on the IOU itself or on a separate piece of paper, and you might also have to tell your friend so that he could pay the new owner instead of you. This system is comparable to the registered form for bonds.

You might have some third person, say a mutual friend Ed, keep a record of the loan and all the payments made, without you receiving any direct document. You would receive only a periodic statement from Ed about the status of your loan. This might be done in cases where there were many such loans. Ed would receive your friend's payments and in turn make these payments to you. This procedure is comparable to the book entry form for bonds.

BEARER BONDS

Bearer bonds are always issued in certificate form, with small detachable coupons for the interest payments. The bearer, presumed to be also the owner or his agent, cuts off each coupon as it becomes due and presents it to his bank for payment. The coupon travels through the banking system, much like a personal check, to the bank responsible for making the actual payment. This bank, called the *paying agent*, sends the interest to the bearer's bank, which credits it to the bearer's account. At maturity, the bond itself is presented for the principal payment along with the last interest coupon. If the bonds have a trustee, the trustee is usually also the paying agent. Figures 1.1 and 1.2 are examples of bearer bonds.

The bearer bond is easy to transfer and to lose, so safekeeping is required at all times. Elaborate provisions are maintained for safekeeping of bearer securities. If you have bearer bonds, you should keep detailed records of the actual certificate numbers. Losing a bearer bond requires possible notification to the issuer and the Securities and Exchange Commission (SEC), and time, trouble and expense to obtain a replacement certificate.

Tax law changes in the early 1980s required that municipal bonds issued on and after July 1, 1983, must be in either registered or book entry form for their interest income to be exempt from federal income tax. Partly, this was an attempt to stop the reputed use of tax-exempt bearer bonds for illegal purposes. The United States Supreme Court upheld this law when it ruled against the state of South Carolina, when South Carolina brought suit claiming that this law was unconstitutional. The Supreme Court also ruled at the same time that Congress could tax interest income from municipal bonds if it so desired and that tax-exemption is not protected by the United States Constitution. This constitutional protection had been frequently stated—and believed—by persons in the municipal bond business.

As a result, the number of bearer bonds constantly decreases, although many of them still exist and will continue to exist for many years.

REGISTERED BONDS

Registered bonds exist in certificate form, similar to bearer bonds. The bondholder or his agent holds the certificate, but their certificate contains the name and address of the bondholder or his agent. This person or firm, called the holder of record, does not have coupons to clip and present to the bank. Instead, all payments and bondholder notices are sent to the holder of record. For the many bondowners who have their brokers hold their bonds, the holder of record is the bondowner's broker. The bonds are said to be "in a street name."

The holder of record transfers the bond to a new owner by endorsing it, usually on the back of the bond, or by attaching a comparable paper, such as a power of attorney. This is similar to endorsing a personal check.

Such transfers are done by an agency called a transfer agent. The transfer agent verifies the accuracy and correctness of the transfer, cancels the old certificate, issues a new certificate in the name of the new owner of record, and sends the new certificate to the new holder of record. Future interest payments and communications to bondholders will go to this new holder. The new holder may be the actual owner, or may be an agent for the owner. Examples of such agents are brokerage houses, who maintain custody of securities actually owned by their customers.

Many large, well-managed banks act as transfer agents; other transfer agents for municipal bonds include the issuers themselves. Sometimes the Treasury Department of a state will act as transfer agent for issues of a state and its political subdivisions. For example, the Treasurer of the State of California is the transfer agent for the California HFA notes shown in Chapter 1.

Transfer ease depends on the transfer agent. Some transfer agents have established a reputation for excellence; others have the opposite reputation. Bonds of the latter sometimes trade cheaper in the market to compensate for the difficulty of transfer. Most transfer agents, however, especially the large and well-established firms, have few problems in transferring bonds on their books. Usually, they provide transfer services to many corporations as well as to municipalities.

The SEC has a transfer regulation known as the 72-hour rule: 90 percent of all bonds must be transferred within 72 hours of the time they are presented to the transfer agent. This does not explicitly apply to municipal bonds, since they are exempt securities under the terms of the Securities Exchange Act of 1934, but transfer agents who do both municipal and corporate security transfers must apply the rule to all of their transfer operations, including municipal bond transfers. Transfer agents that transfer only municipal securities are not affected by the rule; usually these are government agencies that act as transfer agents only for issues of the government and its agencies.

Most municipal bond investors keep their bonds with their securities broker or municipal bond dealer. The broker provides safekeeping of the certificate and additional services, including prompt crediting of interest and principal to the owner's account and notification of calls and other information to bondholders. Usually the broker provides these at little or no cost to the investor. In fact, most brokers encourage customers to keep their bonds with their broker.

Many investors, however, like to have their actual bond certificates in their possession. If the bonds are available in bearer or registered form, then the investor can usually receive the actual certificates if he or she wishes.

If you have bearer bonds, you may be able to convert them to registered form. You would then receive interest and principal payments directly, and you would also receive all bondholder information and notices directly from the trustee. Many bondholders prefer the registered form, and many trustees now work with holders of bearer bonds to convert them to registered form. This reduces work for the trustee and also creates a happier customer. You should check with the bond trustee to see whether your bearer bonds can be converted.

BOOK ENTRY BONDS

Book entry bonds exist in two possible forms: *certificated* (immobilized certificate) form or *book entry only*. Both forms require the existence of a depository. A depository stores the certificates, maintains all books and records, and makes all payments to its participants. The participants include banks, brokerage firms, and other clearing agencies. The participants, in turn, keep all records on their books for their clients, which may be other banks, brokerage houses, trustee accounts, or the actual owners of the bonds. They send each client a periodic statement listing his or her holdings.

Certificated Book Entry

If the depository holds a certificated, or immobilized, book entry issue, the issue has either bearer or registered certificates and the depository will send a certificate to the owner if one is requested. Most bondholders are content that the depository continue to hold the certificates and send the interest and principal payments to the depository participants. For most individual bondholders, this will be their broker. These participants in turn forward the payments to the bondholders. Even many bearer bonds are now held at a depository in certificated form.

Pure Book Entry

Book entry only, also known as *pure book entry*, has no certificates at all available to the investor. Instead, the depository holds one certificate for each maturity of the new bond issue, or for the entire issue. No other certificates exist, or ever will exist, and the owner of the bond cannot receive a certificate. The owner does, however, receive a statement from his broker stating ownership of the bonds.

Several depositories that handle municipal bonds, but Depository Trust Company (DTC), located in New York City, is the largest one and has about 95 percent of all municipal bond depository business. Its participants included, at the end of 1993, 343 broker-dealers, 163 banks, and 9 clearing agencies, for a total of 515 participants.

Book entry only continues to increase its share of municipal new issue. During 1993, about 75 percent of municipal new issue volume distributed through DTC was book entry only, up from about 70 percent during 1992. Almost all large municipal issues are book entry only, and many brokers encourage their customers to use this method. Many of the smaller issues continue to be in registered form, so that, although more issues are in registered form, the majority of the par amount is now issued in pure book entry form. If you buy a new issue, the chances are very good that it will be available only in book entry form, and you will not get a certificate.

CHAPTER 3

Making Contractual Changes to the Bond's Cash Flow

Suppose the friend who borrowed the five dollars from you until payday returns the money to you before payday. He has paid off the loan ahead of schedule. For bonds, this ability to pay ahead of schedule is called the *call feature*, and the act of paying ahead of schedule is called *calling the bonds*.

You might ask your friend for your money back sooner than payday. For bonds, this feature is called the *put option*, and the act of getting the money back is called *putting the bonds*.

If the borrower is paying you interest, the interest rate might change. For bonds, this is called a *variable-rate bond* or a *variable-rate demand obligation* (VRDO).

The borrower may give the money to Ed, the third party, ahead of time and ask Ed to pay you on payday. For bonds, this act is called *defeasing the bonds*.

The borrower might refuse to return your money to you. For bonds, this is called an *act of default*.

HOW THE FUNDS FLOW CAN CHANGE

Once issued, the bond has a scheduled flow of funds, interest and principal payments, until maturity. The terms of the bond contract might allow changes to this flow of funds. These changes could be done in one or more of four ways: calling the bonds, putting the bonds, changing the interest rate paid on the bonds, or defeasing the bonds. A fifth change in the flow of funds is default; the bond contract might define the conditions of default.

The Call Feature

The issuer repays some or all of the bonds ahead of schedule. The issuer need no longer pay interest on his debt; of course, he no longer has the use of the money.

The Put Option

The buyer asks for repayment of his bonds ahead of schedule. The bondholder might do this to make an investment at a higher interest rate.

Variable-Rate Bonds

The interest rate varies from time to time, based on the contract. This is similar to variable-rate mortgages, which are now a widely used home financing technique.

Defeasance

The issuer arranges for the bond issue to be paid from some other source of funds than its own and may no longer have any responsibility for payment itself. The issuer might do this to refund an issue at lower rates or to eliminate onerous indenture requirements.

Default

The issuer does not make all the legally required payments and may not even pay interest and principal when due. The acts which constitute default are either defined by law or stated in the indenture. Most acts of default are involuntary.

HOW TO USE CALL FEATURES

The call feature allows the issuer to repay some or all of the bonds ahead of schedule. The issuer notifies the bondholders that their bonds are being redeemed ahead of time and states the exact terms of the redemption. The owners receive their principal back. They may receive a small additional payment, the *call premium*, and they will receive interest up to the redemption date. No further interest will be paid on the bonds after they have been called. The issuer need no longer make payments on the bond issue; however the issuer no longer has use of the borrowed funds.

There are three main types of call features for municipals: the *optional redemption,* the *mandatory sinking fund,* and the *extraordinary redemption.*

The Optional Redemption

The optional redemption allows the issuer, at his or her option, under the original terms of the bond contract, to repay part or all of the original loan before maturity. The terms of this option will be stated in the indenture, in the official statement, and on the bond certificate, if a certificate form exists.

Most municipal bonds have an optional call feature. A typical recent call feature allows the issuer to call, or repay, the bonds after ten years at a price of 102 percent of par, after eleven years at a price of 101 percent of par, and at par after twelve years. The price is called the call price, and the amount over par (2 percent, 1 percent, and 0 percent, respectively, in the above examples) is called the call premium. Thus, in the above example, the owner of a $5,000 bond would receive $5,100 after ten years (102 percent of $5,000); $5,050 after eleven years (101 percent of $5,000); or $5,000 after twelve or more years (100 percent of $5,000), if the bond were called at those times, respectively. The call premiums, in dollar amounts, would be $100, $50, and $0 respectively. Note that in this example, the original maturity date of the bond doesn't matter; only the call date and price matter.

For example, in the New York State bond shown in Chapter 1, the first call date is June 1, 1997, and the call price is 100.00. The call premium is zero.

The Mandatory Sinking Fund

A sinking fund, or "sinker," is a series of scheduled prepayments which repays all or part of a bond issue before the final maturity of the bonds. Almost all municipal bond sinking funds simply call bonds for redemption; they are said to be "called for sinking fund purposes." The calls are almost always at par. When the sinking fund provisions take effect, and the sinking fund starts actually to call bonds, the bonds are said to have an "active sinker."

For example, suppose a bond issue is sold in a total amount of $1,000,000, due in 20 years. It might have a mandatory sinking fund, starting in eleven years, repaying $100,000 per year. Only interest will be paid for ten years. Starting in the eleventh year, the issuer will call $100,000 face amount of bonds at par for the sinking fund; no further interest will be paid on the bonds that are called after their call date, but of course interest continues on the bonds that are not called. The amount of the issue outstanding will go down by $100,000 per year. At maturity, in twenty years, only $100,000 remains to be paid. The sinking fund has prepaid $900,000 of the bonds before maturity. Note that the issuer could also call additional bonds under the optional redemption provision, if the bonds have such a provision. Such simultaneous calls sometimes occur, especially if the bonds have been advance refunded.

A sinking fund might also be compared to the operation of a standard monthly payment home mortgage. Each monthly mortgage payment pays interest and reduces the mortgage principal; by the time the term of the mortgage is up, possibly in thirty years, the last payment pays off the final amount due on the mortgage. The monthly payments are determined by the original mortgage contract.

Sinking funds may operate without actually calling bonds. The indenture may allow the issuer to satisfy the sinking fund requirements by buying bonds in the open market. The issuer would naturally do this only if the bonds traded at prices under the sinking fund call price; usually, the call price is par, so the bonds must trade at prices below 100 (below par). However, not all sinking funds are allowed to do this; some must actually call outstanding bonds at par, even though the fund might actually be able to buy bonds at a lower price. Buying the bonds in the open market will provide some market support and result in a higher trading price for the bonds. The bond indenture sets up the rules that the issuer and the trustee agree to follow in satisfying mandatory sinking fund requirements.

Example 1. The Port Authority of New York and New Jersey has a large number of different issues of bonds outstanding. Most of these issues have a sinking fund, and many of these sinking funds are now active. The Port Authority may meet sinking fund obligations either by calling bonds or buying them in the open market. If the bonds trade above par, the Authority will call them at par for sinking fund purposes. If the bonds trade under par, the Authority will buy them at the lower price, for sinking fund purposes. For bonds trading at around par, both methods may be used.

Example 2. On February 18, 1969, the Kentucky Turnpike Authority sold a series of bonds, including some 5 $7/8$ percent bonds due on July 1, 2008. The bonds have all been escrowed to maturity; that is, funds have been set aside with a trustee to make the required bond payments. The sinking fund for this issue is now active. The indenture allows the Authority to call the bonds for sinking fund purposes or buy them in the open market. The Authority would presumably buy them in the open market if the market price was lower than par. However, the bonds have been advanced refunded. The securities in the escrow account to secure bond payments provide interest and principal to match the requirements of the issue. These payments are made at the same time that the sinking fund payments are required to be made. The Authority could, in theory, buy bonds in the market if they were available, but the Authority decided that the savings would not be large enough to undertake this kind of activity. Therefore, the Authority instructed the trustee to call bonds at par, even though the bonds might be trading at lower prices. In this case, the indenture does allow the Authority to purchase the bonds, but the Authority has decided not to for operational reasons. The lucky owners of bonds called for sinking fund purposes received par for bonds which might be trading at a much lower price.

The Extraordinary Call

The extraordinary call occurs when one of a number of unexpected events occurs. Typical of these are the following:

- Interest on the bonds is declared taxable by the Internal Revenue Service. This rarely happens, and only when the Internal Revenue Service has serious doubts that the issuer has complied with the rules for bonds to be exempt from federal income tax.

- The property that secures the bonds is condemned and purchased for public use and no plans are made to replace it using the proceeds of the condemnation. The proceeds of the condemnation are used to call the bonds. For example, the government might condemn a piece of property to build a new road or similar project, or might simply take over an existing property for public use. If the managers of the condemned property have no plans to build a new facility, they would call the bonds, using the extraordinary call feature.

- The property that secures the bonds is damaged or destroyed, no plans are made to replace it, and the insurance proceeds are used to call the bonds. This might happen when a storm or earthquake damages or destroys the property, and the managers decide not to rebuild. The insurance proceeds would be used to redeem the outstanding bonds, using the extraordinary call feature.

- The public enterprise supporting the bonds has excess funds from certain sources not needed in the operation of the enterprise, or not expended in the development of the enterprise and is allowed, or obligated, to use these funds to redeem bonds. For example, sometimes only part of the funds raised are used to build the project financed by the issue. Sometimes the issue finances an activity such as home mortgage lending or student loans, and not all the funds are expended on this activity. The funds not so expended may, and under the terms of the indenture perhaps must, be used to call the bonds.

The third example in Chapter 1, the California Housing Finance Agency note, has an extraordinary call feature. Any proceeds from selling the note issue which are not spent to buy mortgages are used to redeem the notes at par under the extraordinary call feature.

HOW A BOND IS CALLED

Whatever the reason for the call, the investor receives notice if his or her bond is called from either the trustee, if there is one, or from the issuer, or both.

Call notices for bearer bonds are published in several newspapers, usually including *The Bond Buyer*, and a newspaper published in the local area of the issuer. The issuer can give no other notice, because he does not know the actual owners of the bonds.

Call notices for registered bonds are sent directly to the bondholder of record. Sometimes a certificate will be for a large par amount, only a portion of which is called. For example, a certificate might have been issued for $50,000 par amount, of which only $5,000 was called. In this case, the bondholder will still hold $45,000 of bonds.

Call notices for book entry only bonds are sent to the depository, which in turn notifies its participants who hold the bonds, who in turn notify the beneficial owner of the bonds. In this case, the bondholders will have no certificates. The participants of the depository must somehow allocate the called bonds among their accounts who hold the bonds. This is usually done by a lottery, conducted by the participant of the depository. The participant simply allocates the called bonds among all the bonds held by its customers in a random way. Frequently, computer programs are used for this.

For example, suppose the customers of a dealer own $100,000 face amount of bonds, and $10,000 face amount of bonds have been called. The dealer will select which bonds, in multiples of $5,000, will be called, and notify the customers of those bonds that their bonds have been called.

HOW THE INVESTOR SHOULD MANAGE CALL FEATURES

You should know all the call features of your bond. Your bond salesman should be able to explain them to you. The final official statement for your bonds will state the call features. When you get the final official statement, be sure to study at least the part on call features.

If you have actual physical possession of your bearer bonds, rather than have them with your broker, call notices present a problem. You must present the bond to receive your principal if the bond is called, but you cannot receive the notice because in the case of bearer bonds the issuer has no record of your ownership. As a result, you may miss the call and won't receive notice until you present the next coupon, when you will be told that your bond has been called. You will then receive the principal and call premium, but you will have missed six months of interest, as well as the possibility of making other investments during the past six months.

Almost all bearer municipal bonds now outstanding have a call feature, and in many cases the issuer may call them now. This is because virtually no municipal bearer bonds have been issued since July 1, 1983. Most municipal bonds have a call feature. A common call feature allows the issuer to call the bond after ten years from issue date. This would make most bearer bonds callable by July 1, 1993. For bearer bond owners, this makes the call notice a significant present problem.

There are several solutions to this problem. You can keep in touch with the issuer or the trustee and make sure that you receive all call notices. You could ask the issuer or the trustee to send you a copy of all call notices.

You might be able to convert your bearer bonds to registered form, so that your bond certificate will be in your name, and call notices will automatically be sent to you. Many issuers and trustees now cooperate in this activity, because it reduces and simplifies their workload. If you can do this, you will receive all notices, because the issuer now has your name and address. You will also receive interest payments directly from the paying agent, which might be more convenient. Of course, you now no longer have a bearer bond, but a registered bond instead.

You may not be able to put your bearer bonds into registered form. The transfer may not be permitted by the indenture, or may not be allowed by the applicable state law. Even if the transfer is possible, you may simply find that it is too expensive or difficult to be worthwhile.

You could subscribe to one of several call notification services, or you could simply subscribe to and read the papers likely to print the notices.

The easiest solution is probably to put your bonds in registered form, but if you want to keep bearer bonds, or your bonds cannot be put in registered form, you would probably want to keep in touch with the issuer or trustee.

Bearer bonds held for you by your broker don't present a problem; the broker takes all the responsibility and does all the work to follow call notices. Usually the broker does not charge a fee for this service above the normal account maintenance charge, if there is one.

You should know whether your bond has a mandatory sinking fund and whether it is active. The call notices are given in the same way as optional call notices. However, you know that a certain number of bonds will be called, and that the call will take place. You should make your plans accordingly.

You don't have to be concerned with extraordinary calls, with one important exception: mortgage revenue (or housing finance) bonds. These bonds usually can be redeemed from funds not used to purchase mortgages, or from prepayments of mortgages financed by the bonds. In times of decreasing interest rates, such as occurred during 1992 and most of 1993, people refinance their mortgages, resulting in large prepayments of mortgages. These in turn result in large early redemptions of the bonds which financed the mortgages. These redemptions take place under the extraordinary call features of the bonds and have resulted in large early calls, at par, of long-term housing bonds. If you have these bonds, you should be aware of the existence of the extraordinary call feature and its importance to them. The extraordinary call feature also prevents housing bonds and mortgage revenue bonds from ever selling at very high prices. As a result, you do not receive the capital gains on these bonds in times of low interest rates that you receive on most other long-term bonds. The municipal security example shown in Figure 1.3 is a mortgage revenue note and has an extraordinary call feature.

Zero-coupon bearer bonds that are callable present a special problem. The issuer may call them many years before maturity, but you won't know about it. You could present your bonds at maturity, only to discover that they had been called years before, and you will receive only a small fraction of the final maturity value. In these cases, you should either convert your bonds to registered form, or maintain annual or even semiannual contact with the issuer or the trustee, to make sure that you know when and if your bonds are called.

If you are an individual investor, you are likely to buy long-term revenue bonds for your own portfolio, for several reasons. The longer term provides a higher yield, and these bonds are among the most common bonds in the new issue marketplace. However, these bonds are almost certain to have an optional call, probably have a mandatory sinking fund, and may have extraordinary call provisions as well. You should make sure you know all of these provisions for your bonds and are prepared to manage the call features.

HOW TO USE PUT OPTIONS

The put option allows you to demand your money back from the issuer; you can "put" the bond to the issuer. To do this, you notify the issuer, under the terms of the original bond agreement, that you wish to return the bond to the issuer and receive your principal. No interest will accrue on your bond after the put date. The issuer may need to borrow the money to do this, so the put feature is frequently combined with another source of funds, such as a loan agreement or letter of credit with a third party.

The procedure is comparable to a case where the bank which lent you money to buy your house demands its money back after you have bought the house.

Naturally, you would usually want to put your bonds only if you have other uses for the money, such as investing at higher rates. The put feature allows you to do this and protects you from a price decline of the bonds; indeed, this was one reason that put features were added to municipal bonds.

The most common bonds with a put option are United States Government Savings Bonds. These bonds allow the owner of the bond to redeem them at any time after six months from the date of issue, at prices stated on the back of the bond certificate. The redemption prices include interest earnings from the purchase date to redemption date. This feature has always added to the popularity of this investment.

You should know the put feature of your bonds, if they have one. If you want to exercise the put, you must make sure that you comply with the terms of the contract. This usually requires you to give notice and tender your bonds (send them to the trustee). You must do all of this in accordance with the terms of the indenture. Failure to do this may result in failure to exercise the put option, and may result in a decline in the value of your bonds.

You should also understand that the put option is a valuable feature of your bond, and you may have accepted a lower yield on your bond to get it. Benjamin Graham wrote in his famous book *The Intelligent Investor*, first published in 1949, that the redemption feature (or put option) on United States Savings Bonds is worth an additional $1/_2$ percent in yield, in his opinion.[*]

The put option will keep up the price of your bond in declining markets. You have given up something for that feature, and you should understand that you have made that trade.

HOW VARIABLE-RATE BONDS WORK

The interest rate paid on variable-rate bonds, also frequently called variable-rate demand obligations (VRDO), fluctuates, according to the contract, as market interest rates fluctuate. The rate paid may bear some relation to a published market interest rate, such as a Treasury bill rate, or may be established at auction by a trustee. The rate may change as often as daily or as infrequently as annually. However the rate is established, the market price of this bond should always stay about par, while the interest paid fluctuates with the market. This is the purpose of these bonds and the reason they were set up in the first place. The variable rate, with resulting stable market price, is not simply a feature of the bond. It is the main purpose of the bond. For this reason, variable-rate bonds are covered in more detail in Chapter 5.

HOW DEFEASANCE WORKS

Defeasance occurs when the issuer makes other arrangements to pay the bonds. This is done by placing in a special trust fund, called an escrow fund, sufficient securities to pay the interest and principal on the bonds as they come due. Almost always, the securities placed in the trust account are United States Treasury securities, but very occasionally other securities are used instead. Future inter-

---

[*]Graham, Benjamin. *The Intelligent Investor.* p. 129. New York: Harper & Brothers Publishers. 1949.

est and principal payments on the bonds are made by the trustee from the escrow fund; the issuer no longer makes the payments.

Why an Issuer Will Defease Bonds

An issuer may have several reasons for doing this. For example, the issuer may save money by offering new bonds at a substantially lower interest rate than the bonds being defeased, and many refundings are solely for this purpose.

The issuer may also refund outstanding bonds to eliminate restrictive or obsolete features of the indenture or add new features that allow the issuer to do things he couldn't previously do. These might include using new techniques to reduce or eliminate reserves; eliminate liens on property; get explicit permission to issue previously forbidden kinds of securities, such as zero coupon bonds; or do previously forbidden activities, such as new construction or changes to the project.

For example, our local bridge authority (LBA) might have an indenture for its original bond issue which said that only one level of roadway would be permitted for the bridge. Suppose the bridge prospers and traffic grows to more than can be handled by one roadway. The LBA might want to add a second roadway. This would not be allowed under the terms of the original indenture.

The LBA might decide to issue new bonds to pay for the additional roadway and also to defease the original bonds. This would mean that the original bonds were deemed to have been repaid under the terms of the original indenture and that the restrictions of the original indenture would no longer hold. The LBA could then build the second roadway.

How Call Features of Defeased Bonds Are Handled

Sometimes defeasance is accompanied by the exercise of the call feature (if the bonds are callable), even if the first call date is some time in the future. In such cases, the bonds may be "advance refunded," or "pre-refunded."

An advance refunded or pre-refunded bond has had provisions made for its payment by the sale of another bond issue. The refunded bonds (the old issue) will have part or all of the proceeds of the refunding bonds (the new issue) placed in a special account, with a trustee appointed to invest the proceeds and use the securities in the account to pay interest and principal as due on the refunded bonds. The new issue is planned to provide enough funds so that enough securities can be bought to provide the interest and principal when due on the old issue.

If the refunded bonds are called, a call notice will be issued and the bonds will be redeemed on the call date at the call price, as specified in the original indenture or other bond agreement.

Rarely, funds to repay outstanding debt are advanced from sources other than the sale of refunding bonds. The bonds which have been provided for in this way would usually be considered advance refunded, even though no refunding issue exists.

Advance refunded bonds would also be considered escrowed, because they have securities placed in trust to ensure payment until either they mature or until an earlier call date. A trustee is appointed and makes interest and principal payments on the securities from the trust until the bonds are redeemed or mature as planned. The issuer no longer has direct responsibility for making payments on the escrowed bonds.

What Escrowed to Maturity (ETM) Means

Bonds that are escrowed to maturity are escrowed, as described above, but interest and principal payments will be made until the bonds mature, as planned.

Bonds which have a mandatory sinking fund will have sinking fund payments made, as described in the original offering or indenture. The original terms of sinking fund operations are followed. The Kentucky Turnpike bonds described previously are in fact escrowed to maturity (even though they could in theory be called), and the mandatory sinking fund is now active.

When bonds are called, the trustee of the escrow fund will pay interest and the call price from the funds in the escrow account.

Sometimes the bonds are callable, but the issuer formally waives (defeases) the right to call them. These bonds are also said to be escrowed to maturity. The trustee will pay interest and maturity payments, as due. The call will not be exercised.

Sometimes the bonds have a call feature, but the call has neither been exercised nor formally waived. An open question exists about whether the issuer still retains the right to call the bonds, even though they may already have been escrowed to maturity. Frequently, the bonds have traded as though they would not be called; calling the bonds would result in a large decrease in their value. On the rare recent occasions when the issuer tried to call bonds which had been escrowed to maturity, pressure from the municipal bond community forced the issuer to refrain from calling the bonds. For example, a few years ago, the Kansas Turnpike tried to call some of its bonds which it had previously escrowed to maturity. The municipal bond industry was able to stop this effort to call the bonds.

However, many knowledgeable persons think that the issuer always has the right to call the bonds unless he has explicitly given up the right.

Defeased bonds which have been escrowed by United States Treasury bonds should have a AAA rating (the highest), if a rating has been applied for.

If your bonds are defeased when you buy them, you should have been so informed by your salesperson. If they are escrowed to maturity and the issuer has not formally waived his right to call the bonds, you should at least be aware of his theoretical possible right to do so, the resulting possible decline in the value of your bonds, and the possible reduction of the time during which you will receive interest payments. You should also know whether your bonds have been defeased by United States Treasury securities or by some other kind of security.

WHAT DEFAULT MEANS

Default occurs when the issuer fails to fulfill some of the obligations of the contract. These obligations are defined in the contract, and the obligations and acts of default are specified in the indenture, if one exists.

Clearly, failure to pay interest and principal when due is an act of default. But other failures to make payments can also be acts of default. For example, failure to make other payments, such as sinking fund payments or payments to other fund accounts might be acts of default, even though no individual bondholder suffered loss because of the failure. These might also include failure to make payments to reserve accounts required by the indenture and failure to keep these accounts at the levels promised. The bond trustee has the responsibility of making sure that all payments are made according to the contract and to take whatever steps may be required to safeguard the interests of the bondholders.

For example, if the local bridge authority failed to make the required monthly payments into the bridge painting fund, this failure might be an act of default. The trustee would be required to take whatever actions it might consider necessary to force the LBA to make the required payments.

If your bonds are in default when you buy them, you should have been told about that. Municipal bond defaults rarely come as a surprise to most observers; if the issuer of a bond you buy is in poor financial condition, you should have been informed about that.

Some investors buy defaulted bonds, hoping that the eventual workout price will yield them a large profit. Investors who do this are operating in areas far beyond the scope of this book.

CHAPTER 4

How Recent Bond Market Changes Will Affect Your Investment

Since the mid-1970s, the fixed income market, comprised of bonds and other fixed income instruments of all types, has had three major changes. First, interest rates rose to historically very high levels from 1980 to 1982, and then declined gradually back to about what they had been before the rise. Second, the market now has much greater fluctuations in rates than previously; bond market volatility has increased. Third, the market is composed of more and better informed investors.

EVALUATING THE RISE AND DECLINE OF INTEREST RATES

Interest rates had been generally rising since the mid-1940s, but they went into a steep rise starting about 1978–1979, and

reached a peak in 1980-1981. Some rates, such as those on municipal bonds, more than doubled. For example, municipal bond yields,
as measured by the Bond Buyer Average, a widely used reliable
index, went from the 5-to-6-percent range in the early 1970s to the
9-to-13 percent range in the years 1980–1982; in late 1993, it had
returned to about 6 percent. Long Treasury bond yields rose from
the 7-to-8 percent range in the early 1970s to as high as about 15
percent; in late 1993, they were back to about 6 percent. By mid-
1994, they had reached about 7.5 percent.

These rate increases resulted in enormous market losses. For
example, a municipal bond paying 6 percent interest and maturing in
twenty years, originally offered at a price of 100 percent of par, could
have sold to yield 10 percent, with a price of about 70 percent of par,
a decline of about 30 percent from its original offering price several
years earlier. A municipal bond paying 6 percent interest and maturing in thirty years, also offered at a price of 100 percent of par, could
have sold at a price of about 64 percent of par, a decline of about 36
percent from its original offering price several years earlier. These
were catastrophic declines by traditional bond standards, yet they
were common losses in just the few years from about 1978 to about
1981 to investors in bonds or fixed income investments of any sort.

In the other direction, since the early 1980s, bond prices have
generally moved up, with interest rates moving lower, so that some
long-term United States Government bonds, which were issued at
prices of about 100, were trading in late 1993 as high as 160.

WHAT INCREASED VOLATILITY MEANS TO YOU

Bonds now fluctuate more in price than they did before the late
1970s. This is quite different from a simple rise and decline. Bond
yields could have stayed unchanging at 6 percent, then moved
quickly to 12 percent and remained unchanged. This isn't what happened. Bonds did not just move upward in yield (downward in
price). They also fluctuated much more than previously, and this is
a development since the late 1970s.

This rise in volatility has had enormous consequences in all
fixed income markets, and although prices have recovered to about

their levels of the mid-1970s, the increased bond market volatility appears to be here to stay. For example, from early February, 1994, to mid-July, 1994, the long United States Treasury bond moved from a yield of about 5.80 percent to a yield of about 7.50 percent, an increase in yield of about 1.70 percent, or 170 basis points. This was an enormous decline in the market in just over five months. The long United States Treasury bond was down about 15 percent in price. This was approximately twice the much more widely publicized decline in the stock market during the same time period.

This increase in volatility is so noticeable that it has been frequently commented on by bond market participants, commentators, and analysts. For example, for a recent analysis of the new volatility of fixed income markets, and the degree to which they are interrelated, see the front page article in *The Wall Street Journal* for Friday, May 20, 1994.

TRAINING MORE AND BETTER INFORMED INVESTORS

Before the mid-1970s, investors generally were not well informed about the variety of bond investments available to them. Many of these investments could be made only with difficulty compared to many common stock investments. Most buyers of municipal bonds were banks and insurance companies, and most buyers of marketable government securities were also banks and insurance companies.

The changes in the fixed income market made it more important that investors understand more and manage better their fixed income investments. Many investor educational advances have been made, consisting of books on investment (including bond investment), educational seminars by investment firms and others, and individual efforts by securities salespeople. Investment firms especially have made major efforts to educate their customers about investments in bonds, especially municipal bonds. This has resulted in establishment of whole departments dedicated to investor education in this field.

For example, according to the Federal Reserve System, in 1970 about 31.9 percent of outstanding municipal bonds were owned by households (this figure includes unit investment trusts). This percentage stayed relatively constant until 1981, when about 30.8 percent of outstanding municipals were owned by households (including unit investment trusts); an additional 1.3 percent were owned by mutual funds and 1.1 percent by money market funds, both of which are largely owned by households.

In 1970, about 48.6 percent of outstanding municipal bonds were owned by commercial banks, with an additional 11.8 percent owned by property and casualty insurance companies, according to Federal Reserve System statistics.

By the end of 1992, the amount of municipals held by households had increased to about 52 percent of the total, and, if mutual funds and money market funds are included, households, or retail, owned about 75 percent of outstanding municipal bonds.

At the same time, the percentage of municipals owned by banks declined substantially, to about 8.5 percent of outstanding municipals in 1992. Ownership by property and casualty insurance companies rose and then declined again, and was about 12 percent of outstanding municipals in 1992.

Thus in the twenty-two years from 1970 to 1992, the percentage of municipals owned by banks has declined by over 80 percent, while households and investment vehicles largely owned by households (unit investment trusts, mutual funds, and money market funds) now account for about three-quarters of all municipal ownership. Figure 4.1 shows the trends of municipal bond ownership during the last twenty-five years.

EVALUATING THE RESULTS OF THESE MARKET CHANGES

One measure of security risk is the extent of the security's price fluctuation. Since bond prices fluctuate more than previously, they are now a riskier investment, even if the risk of default has not increased. This increased risk has been combined with greater returns and more

Figure 4.1

Public Securities Association
Trends in the Holdings of Municipal Securities
1970 - 1994:Q1

	Total Amount Outstanding	Households		Mutual Funds		Money Market Funds		Closed-end Funds		Bank Personal Trusts		Commercial Banks		Property & Casualty Insurance Companies		Other*	
		Amount	% of Total	Amount	% of Total	Amount	% of Total	Amount	% of Total	Amount	% of Total	Amount	% of Total	Amount	% of Total	Amount	% of Total
1970	144.4	46.0	31.9%									70.2	48.6%	17.0	11.8%	11.1	7.7%
1971	161.8	46.1	28.5%									82.8	51.2%	20.5	12.7%	12.4	7.7%
1972	176.5	48.4	27.4%									90.0	51.0%	24.8	14.1%	13.4	7.6%
1973	191.2	53.7	28.1%									96.7	50.5%	28.5	14.9%	12.4	6.5%
1974	208.0	62.2	29.9%									101.1	48.6%	30.7	14.7%	14.0	6.7%
1975	223.0	67.2	30.1%									102.9	46.2%	33.3	14.9%	19.6	8.8%
1976	243.9	73.7	30.2%	0.5	0.2%							106.0	43.5%	38.7	15.9%	25.0	10.3%
1977	273.6	79.8	29.2%	2.2	0.8%							115.2	42.1%	49.4	18.1%	27.1	9.9%
1978	313.5	94.0	30.0%	2.7	0.9%							126.2	40.3%	62.9	20.1%	27.7	8.8%
1979	341.5	102.0	29.9%	4.0	1.2%							135.6	39.7%	72.8	21.3%	27.1	7.9%
1980	365.4	80.0	21.9%	4.4	1.2%	1.9	0.5%					135.6	39.7%	72.8	21.3%	27.1	7.9%
1981	398.3	100.8	25.3%	5.1	1.3%	4.2	1.1%			22.5	6.2%	148.8	40.7%	80.5	22.0%	27.3	7.5%
1982	451.3	124.1	27.5%	8.0	1.8%	13.2	2.9%			21.9	5.5%	154.0	38.7%	83.9	21.1%	28.4	7.1%
1983	505.7	159.4	31.5%	13.4	2.6%	16.8	3.3%			29.2	6.5%	158.3	35.1%	87.0	19.3%	31.5	7.0%
1984	564.4	186.3	33.0%	19.1	3.4%	23.8	4.2%			33.1	6.5%	162.1	32.1%	86.7	17.1%	34.2	6.8%
1985	743.0	255.2	34.3%	33.5	4.5%	36.3	4.9%			37.9	6.7%	174.6	30.9%	84.7	15.0%	38.0	6.7%
1986	789.6	242.9	30.8%	65.3	8.3%	63.8	8.1%	1.0	0.1%	48.6	6.5%	231.7	31.2%	88.2	11.9%	48.5	6.5%
1987	873.1	332.8	38.1%	70.7	8.1%	61.4	7.0%	2.0	0.3%	59.1	7.5%	203.4	25.8%	101.9	12.9%	51.2	6.5%
1988	939.4	391.8	41.7%	78.7	8.4%	65.7	7.0%	3.3	0.4%	63.5	7.3%	174.3	20.0%	124.8	14.3%	42.3	4.8%
1989	1,004.7	442.2	44.0%	93.6	9.3%	69.4	6.9%	7.1	0.8%	67.8	7.2%	151.6	16.1%	134.1	14.3%	42.6	4.5%
1990	1,062.1	468.9	44.1%	109.1	10.3%	83.6	7.9%	12.2	1.2%	75.1	7.5%	133.8	13.3%	134.8	13.4%	43.6	4.3%
1991	1,131.6	503.8	44.5%	137.1	12.1%	89.9	7.9%	14.0	1.3%	82.5	7.8%	117.4	11.1%	136.9	12.9%	49.7	4.7%
1992	1,197.3	508.9	42.5%	173.4	14.5%	94.8	7.9%	28.1	2.5%	91.6	8.1%	103.2	9.1%	126.8 **	11.2%	51.1	4.5%
1993	1,257.8	480.8	38.2%	217.9	17.3%	103.4	8.2%	39.9	3.3%	97.6	8.2%	97.5	8.1%	134.3	11.2%	50.9	4.3%
1994:Q1	$1,270.0	$478.2	37.7%	$221.0	17.4%	$114.9	9.0%	$55.1	4.3%	$112.3	8.8%	$99.8	7.9%	$139.4	11.0%	$49.3	3.9%

* Includes non-financial corporations, state & local government general funds, savings institutions, life insurance cos, private pension funds, state & local government retirement funds, and broker\dealers.

** A series break in 1991 distorts comparisons to prior-year figures of property & casualty insurance companies.

Source: Federal Reserve System, Public Securities Association
All Amounts in Billions

MUNI 7094, XLS; 8/9/94

investor interest in bonds, especially since current returns from bonds are so much greater than those from common stocks. For example, in late 1993, the United States Treasury bond maturing in thirty years yielded about 6 percent, or about twice as much as the return from the Dow-Jones or Standard & Poor's common stock averages.

Bondholders had market operating losses, at least temporarily, with resulting operations losses to business investors. Many banks owned large amounts of long-term fixed income securities, including mortgages and similar securities as well as bonds. The losses on their securities resulted in large operating losses, and these in turn resulted sometimes in the loss of independence of the bank. Many savings banks in New York City were taken over by other banks as a result of these losses; some of these takeovers were forced by the bank regulating authorities. In some cases investors have recovered these losses, and even some profits have been shown as interest rates are back to where they were some twenty years ago.

Substantial bond portfolio losses have also occurred in the first half of 1994, as long-term interest rates, measured by the long-term treasury bond, increased by over 150 basis points, and the longest-term treasury bond fell over 15 percent in price.

If you invest in bonds, you should understand that increased bond market volatility means that your bond investments have increased market risk, even if you invest only in the very highest grade of bond. That gives you an opportunity to take advantage of market swings if you want to do so. However, it also means that you may see lower prices for your bonds, even if you don't need to sell them. A 15-percent price movement in the bond market, such as occurred in the first half of 1994, now happens occasionally, and you should be prepared for that kind of fluctuation.

You should also remember that your bond may fluctuate based on other developments. Credit risk is still a factor in bond prices, and other factors exist as well. For example, a few years ago, a large firm sold tax-exempt variable-rate bonds, which the Internal Revenue Service ruled were subject to Federal income tax. The bonds promptly declined about 10 percent in price. They were eventually redeemed at par, and the results were unpleasant rather than serious for the buyers of these bonds. You should understand that other risks than market risks exist for all fixed income investments.

Resulting New Issue Volume Increase

Partly as a result of the increased volatility, new issues of all types of bonds have increased. Refundings (repayments of old bonds by issuing new bonds) have increased, as issuers take advantage of lower interest rates and exercise the call features of their outstanding bonds to save interest costs. For example, during 1993, refundings of municipal bonds were about $150 billion, or about 60 percent of total new issue of about $250 billion. For another example, during 1993, many homeowners refinanced their mortgages, resulting in a large increase in issuance of mortgages that would not have occurred in normal markets.

HOW THE MARKET HAS RESPONDED TO THESE CHANGES

Issuers, investors, and investment bankers responded to these market changes in several ways. Changes were instituted in the bond contract, some of them highly successful. Investors also changed their investment behavior in a reaction to the changes.

Contractual Responses to the Changes

The rise in interest rates and the resulting large decline in bond prices caused some investors to realize that they had to maintain a stable value to their portfolio, even if they had to give up something to achieve this. They would be willing to give up fixed income if they could obtain stable value portfolios.

If you decide to accept fluctuating income in exchange for portfolio stability in value, you should understand that your income could fluctuate considerably. For example, income from money market funds has recently been half or less of what it was a few years ago, although it has been increasing during the first half of 1994. Some persons, especially retired persons, now have much lower incomes than previously and in some cases may have suffered some resulting hardship and possibly had to sell securities to pay household bills. You should make sure that you must have a fixed-value portfolio and that you can tolerate the resulting income fluctuations; otherwise, you might find yourself with larger income reductions than you can afford.

The following are three ways to achieve stable value: put bonds, variable-rate bonds, and bonds having a shorter term to maturity.

Put bonds.

The put bond has a feature, discussed earlier, which allows the owner of the bond to sell, or "put," the bond back to the issuer and regain his or her original investment. Naturally, the investor would only want to do this to increase his income (or portfolio value). This would be possible only if interest rates are higher (bond prices lower) than when he or she first bought the bond. In buying a bond with this option, the investor is protected against price declines with the ability to regain the investment at the time provided by the put option. The investor can abrogate the contract and regain his money. To obtain this option, the investor usually accepts a somewhat lower yield than he would get on the same bond without a put option. Remember that if you buy put bonds, you are usually giving up income in exchange for this option. You should make sure that the value of the option is high enough to make the income reduction worthwhile.

While United States Savings Bonds, with their put feature, have been offered since 1940, and the United States Treasury sold notes with a put option in the 1950s, only since about 1980 has the put option been widely available to municipal bond investors.

Variable rate bonds.

Many homeowners have a variable rate mortgage on their homes; the interest rate on the mortgage fluctuates up and down as interest rates fluctuate. The mortgage interest rate has a predetermined relationship to some readily available market rate and is adjusted periodically, usually annually. The mortgage rate is said to be "tied" to this market rate. Typical market rates are the one-year treasury borrowing rate, the prime rate banks charge their preferred customers, and the long-term treasury bond rate.

A variable rate bond works in a similar way. It pays interest that varies according to the market level. The interest paid has some predetermined relationship either to specific actively traded securities or to widely known, publicly available, and reliable indexes of interest rates. It will go up when rates go up and go down when rates go down. The result is a bond which should always have a price of about par. The investor has achieved the goal of a bond with a price of par, but has paid a price for this: the price is variable income. The investor also has a different contract than with the put bond: he or she cannot necessarily abrogate the contract and receive money back; there is only a change in interest payment to assure a price of around par. The original term of the bond remains unchanged.

If the investor wants the money back, the bond must be sold; he should be able to obtain about par when he sells it. Variable-rate bonds usually have the right to put the bond back to the issuer. The expectation, however, is that the rate will be changed to keep the bonds outstanding. Note also that the investor has given up the chance of capital gain if interest rates fall, as well as continuance of a high coupon income. The original term of his bond remains unchanged. Most individual investors probably buy variable rate bonds through the mechanism of the tax-exempt money market fund. (Variable-rate bonds are discussed more fully in Chapter 5.)

Bonds having a shorter term to maturity.

In this case, the investor buys a bond that will mature in a short time. This short maturity results in prices that will fluctuate much less as yields fluctuate. This is shown in more detail in Chapter 7. The investor has a security that won't fluctuate as much in price. However, it will mature sooner, and the investor must reinvest the principal at the rates available at that time, whatever they are. The trade-off that the investor makes is once more a variable income return in exchange for a stable principal value.

If you invest in short term obligations, you should understand that you will have to reinvest the proceeds when your present investments mature and that interest rates could easily be lower at that time. This happened to many investors during the late 1980s and early 1990s.

Behavioral Responses to the Changes

Investors in fixed income securities have also changed their investment behavior in important ways as a result of these market changes. The major changes are disintermediation and increased trading.

Disintermediation.

Disintermediation is the direct ownership of securities, rather than ownership through a financial intermediary. It usually occurs through the ownership of United States Treasury obligations, which can easily be bought and sold, including purchase directly through the Federal Reserve Bank, which operates as an agent for the United States Treasury.

Many years ago, fixed income investors bought products and services offered by institutions which were in the business of making such offerings. The intermediaries consisted primarily of savings banks, savings departments of commercial banks, savings and loan associations, and life insurance companies. The savings consisted of actual savings accounts in savings banks, commercial banks, savings and loan associations, or the savings portions of permanent plan life insurance, usually either whole-life insurance or a limited term payment or endowment plan. The returns were smaller than could be otherwise obtained, but they were guaranteed, at least for a period of time, and the investor could count on receiving them. The institution acted as a financial intermediary between the investor and the investments.

These intermediaries sometimes also provided other guarantees. The life insurance companies provided investments regulated by the states, and their surpluses provided an additional margin of safety for the policyholders. The income of the investment portion of the permanent plan insurance policies was not taxed, at least until the policy was redeemed. If the policy was exchanged for an annuity income, taxes might be further deferred.

Bank deposits and deposits in savings and loan institutions were usually insured by an agency of the United States Government, either the Federal Deposit Insurance Corporation or the Federal Savings and Loan Insurance Corporation, as appropriate, and were regulated by one of several governmental agencies. Banks and savings and loan organizations also had reserves, which provided an additional margin of safety.

In the early 1980s, investors discovered that they could obtain yields of 10 percent or more by buying United States Treasury obligations with funds that might have been yielding only 3 percent in savings accounts in banks. In fact, long lines formed at the New York Federal Reserve Bank on days that the United States Treasury offered new issues of securities. These lines, and the reason for them, were widely publicized in daily newspapers, further increasing investor knowledge and interest in direct purchase of United States Treasury obligations. Some investors doubled or even tripled their income. This income, as income from United States Treasury securities, was also exempt from state income taxes as well. In some states, such as New York, this was an important savings.

At the same time, widespread interest developed in specialized mutual funds which appeared to offer directly comparable services to those offered by banks. The most important of these were money market mutual funds.

Money market mutual funds invest in short-term securities of high quality. The price of fund shares, usually $1.00, hardly ever fluctuates, although at times of extremely high interest rate change some fund share prices have changed a little. Dividends are declared daily, and income is paid monthly to the shareholder. The investor can almost always obtain his or her money back from the fund upon request.

These funds offer a high degree of safety and flexibility to the investor and have proved extremely popular. Almost all mutual fund families offer a money market fund, and most offer both taxable and tax-free money market funds. Tax-free money market funds invest in municipal securities, and income is exempt from federal income tax.

Tax-free money market funds specializing in securities of a specific state, such as New York, exist. These are attractive to investors who are resident of that particular state, because income will be exempt from state income tax as well as from federal income tax.

At first glance, these funds appear identical to savings accounts. Actually, they differ in several important ways.

The bank interest income is stated and usually does not change frequently. The bank's net income is earned after deducting savings account interest from bank gross revenues. Money market fund income is determined directly by money market fund earnings; the investor gets what the fund earns, less the manager's charge for managing the fund. Income usually changes every day, and fund dividends are usually declared every day. Funds usually pay distributions monthly.

Banks have surpluses, and bank deposits are protected by insurance from a federal agency. Money market funds have no surpluses, and they are frequently not protected by insurance, except the normal security insurance. A possible loss in a bank will be absorbed by the bank surplus, by the bank's owners, and by the insuring agency. A possible loss in a money market fund will be absorbed by the fund investors or the fund sponsors. This important point was highlighted during the first half of 1994, when several funds had large losses; these losses were reimbursed by the firms which sponsored the funds. If you invest in money market funds, you should understand that the fund sponsors are not required to do this and may not necessarily reimburse funds for such losses in the future. Some observers believe that investors may have received a cost-free (to them) warning of possible dangers in these funds.

In fact, in late September, 1994, the sponsors of a relatively small money market fund declined to absorb the fund's investment losses. Investors apparently will lose about 6 percent of their investment. Some observers believe this could still be viewed as a low-cost warning.

Note that some banks offer insured money market funds.

Target funds invest in securities of a particular maturity year. For example, a target fund might invest in securities maturing in the year 1997; all its investments will mature in that year. Investors in that target fund are investing in securities maturing in 1997, and they could consider their investment in the fund as a bond that matures in 1997.

Trading increase.

Trading volume in the secondary market is hard to measure, especially in municipal securities, but there seems to be little doubt that trading volume has increased enormously during the last twenty years.

Registered and book entry forms.

The use of registered and book entry forms has allowed the markets to handle the increased volume. The securities industry has not had the securities transfer problems which plagued it during the 1960s, even with the recent large increase in trading and new issue volume.

Increased investor interest in bonds has resulted in many books and publications for bond investors. At the same time, buying bonds is much easier and less mysterious. The Treasury Direct service, offered by the Federal Reserve System as a means of buying United States Treasury obligations at the initial offering makes buying these securities much easier. Many firms have increased staff serving municipal bond investors, and many firms specialize in offering municipal bonds to individual investors.

CHAPTER 5

Other Municipal Security Contracts and Related Features

In the first four chapters we discussed the bond contract and some of its features. That discussion applied to all bonds, including municipal bonds. This chapter discusses some municipal securities other than bonds, and municipal derivatives. It also discusses contractual features of municipal bonds.

Not all municipal securities sold to investors are bonds; some are municipal notes, some are certificates of participation, and some may be tax-exempt commercial paper. Many contractual variations exist for each of these different municipal securities. This chapter outlines the different basic features of these various securities.

If you buy any sort of municipal security, you should know the actual nature of the security you are buying. Your salesperson should

explain the contract to you and explain to you whether you are buying a bond, note, certificate of participation (COP), tax-exempt commercial paper, or some other contract. Make sure you understand what
you are buying and that you understand the nature of the contract. You
should know the features that affect you, whom to ask in case of questions, and where to find information about your investment.

Most municipal securities issued are bonds. They are issued
under the laws of the state of the issuer. They are generally of long
term, ranging up to forty years to final maturity, although some
bonds have original maturities of less than one year. These are
almost always the first maturity of a serial issue composed of a number of maturities, possibly as many as thirty or more annual maturities. Municipal bonds are the main subject of this book.

NOTES

Notes are generally of short term, usually under one year to
maturity, but sometimes as long as two or three years to maturity.
Notes are issued under a different law than bonds, with somewhat
less stringent requirements. The guaranty of payment may also differ. For example, when New York City defaulted on its notes in 1975,
it continued to make all required payments on its bonds. The value
of the bonds fell sharply due to the default on the notes and uncertainty about continued payment on the bonds, but the bonds continued to be paid.

Notes are usually issued to meet short-term financial needs.
They may be issued in anticipation of receipt of taxes (tax anticipation notes, or TANs), revenues (revenue anticipation notes, or
RANs), both taxes and revenues (TRANs) or of issuance of bonds
(bond anticipation notes, or BANs). Sometimes, when notes mature,
the anticipated source of repayment has not materialized, so a new
set of notes may be issued to pay the old ones at maturity; the notes
are said to be "rolled over." Usually there are limits as to how often
this may be done; for example, in New York State, bond anticipation notes must be rolled over into bonds in two years. Continual
note rollover is generally considered bad financial practice, and it
may be financially unsound as well. Long-term financial needs

should be met by long-term financing. Short-term financing should meet only short-term financial needs. Use of short-term financing techniques to meet long-term needs has sometimes resulted in much higher interest rates, if interest rates rise, or in actual lack of availability of funds in periods of tight money.

CERTIFICATES OF PARTICIPATION

A Certificate of Participation (COP) is a security that represents an interest in payments which the issuer has promised to make, but which are subject to annual appropriation by the issuer's governing body. The issuer must actually appropriate the funds each year.

Usually, the security is a lease of real estate, equipment, or a similar piece of property. Examples are office buildings, trucks, and computer equipment. COPs offer a convenient way for the issuer to obtain property easily and conveniently, and pay for it on the installment plan.

However, this lease sometimes need not be continued if the issuer does not wish to continue with it. Sometimes voter disapproval may lead to a referendum on whether to continue paying the COPs. This adds an element of risk not present in bonds. COPs can be insured. If the COPs are insured, there is, of course, protection from the bond insurance company.

Any buyer of a COP should understand that he or she has not bought a bond and does not necessarily have the protection and security provided by a bond. If the annual appropriation is not made by the issuer, the security owner might not, and probably will not, be paid.

For example, Brevard County, Florida, leased a new operations center, which was financed by an issue of COPs. The COPs were also insured by Municipal Bond Insurance Association (MBIA), a leading bond insurance company. A group of citizens in the county brought forward a citizens' initiative referendum to cancel the lease which the County had made for the center. Some citizens did not like the building or its location. Others did not like the fact that the building had not been voted on by the citizens of the county. The referendum was widely reported on in the municipal bond business press. MBIA, with financial help from other major bond insurance firms, led an active fight against the referendum; they would, of course, have had to continue payments on the COPs if Brevard County did not continue the payments.

The referendum lost, but not by much. Although these particular COPs continue to be paid, the whole episode indicates the risks of investing in COPs. If your COPs are insured, all may be well. Still, any investor should make sure he is being fully compensated for his recognized risk.

TAX-EXEMPT COMMERCIAL PAPER

Tax-exempt commercial paper (TXCP) is a short-term instrument with maturities up to 270 days, although thirty to sixty days is usual. It is issued for short-term financing purposes, sometimes in place of notes. TXCP is a coupon-bearing, bearer instrument, with next-day delivery. It is usually bought by large institutions, rarely by individual investors. It is not a bond, and it is issued under a different set of laws.

Tax-exempt commercial paper may be used as a substitute for issues of notes (RANs, TANs, TRANs, and BANs), and used as part of an overall cash management procedure. It usually offers the issuer more flexibility than the issue of notes.

Tax-exempt commercial paper may be used by large issuers as a means of financing continuing construction or development projects. The issuer issues TXCP continually to finance the construction as it occurs. Periodically, as required, the issuer sells long-term bonds and repays the TXCP. Meanwhile, long-term reserve investments remain untouched by the needs of the capital development program, and continue to earn their regular income.

Finally, TXCP may be used as a source of permanent financing, and simply rolled over upon maturity.

VARIABLE-RATE BONDS

A variable-rate bond, or, as it is frequently called, a variable-rate demand obligation (VRDO), is a bond whose coupon rate may be changed during the life of the bond. The interest rate is reset periodically to market rates applicable at that time. The bond contract, as contained in the bond indenture, states the method of resetting the rate, including the amount, timing, and limits. A wide variety of contracts are possible and, in fact, exist. Interest rate changes may occur with frequencies ranging from daily to semiannually or even annually, depending on the bond contract. The contract also usually has some security agreement that provides liquidity.

The variable-rate bond gives the investor a long-term contract, while avoiding the possibility of price declines intrinsic in fixed rate long-term bonds. However, to achieve this, the investor gives up the higher yield possible from a fixed rate bond.

The issuer obtains the advantage of a lower, short-term rate, while avoiding the possible problem of put bonds, which might be put back to the issuer under unfavorable circumstances.

Although a wide variety of contracts exists for variable-rate bonds, the newer issues generally follow a pattern, with four main features:

1. The holder of the security can demand payment at times predetermined by the contract. This put feature allows the holder to treat the contract as a short-term contract, even though the expectation and usual practice is for the holder to accept a revised interest rate on the security.

2. The interest rate paid on the bond changes at set intervals according to the market. It might be tied to an index, set by a third party, or set by an auction process.

   Typical indices used for this purpose include the Bond Buyer index, one of the J. J. Kenny indices, one of the PSA indices, or one of the United States Treasury rates, such as the 90-day bill rate or the long-term bond rate. The interest rate paid on the bonds is set to bear some relationship to the index. For example, the rate might be set at the latest 90-day bill rate, minus 35 basis points.

   The rate might be set by an auction process. This is commonly used to set the rates of municipal variable-rate derivatives, and sometimes for the variable rate bonds as well. The rate is set at a level which will ensure that all the bonds are resold.

Finally, the rate might be set by the underwriter or other financial advisor at a level appropriate for that bond.

3. A security agreement provides assurance that the owner's demand will be met. This is frequently in the form of a letter of credit or a purchase agreement with a major commercial bank.

   Variable-rate bonds are frequently also coupled with a remarketing agreement by the underwriter to find a buyer on a "best efforts" basis if the bondowner wants to sell. Although no guarantee is made of actually locating a buyer at a price acceptable to the seller, the underwriter can usually find one. The expectation is that the underwriter will find another buyer and that the standby security agreement will not be needed.

4. Frequently the variable-rate bond can be converted to a fixed-rate bond by the issuer. The issuer must meet certain conditions of notice and timing to do this. The security holder must tender his security, but usually may accept the new fixed-rate security in exchange. The standby security agreement almost always expires when the conversion to a fixed rate security is done.

   Variable-rate bonds allow the owner to have a long-term instrument which will always sell around par. These securities are popular with tax-free money market accounts for that reason, but they will also appeal to many individual investors. However, in return for a security always worth about par, the investor accepts fluctuating income; in times of declining interest rates, such as occurred during 1993 and through January, 1994, the investor's income will decline. This decline could be quite large.

MUNICIPAL DERIVATIVES

The discussion of this fast-moving field may be obsolete by the time it is printed, but any book on municipal bonds should cover municipal derivatives to some extent.

We will discuss three topics: (1) floaters and inverse floaters; (2) detachable call features; and (3) interest rate swaps.

Derivatives, especially floaters and inverse floaters, were originally developed by enterprising underwriters for the municipal bond mutual fund industry and sold to that industry. Few, if any, derivatives have been sold to individual investors. However, that too could change at any time. Already, sales to individuals have been proposed at major municipal bond firms, although the firms have always rejected these proposals so far.

Municipal bond mutual funds have found that inverse floaters allow them to maintain a high yield in times of falling interest rates, because inverse floater interest payments rise when bond yields fall. This, in turn, allows the funds to remain competitive, because many municipal mutual fund investors choose mutual funds based on the current yield of the fund. Of course, in times of rising interest rates, such as the first half of 1994, inverse floaters no longer help the mutual funds. In fact, the income declines and the price of the inverse floater also declines, a double hit to the funds.

Floaters and Inverse Floaters

Variable-rate bonds were discussed in the previous section. A floater, or floating rate bond, as a derivative, is a variable-rate bond that results from splitting a fixed rate bond into two parts.

A fixed-rate bond, with a fixed coupon and a final maturity date, may be divided into two parts, called a floater and an inverse floater. The issuer's interest and principal payments remain unchanged during the life of the bond, but the division of interest payments between the floater and the inverse floater may, and almost always does, vary during the life of the bond.

The rate paid on the floater is a variable rate, determined by one of the ways used to set rates on variable rate bonds. A common method is to have a periodic auction of the floaters. The rate paid on the inverse floater is the difference between the fixed rate paid on the combination of floater and inverse floater (which is, of course, the original bond), and the amount paid on the floater. In many cases, the floaters are auctioned anew every thirty-five days, and a new rate is set based on the results of the auction. In addition, a fee is usually paid to the firm conducting the auction; this fee is usually about 0.28 percent per year.

For example, suppose an issuer issues a bond with a 6-percent coupon, maturing in twenty years. The underwriter can create floaters and inverse floaters in the following way: The underwriter takes a certain amount of bonds, say $200,000 face amount. He splits this into two parts, $100,000 face amount of floaters and $100,000 face amount of inverse floaters. The interest paid on the floaters is determined according to a method used for variable rate bonds. The inverse floaters receive what is left over from the 6 percent paid on the total amount ($200,000) of bonds. Both the floaters and the inverse floaters are separate securities, so both, along with the original bond, receive their own CUSIP number.

For example, suppose the initial rate set on the floaters was 3 percent. The $100,000 face amount of floaters receives $3,000, representing 3 percent of the face amount of the bonds. The total interest paid on the $200,000 face amount of bonds is 6 percent of $200,000, or $12,000. The inverse floaters will receive what is left over, or $9,000 in this case, less the small auction fee. When the bonds mature or are called, the bondholders will receive the par amount of their bonds.

Suppose interest rates fall so that the inverse floaters receive only 2 percent. They will receive $2,000, and the inverse floaters will receive $10,000.

But suppose interest rates rise, as they started doing in February, 1994. Suppose the applicable short-term rates rise to 4 percent. The floaters will receive $4,000, and the interest paid on the inverse floaters will fall to only $8,000. Thus in the case of rising rates, not only will the income from the inverse floaters decline, but the price of the inverse floaters will decline as well, along with bond prices generally. The price of the floaters should remain about par.

The underwriter need not restrict the amount of floaters to $100,000 as in the above example. He could, for example, create $180,000 in floaters and only $20,000 face amount of inverse floaters. These are called leveraged floaters, and the inverse floater interest payments go up and down much faster with the market than the rates of regular inverse floaters.

Usually the floaters and the inverse floaters may be linked to recreate the original securities, and the recreated securities may be delinked again to recreate the original floaters and inverse floaters.

Floaters and inverse floaters need not be created at the time of issue. An underwriter can create floaters and inverse floaters at any time. He buys a block of bonds in the secondary market, or from a new issue syndicate, and sets up the mechanism to create floaters and inverse floaters, or even leveraged floaters. Theoretically, this could be done with blocks of any size, but usually blocks of $10,000,000 par amount or more are used to make the transaction worthwhile.

How to evaluate an inverse floater

Suppose you own an inverse floater. How much is it worth, assuming that you know the value of the underlying bond?

At issue time, the bond is usually worth about 100 percent of par, and both the floater and the inverse floater are also worth about 100 each. Suppose the bond rises in price to 110. If you had $200,000 of the original bond, the value would be $220,000. The floater always has a value of about par. In this case, the floater would be worth about $100,000. The inverse floater would be worth the difference, about $120,000, or a price of about 120. The floater and the inverse floater can always be linked, so there will always be a connection in price between the value of the derivatives and the value of the underlying bond.

This does not mean that a trader providing a bid would necessarily bid you the value you have just calculated. The value is only an evaluation, an idea of approximately where the bond would sell in the marketplace. In fact, owners of inverse floaters have recently complained that the bids they receive don't equal what they think the bonds are worth, and occasionally they don't receive any bids at all.

Suppose the price of the bond goes down to 90. In this case, the underlying bonds are worth $180,000. The floater is still worth $100,000, so the inverse floater is worth about $80,000, or a price of about 80. Note that the inverse floater moves in the same direction as the bond market, but at a much faster rate; we say that it is much more volatile than a regular bond. Leveraged inverse floaters are, of course, even more volatile.

Summarizing, to compute the theoretical price of an inverse floater, obtain the market price of the underlying bond; this could be simply an evaluation from one of the bond evaluation companies. Multiply it by two. Deduct 100. The result is the evaluation price of the inverse floater. In the experience of the author, the results are within the reasonable range, considering the difficulty of finding bids for this kind of security.

Detached Call Options

Most municipal bonds have a call feature, which gives the issuer the right to redeem the bond before maturity by paying the call price and accrued interest to the call date. Usually, the issuer retains the right to call the bonds.

But suppose the issuer were to sell the right to call the bonds. If he did that, he would have created a municipal derivative called a *detached call option.*

If the issuer sells the call feature, he can no longer call the bond; the bond has become noncallable from his point of view. The issuer has given up an important option; however, he has been compensated for this by the price he received for the call.

The buyer of the call can call the bond under the terms of the contract and may wish to do so when the call feature becomes effective. If the call buyer is also the bondholder, the bonds are noncallable for as long as he or she owns the call feature; no one else can call the bonds.

If the issuer does not sell the detached call option at the time the bond is issued, he may not be able to sell it later. The proceeds of the sale of the call option are part of the proceeds of the issue. If the call feature is sold later, the issue may then violate arbitrage restrictions, and possibly other regulations as well. Very few detached call options have been sold.

Interest Rate Swaps

Suppose you have an obligation to make an interest payment each month, and the payment is variable, so that the size of the payment depends on the market level of interest rates. You would prefer to make a constant interest payment. To do this, you make an arrangement with another person to pay a fixed rate of interest each month and he or she pays to you a variable rate of interest each month. You set the terms of the deal so that the payment you receive is identical to the variable amount you must pay each month.

Each interest payment is based on the same fixed amount of money, the *notional amount.* This amount has never changed hands; it is only an amount which determines the size of the interest payments that you and the other person pay to each other. In settling up each month, each of you owes the other some money, so the one owing the larger amount pays the difference to the other.

You have just converted your variable rate payment into a fixed-rate payment. The variable amount you receive will just equal the amount you have agreed to pay, and you will be left with the net fixed-rate payment. You have, in effect, made an interest rate swap.

In most cases, you are obligated to pay your contracted amount to the other party, and he or she pays the contracted amount to you. But suppose the other party defaults? You may still be obligated to pay, even though you are not receiving any payments in return. Therefore, the credit of the other party, or *contra-party*, is important to you, as your credit is important to the contra-party. Since interest rate swaps can continue for many years, long-term credit concerns are a major factor in entering into these transactions.

The variable rate part of the interest rate swap is frequently linked to indices. A common set of indices used for these is a set put out by the Public Securities Association (PSA), and published every day in the *Bond Buyer.*

TAX-EXEMPTION OF MUNICIPAL SECURITIES

The tax-exempt feature of municipal securities is probably the most widely advertised and best-known feature of these securities. However, this feature has limits. If you invest in municipals, you should understand these limits.

These securities are generally exempt from the federal income tax. However, not all municipal securities are exempt from this tax.

A few (taxable municipals) are subject to federal income tax; as much as 5 percent of annual issuance is subject to federal income tax.

Some municipal bonds are exempt from federal income tax, but are still subject to the alternative minimum tax (AMT); these are generally bonds issued for a private purpose, after August 7, 1986. You should know whether your bonds are subject to AMT. Your salesperson should tell you whether they are so subject, and information reports from reporting agencies will also tell you this. This feature will also be stated in the official statement, and will usually be stated on the bond certificate.

Tax-exemption is not protected by the United States Constitution. Until recently, many people in the municipal industry thought that tax-exemption was so protected. In 1986, the State of South Carolina brought suit contesting the new federal requirement that municipal bonds be in registered or book entry form for the interest to be exempt from federal income taxes. The Supreme Court of the United States decided against South Carolina in that suit, but at the same time also ruled that Congress had the right to tax municipal bond interest if it chose to do so. Few people think that Congress is likely to do this, but it is now clear that Congress has the right to do it, and that the tax-exemption of municipal bond interest is not constitutionally protected.

Most states exempt interest income of bonds issued by the state and its local governments from state income taxation. Six states tax interest income of their own obligations. Almost all states that have a state income tax subject interest income from out-of-state securities to their state income tax. For high-tax states such as New York, this makes bonds issued within the state much more attractive than those issued outside of the state. You should know whether your state is one of the few that taxes the interest income of its own issues. If it is, bonds issued within the state may not have any particular tax reason for purchase.

A few issuers, those which have Commonwealth status, are exempt from income taxation in all states as well as from federal taxation. The largest issuer right now is Puerto Rico, but issues of Hawaii and Alaska, before they became states, if any are still outstanding, are exempt from both federal and local taxation, as are bonds of comparable other, smaller issuers, such as United States Virgin Islands, Guam, and a few others.

The tax-exemption of these securities applies only to income tax. They are still subject to capital gains taxes, personal property taxes, estate taxes, and other taxes as prescribed by law. These laws change frequently, and are beyond the scope of this book.

Don't let the tax-exempt feature cause you to disregard other important features of your bond or cause you to overlook other features which might make the bonds questionable investments. The municipal bond industry has promoted tax-exemption heavily. For you, tax-exemption should be just another feature of your bonds. Most municipal bonds would still be attractive investments even if they were not tax-exempt; they would just have to pay a higher interest rate. After all, few corporations have the power to levy taxes, nor do many businesses offer essential public services that no one can do without and for which the business can charge any reasonable price it wishes to charge.

Don't be afraid to consider taxable municipals as an investment, if they otherwise meet your requirements. As these bonds increase in number, investors are increasingly becoming aware of them and municipal dealers are increasingly offering them to their customers. One well-known dealer in the New York City area is now actively promoting a taxable municipal fund. For many accounts, such as retirement accounts, which are tax-sheltered, taxable municipals and mutual funds containing taxable municipals might be quite suitable, although there would be little point in buying tax-free municipals for such accounts, since usually all distributions from such accounts are subject to federal income tax.

UNDERSTANDING ORIGINAL ISSUE DISCOUNT AND MARKET DISCOUNT

Suppose you buy a bond at time of issue which matures in twenty years, and for which you pay a price of 80. Part of your income over the years will be the coupon income you receive, but another part of your income will be the gain you receive when your bond matures. You will have a 20-point gain, assuming you hold the bond until maturity.

This discount you received when you bought the bond is called *Original Issue Discount*. It is considered interest because it is considered a payment for the use of your capital which you invested when you bought the bond. Special Internal Revenue Service regulations apply to original issue discount, and these regulations change from time to time. If you own a bond which has original issue discount, the discount interest accrual applies to you for the time you own the bond, even if you didn't buy it at the original offering.

For municipals, this would be municipal interest, which would usually be exempt from federal income taxation. However, the accrual of the discount might affect the cost basis of your bond.

If the bond's income is taxable, such as income from treasury or corporate bonds, the accrual might also be taxable, and taxes would be payable, even though no cash income was actually received.

At one time, original issue discount was accrued using a straight-line method. Now, a yield-basis method is likely to be used. Both of these methods are discussed in the chapter on financial mathematics.

The Internal Revenue Service regulations that apply to original issue discount change from time to time. A discussion of these is beyond the scope of this book. Your tax advisor or accountant should be able to advise you fully on original issue discount and its tax treatment.

Many bonds now outstanding were sold with a discount so small that the OID regulations don't apply. They are said to come in under the *de minimus* rule. One rule commonly applied was that a discount of less than $1/4$ point for each year until maturity was not original issue discount. For example, a bond with twenty years to maturity which sold at issue at a price higher than 95 would not have the OID regulation applicable. If this applies to bonds you own, you should know about it.

If you own OID bonds, you should know it, and you should consult with your accountant on how to report this on your income tax return.

If you buy a bond which was issued at par, but declined in the market before you bought it, you have bought a bond which has market discount. Special Internal Revenue Service regulations also apply to market discount. You should know that your bond has market discount, and you should consult with your tax advisor on how to treat this market discount for tax purposes.

CUSIP (COMMITTEE FOR UNIFORM SECURITIES IDENTIFICATION PROCEDURE) NUMBERS AND THEIR USE

Suppose you wanted to refer to a particular security, say American Telephone and Telegraph Common Stock. You might call it by the full name (above), you might say *AT&T,* you might abbreviate it *A. T. & T.,* you might write *Am Tel and Tel,* and you might even use the New York Stock Exchange ticker symbol *T.* All of these would refer to the same security. You can easily see that many different security firms, working with the same securities, would have many different ways of referring to the same security. You can also see that if they wanted to work together to identify securities that they transferred between themselves in the course of trading, they would need a common way of referring to the securities. This need became particularly apparent during the securities transfer problems that developed during the late 1960s. A committee was formed to establish a uniform way of identifying securities. The result was the CUSIP number, named for the Committee for Uniform Securities Identification Procedure. Every security has a unique CUSIP number identification.

CUSIP numbers are assigned by the CUSIP Service Bureau, part of Standard & Poor's, which is part of McGraw-Hill, under contract with the American Bankers Association. The CUSIP Service Bureau publishes annually a complete directory of CUSIP numbers, in two large blue volumes, as well as a shorter volume restricted to corporate securities, and periodic updates as new CUSIP numbers are assigned. The vast majority of CUSIP numbers (about 95 percent) are assigned to municipal bonds.

The CUSIP number consists of a total of nine numbers and letters. The first six numbers (or letters) identify the actual issuer of the security. The next two numbers or letters identify the particular security of the issuer. The last number is a check digit, used for processing purposes to help ensure the accuracy of the first eight digits.

The first six digits are called the base number. Each issuer has its own base number. Some issuers, such as New York City, which have issued many securities, require more than one base number, but these are rare. Most issuers have only one base number.

The next two digits, numbers seven and eight, identify the particular security of the issuer. For municipal bonds, these identify each different bond the issuer has issued. For municipals, these are letters or a letter and a number. For example, if an issuer has issued three bonds, and these are its first issues, the bonds might have *AA*, *AB*, and *AC* respectively as the seventh and eighth digits of the CUSIP numbers assigned to the bonds.

The ninth digit is used for check purposes. Some firms don't bother with the ninth digit.

MSRB Rule G-34 requires that a CUSIP number be assigned to all new issues of municipal bonds, with minor exceptions.

Figure 1.2, the Allegheny County IDA bond, shows its CUSIP number printed on the bond. The CUSIP number is *017292DQ3*. The base number is *017292*. All bonds issued by Allegheny County Industrial Development Authority will have this base number. *DQ* identifies this particular bond; of all the bonds issued by Allegheny County Industrial Development Authority, only this bond has seventh and eighth digits of *DQ*. The check digit is *3*.

If you buy a municipal bond, the CUSIP number should be printed on your confirmation, in compliance with MSRB Rule G-15. You should know the CUSIP numbers of all your bonds. They provide complete, unique identification of your securities. You probably won't need to bother with the check digit, although your broker may ask you for it when you sell your bonds.

Understanding the Importance of United States Treasury Obligations

United States Treasury obligations are important to all bond investors anywhere in the world for a variety of reasons. The U.S. Treasury is the largest issuer of securities in the world; the securities are of the highest quality; they are widely held, actively traded, and extensively reported; many other securities trade in some relation to Treasuries; and they are actively used for hedging purposes.

Over 4 trillion dollars worth of United States debt is outstanding, with new issues at least every week. This debt is of the highest quality. For national government debt, this does not mean that the debt will be paid; modern government finance allows any national government to pay its debt by simply printing the money to pay it. In the words of Benjamin Graham, "the question is not whether the investor will get his money, but what the money will be worth when he gets it."[*] Compared with the rest of the world, the United States has an excellent record of maintaining the value of its money, in spite of continuing concerns with inflation in the United States. Indeed, in some countries, United States currency has actually circulated as a medium of exchange in preference to the local currency, because United States money has maintained its value so much better than the local currency. In some countries, prices have been advertised in United States money, although local government authorities have usually stopped this practice.

The value of United States money has been maintained for years; a wealthy person in the United States 100 years ago, say with $1,000,000, would still be considered wealthy today. Few other countries can make this statement, and in most countries the value of money has been wiped out several times over. This includes nations which were world powers as recently as 1900.

The debt is widely held. All over the world, United States Treasury debt is regarded as a premier investment. As a result, worldwide active trading markets exist. If an owner of United States Treasury obligations wants to sell them at 2:00 A.M., he or she simply calls one of the Far Eastern markets and makes his trade. Some New York firms now maintain twenty-four hour trading desks, so you might not even have to make a long distance call. The securities can be easily bought or sold, in large or small amounts, at small trading cost. They are truly among the world's best investment vehicles.

Many other securities trade in relation to Treasuries; we say they "trade off" Treasuries. Some securities, such as various derivative products, are explicitly priced relative to Treasuries of comparable maturity. Other securities, such as corporate bonds and Government National Mortgage Association (GNMA) securities, trade in their own markets, but their trading levels are compared to those of Treasuries of comparable maturity. Frequently reports of new issues of corporate bonds or GNMA obligations will report on the relation of the yield of the new securities to yields of comparable maturity Treasuries.

---

[*]Benjamin Graham, *The Intelligent Investor*, pp. 127–28. New York: Harper & Brothers, Publishers, 1949.

Treasuries are sometimes used to hedge positions in these securities, even though they are not always a perfect hedge. For an analysis of recent hedging of securities other than Treasuries, especially mortgage-backed securities with Treasury obligations, and the problems it can cause, see the front page article in *The Wall Street Journal* for May 20, 1994.

HOW TREASURY OBLIGATIONS CAN INFLUENCE TRADING STRATEGIES

Sometimes actual trading strategies are implemented by portfolio managers using these relationships. For example, some years ago, portfolio managers would sometimes trade Bell System (American Telephone and Telegraph Company and its subsidiaries) bonds, almost all of which at that time had the highest ratings, with Treasuries. When the Bell System bonds traded close to Treasuries, they would sell the Bell System bonds and buy Treasuries; when the spreads opened up, and Bell System bonds traded considerably cheaper than Treasuries, the portfolio managers would sell their Treasuries and buy Bell System bonds again.

Yield levels of municipal securities are also frequently compared to those of Treasuries, and trades are frequently suggested based on these relative levels. When municipal yields are high compared to yields on Treasuries of comparable maturity, investors may obtain tax-free yields comparable, or close to, the taxable yields on Treasuries. Many investors may find this attractive and make the swaps.

For example, one large retail brokerage firm publishes the ratio of municipal bond yields to United States Treasury yields of comparable maturity. On May 17, 1994, these yields ranged from about 70 percent of Treasury yields for bonds maturing in two years to about 82 percent of Treasury yields for long-term bonds. These ratios indicate that for most investors, short-term municipals were not particularly attractive, but long-term municipals did provide an attractive after-tax return compared with United States Treasury bonds.

If you have any bond investments at all, you should follow the United States Treasury market regularly to have some idea of the level of interest rates, as set by the world's most important fixed-income marketplace. The United States Treasury market is reported daily by most major newspapers. You should always consider Treasuries as an alternative to your municipal portfolio, based on considerations of quality and yield. In fact, a recent government investigation showed that many investors in municipal bonds would actually be better off economically if they owned Treasuries instead of their municipals; the after-tax yield would be greater from the Treasuries. This, of course, does not allow for the investor's desire to have income on which he pays no federal income taxes, as well as for other important, non-economic factors.

EXAMINING THE PUBLIC DEBT OF THE UNITED STATES

Figure 6.1 shows the public debt of the United States, as of December 31, 1993, and is adapted from Chart A30 of the *Federal Reserve Bulletin* for May, 1994. It shows the public debt broken down by marketable debt held by the public, nonmarketable debt held by the public, and government account series debt.

About three-quarters of the public debt is held by the public; that is, it is owned by individuals, corporations, state and local governments, pension funds, and other investors, but not the United States Government or its agencies.

About two-thirds of the debt can be bought and sold by its owners. This is called marketable debt, and it is reported in many daily newspapers. Three types of marketable securities exist: United States Treasury bills, notes, and bonds.

United States Treasury Bills

United States Treasury bills are one of the three marketable instruments of the United States public debt. They have maturities of up to one year and are used for short-term, high-grade investments by a wide variety of investors.

Figure 6.1

PUBLIC DEBT OF THE UNITED STATES

as of 12/31/93

	AMOUNT (BILLIONS)	PERCENT
Marketable		
Bills	714.6	15.8
Notes	1,764.0	38.9
Bonds	495.9	10.9
Total	2,989.5	65.9
Nonmarketable		
Savings bonds	169.4	3.7
SLGS	149.5	3.3
Other	43.5	1.0
Total	362.4	8.0
Total held by public	3,351.9	73.9
Government Account Series	1,150.0	25.4
Total interest bearing debt	4,532.3	99.9
Other	3.4	.1
Total	4,535.7	100.0

Source: Federal Reserve System, United States Treasury Department

Treasury bills (T-bills) are what is called *discount paper.* They have a final maturity date, but no explicit interest is paid or accrued; instead, T-bills trade below par (at a discount) and the owner earns interest when he or she sells the bill for more than the purchase price, or when it matures. The difference between sale price and purchase price is interest and is reported as interest on the owner's income tax return; T-bills do not have capital gains or losses.

Four types of Treasury bills exist: 90-day bills, 181-day bills, one-year bills, and cash management bills. Each week, an issue of 90-day bills and 181-day bills is auctioned on Monday, for delivery and payment on the following Thursday. Thirteen weeks later, a new issue of 181-day bills is sold, and the previous 181-day bills are reopened with a new auction of what are now 90-day bills. Each month bills that mature in approximately one year are sold. Periodically, the Treasury sells cash management bills. Cash management bills are not offered frequently and are not offered to the typical individual investor. They are sold in large amounts, and for short maturity periods.

Treasury bills have a $10,000 minimum amount, with multiples of $1,000 over that amount. If you have enough to buy them, T-bills offer a suitable alternative to bank deposits and money market funds for money you want readily available. They can easily be sold, the income is exempt from state income taxes, and quotes are readily available in many newspapers. However, you will need the minimum amount of $10,000 to buy bills.

Treasury bills are traded on a discount yield basis. The actual discount from par is computed, then deducted from par to compute the actual price.

In mathematical terms,

Discount   =   (Actual days to maturity/360) × (Rate)
Price   =   (100) × (1 – discount)
(Price is expressed as a percentage of par.)

For example, on Monday, May 16, 1994, the United States Treasury sold bills maturing on August 18, 1994, for delivery on Thursday, May 19, 1994, at an average discount yield of 4.22 percent and an average dollar price of 98.933. The calculations work out as follows:

Discount rate   =   4.22 percent
Discount   =   (91/360) × (.0422)

(There are 91 days from May 19 to August 18)

                 =   (.2527778) × (.0422)

$$
\begin{aligned}
&= \quad .0106672 \\
\text{Price} \quad &= \quad (100) \times (1 - .0106672) \\
&= \quad (100) \times (.9893328) \\
&= \quad 98.933
\end{aligned}
$$

Thus, if you bought $10,000 par amount of these bills, for delivery on May 19, 1994, you would pay $9,893.30 on that date and receive your bills. You would receive $10,000 on August 18, 1994, for net interest income of $106.70.

Suppose you sold your bills on July 10, 1994, for $9,950.00. You would then receive interest income of $56.70 ($9,950.00 − $9,893.30).

Treasury bills are sold at auction. Both competitive bids and noncompetitive bids are allowed. Noncompetitive bidders obtain their bills at the average of the awarded competitive bids.

The Federal Reserve System, acting as an agent for the Treasury, determines how many bills it wants to sell. It then deducts the noncompetitive bids to determine how many bills it wants to sell competitively. The competitive bids are then awarded bills in order of decreasing bid prices. Awards are made starting with the highest bid and filling bids in order of decreasing bid price. Finally, all the desired bills are sold. The bidders at the price that results in filling the total amount to be sold do not get their bid filled in full; instead they get partially filled, and the percentage filled is reported in the papers.

The noncompetitive bids are then awarded in full, up to the maximum allowable amount, at the average price of the competitive bids.

Treasury bills are among the most important instruments of Federal Reserve open market operations. Much of the management of the country's money supply is done through buying and selling in this market. The Federal Reserve System tightens money by selling bills, and loosens credit by buying bills.

Treasury bills are quoted on a discount yield basis, in a dealer market. This means that the dealer makes a profit by offering to buy at one price and offering to sell at a higher price; dealers do not charge a commission for executing trades, but buy and sell for their own account. For example, suppose the listing in the Treasury Bills section of the daily United States Treasury market shows:

| Aug 18 | 4.21 | 4.19 | +0.01 | 4.32 |

This means that for the bills maturing on August 18, the dealer will pay a 4.21 discount yield and offer to sell at a 4.19 discount yield. This yield is .01 higher than the closing yield on the previous day, and the bond equivalent yield is 4.32 percent.

If these bills mature in 91 days, the 4.21 bid will give a price computed as follows:

Discount = (4.21) × (91 / 360) = .01064
Price   = (100) × (1.00000 − .01064) = 98.936

The dealer will bid you $9,893.60 for $10,000 face amount of bills.

For bills maturing in 91 days, the 4.19 offer will give a price computed as follows:

Discount = (4.19) × (91 / 360) = .01059
Price   = (100) × (1.00000 − .01059) = 98.941

The dealer will offer to sell these bills to you for $9,894.10 for $10,000 face amount of bills.

Thus, if the dealer buys $10,000 of 91-day bills at 4.21 and sells them at 4.19, he will make fifty cents gross profit on the deal.

You can buy bills from your broker, or you can buy them directly from the Treasury, through the Federal Reserve System, using a method called Treasury Direct. You can submit your bid; you will probably want to bid noncompetitively. Your bank or broker can submit your bid for you, if you wish; they will usually charge a fee, probably about $50.00.

United States Treasury Notes

United States Treasury notes are coupon instruments; that is, they bear interest at a stated rate and pay interest semiannually. Calculations of accrued interest are done on an exact days/exact days basis, using a 365-day year (366 days during leap years). They are now offered only in book-entry form, but in 1994 some older notes were still available in registered form.

Terms to maturity range from two years to ten years at time of issue. Notes do not have a call feature. Notes with a two- or three-year term to maturity at time of issue are available in minimum amounts of $5,000, and multiples of $1,000 over that amount. Notes with four or more years to maturity at time of issue are available in multiples of $1,000, with a minimum amount of $1,000.

The major new issues of notes are a monthly offering of two-year and five-year notes, and quarterly offerings of three-year and ten-year notes. Like Treasury bills, notes are sold competitively and noncompetitively, through the Treasury Direct system.

For example, a recent note issue had a coupon of 7.25 percent and matures in May, 2004. These notes were recently reported in the daily Treasury Bonds and Notes section as follows:

May 04　　n　　7.25　　100-03　　100-05　　+11　　7.24

These securities mature in May, 2004. The code "n" means that they are notes. The coupon rate of the notes is 7.25; interest will be paid semiannually in May and November. The bid price is 100-03, and 100-05 is the offered price. The United States Government bond dealer will bid 100 and 3/32 for the notes, and offer them at 100 and 5/32. These are dollar prices of 100.09375 and 100.15625 respectively. This was an increase of 11/32 from the closing price the previous day. The notes offered a yield to maturity of 7.24 percent; yield and its meaning is discussed more fully in Chapter 7.

Based on the report, for $10,000 face amount of these notes, the dealer will offer you $10,009.38, and sell them to you at $10,015.63, a difference of $6.25. This represents his operating profit on the trade.

Notes constitute nearly 40 percent of the overall public debt and about 60 percent of the marketable debt. They are the major source of short- to medium-term obligations available to you. New issues of notes are available in large amounts, are quite marketable, and don't have call features. This makes them particularly attractive investments for individual investors.

Like Treasury bills, you can buy notes directly using the Treasury Direct system. You will probably want to bid noncompetitively to be sure of getting your notes at market rates. Notes are offered so frequently that you can almost always be sure of buying some at a new offering in the near future.

United States Treasury Bonds

United States Treasury bonds constitute the marketable obligations of the United States Government with the longest available term to maturity, going out as far as thirty years in maturity. Like notes, they are coupon instruments, bearing interest, which is payable semiannually. Also like notes, they use a 365-day year, with accrued interest computed using exact days/exact days.

Many bonds have a call feature, and if they are callable, they are almost always callable at par five years before final maturity.

Bonds have a denomination of $1,000, except that some denominations of $500 exist; these are called "baby bonds," and are almost always for earlier issues.

Like bills and notes, United States Treasury bonds are traded in a dealer market. The dealer makes a profit by the difference between his buying price and his selling price.

For example, the longest-term bond outstanding in May, 1994, matures in August, 2023. It has a 6.25 percent coupon, is not callable, and during May, 1994, was quoted at 85-22 bid and 85-24 asked. The entire report was as follows:

Aug 23   6.25   85-22   85-24   +13   7.46

This means that the bonds mature in August, 2023, and have a coupon rate of 6.25 percent. Note that the code "n" does not appear; these are bonds, not notes. The dealer will bid 85 and 22/32 for the bonds and offer them at 85 and 24/32. These are prices of 85.6875 and 85.75 respectively. This is an increase of 13/32 from the previous day's close. The price offers the investor a yield to maturity of 7.46 percent.

Thus the dealer will bid $8,568.75 for $10,000 face amount of bonds, and offer them for $8,575.00. The difference of $6.25 represents the dealer's operating profit on the trade.

Some bonds are callable. For example, a recent quote showed the following bond:

Aug 95-00   8.375   102-20   102-24   +01   6.15

These bonds have a 8.375 coupon and mature in August, 2000, but may be called at par on or after August, 1995. This early call keeps them from selling as high as they would if they didn't have the call.

Treasury bonds are now offered twice per year, in February and August. Like bills and notes, they are offered using the Treasury Direct system, and you can buy them directly using that system.

You should follow the long-term bond market, at least to keep in touch with the level of long-term yields. As with all other Treasury obligations, you should always consider them as alternatives to municipal bond investments. You can compare their yield directly with the yield of long-term municipal bonds to help determine which is more attractive to you.

Treasury STRIPS

Separate Trading Registered Interest and Principal Securities (STRIPS) created by breaking United States Treasury bonds and notes into their separate interest and principal components and selling these components as individual zero-coupon securities. For example, $1,000,000 face amount of 8 percent bonds maturing in thirty years could be converted into $1,000,000 of thirty-year STRIPS, and $40,000 of STRIPS for each six-month period up to and including the final maturity. Each semiannual interest payment of $40,000 has been converted into $40,000 of zero-coupon securities maturing on the date that the interest payment is due. It is also possible to put these back together again to make up the original bond.

STRIPS can be a valuable investment vehicle. You can make an investment that will automatically reinvest your income, without any further concern on your part. However, STRIPS can have some defects, and you should be aware of them.

You should understand that securities issued at a discount may have their accrual to par treated as taxable interest income. You may be required to report the annual accrual of this discount on your income tax return as interest, and pay taxes on the accrual, even though you don't have any cash income from the investment. This can be original issue discount, or market discount. For this reason, many investors in STRIPS are exempt from federal income tax; these include individual investments in IRAs and Keogh plans, and pension funds. You should discuss this entire problem with your accountant before you make investments in STRIPS or any other discount security. Many individual investors have put STRIPS into their IRAs or their Keogh plans.

You should also understand that a zero-coupon bond is the most volatile bond investment possible and is likely to fluctuate the most widely of all bonds of comparable maturity as the bond market fluctuates. For many investors, this is not a problem, and may even be a desirable characteristic. However, you should be aware of this feature.

NONMARKETABLE TREASURY SECURITIES

Two main types of nonmarketable securities exist: United States Savings Bonds, and State and Local Government Series bonds.

United States Savings Bonds

Two types of United States Savings Bonds exist: Series EE and Series HH.

Series EE United States Savings Bonds are issued at a discount, and interest is paid when the bond matures or is redeemed before maturity; they are zero-coupon bonds. They are the successors to the well-known Series E Savings Bonds, sold from 1940 to 1981. Series E bonds were heavily bought during World War II, when they were known as War Bonds. They helped finance the cost of the war, and they helped control inflation during the war by removing money from circulation.

Investors may buy Series EE Bonds at their local bank, through payroll deductions, and at the Federal Reserve Bank. Savings bonds are available in denominations of $50, $75, $100, $200, $500, $1,000, $5,000, and $10,000. Interest accrues semiannually through an increase in the redemption value of the bond.

For example, in April, 1994, Savings Bonds are sold at 50 percent of face amount, so that a $100 Savings Bond is sold for $50.00. The bonds mature for their full face amount of $100 eighteen years after issue date, for an annual percentage yield of 4.04 percent. Savings bonds held five years or more may earn interest at a market-based rate if the market-based rate is higher than the original rate. This market-based rate is announced each May and November.

Series E and Series EE bonds may have extended maturities, up to forty years in some cases.

Series HH Bonds are current income bonds. They are available in denominations of $500, $1,000, $5,000 and $10,000, and may be obtained only in exchange for Series E or Series EE bonds, or U. S. Savings Notes. They have a maturity of ten years, but this may be extended for another ten years. Series HH pay income at a fixed rate set at the time of exchange. Bonds issued on or after March 1, 1993 earn interest at 4.00 percent per year.

Both series of savings bonds can have tax deferral features.

Savings Bonds are designed to be attractive investments for individuals, and they have proved exceedingly popular since their introduction over fifty years ago. Refer to your local bank, the Federal Reserve Bank, or the United States Department of the Treasury, U.S. Savings Bond Division, Washington, D.C. 20226 for more information on these important securities.

State and Local Government Series

State and Local Government Series (SLGS) are issued to state and local bond issuers to enable them to avoid arbitrage restrictions in the issuance of new bonds. Arbitrage restrictions are set up by the Internal Revenue Service to prevent state and local governments from issuing bonds at low tax-exempt rates and reinvesting the proceeds in higher United States bond rates. SLGS carry interest rates set to avoid violating these arbitrage restrictions. You don't need to worry about State and Local Government Series bonds. A detailed discussion of them is far beyond the scope of this book. The only buyers of these bonds are state and local governments. Highly paid municipal bond investment bankers and lawyers keep abreast of developments in this field and advise their clients on how to use these highly specialized issues in the issuance of new municipal bonds. If you have a public position that requires knowledge of these bonds, you will also have these expert advisors to inform you about them, and this knowledge will be part of the requirements for your performance of your official duties and their performance of their duties.

The Remaining Nonmarketable Debt

The remaining nonmarketable debt is composed of foreign issues and government account series. Foreign issues are held by foreign governments. Government account series are held by the United States Treasury and other federal agencies and trust funds. A large amount of these are held by the Social Security Trust Fund.

Government account series securities won't concern you unless you are a United States Government official involved with the management of these accounts. In this case, you will have plenty of expert advice available from other sources. These securities are beyond the scope of this book.

CHAPTER 7

Applying the Mathematics of Finance to Bond Investments

Any bond investor should have some idea of the mathematics of finance and how to apply financial mathematics to bond investments. Many municipal bonds are traded on what is called a "yield basis," so you should understand the meaning of the term "yield basis" and how the dollar price is computed from the yield basis. Furthermore, you should have some understanding of present and future value calculations and how they work to determine whether a proposed bond investment is likely to work out in a satisfactory manner.

Many fine books have been written on financial mathematics. Much of the subject matter is beyond the scope of this book, but we do present an introduction to basic concepts of the mathematics of finance. We will show how these concepts are used, especially in the calculation of municipal bond dollar prices from the yield basis, and provide a framework for further study.

COMPOUND INTEREST

Interest is compensation for the use of money; in more general terms, it can be considered compensation for the use of capital. Historically, this has been done in a variety of ways. For example, in the ancient Near East, a farmer could borrow wheat from the temple, sow it, and repay the loan after harvest time. More recently, farmers have farmed someone else's land in exchange for a share of the crops. This sharecropping, although it has a poor reputation, can actually provide a good living to the farmer, if the land is good and he can farm it successfully.

For the purposes of this book, we measure both capital and interest in units of account; this can be thought of in either numbers or money, such as dollar bills. Both approaches will produce the same answer, but some people find one more convenient than the other.

These calculations assume that all payments are made when due and all principal is repaid when due. In real life, of course, this doesn't happen; people miss payments, make payments in advance, make partial payments, and a variety of other things. Financial institutions adjust for these in their own ways; sometimes, they charge extra service charges, other times they simply charge a higher rate of interest to offset these extra costs. But in our financial mathematical analysis, we assume that all payments are made like clockwork. Methods of adjusting for discrepancies are beyond the scope of this book.

Any financial mathematical analysis requires the statement of interest rate. This must be stated as a percent per time period. Both the rate and the time period to which it applies must be stated; otherwise, the problem doesn't make sense.

For example, suppose someone comes to you with a proposal which will pay you a gigantic 15 percent return. Upon analysis, you learn that this 15 percent return is after four years; the return doesn't look so large after all. Or suppose you borrow at a low 2 percent cost. After analysis, you learn that this is 2 percent per month; the cost might not appear so low after all. In all financial analysis, you must know both the rate and the time period.

These are not always explicitly stated in the problem. For example, bond yields are usually quoted in annual rates. However, trade custom, and the resulting mathematics, are done in terms of semiannual rates; we say that the rates quoted are nominal annual rates, but compounded semiannually. For example, the long United States Treasury bond was, in July, 1994, quoted at a yield of about 7.60 percent. This does not mean 7.60 percent per year; it means 3.80 percent per semiannual (six-month) period. This is a different annual rate, about 7.74 percent annually, and will produce different answers to financial problems asked.

In another common occurrence, home mortgage rates are almost always quoted at an annual rate, although payments are almost always made monthly. Thus, for example, an annual rate of 7.5 percent really means a monthly rate of 0.625 percent, and all the calculations are made on that basis; this works out to an annual rate of about 7.763 percent. Other problems may have other interest rates and time periods implicit in their statement, either due to trade custom, like the bond business, or to other factors.

Suppose you put $100.00 in the bank and the bank promises to pay you 10 percent per year on your deposit. At the end of the year, you would have $110.00 on deposit in the bank. You have received a 10 percent return on your original investment in the bank deposit. This is a true 10 percent annual return because at the end of the year you have 10 percent more on deposit than when you started. In diagram form, it looks like this:

Year 0 (now)	100.00
Interest	10.00
Year 1	110.00

You could take your $10 and spend it. But suppose you decide to leave the entire deposit in the bank, and the bank continues to pay 10 percent annual interest on the deposit, and you, and the bank, continue to do this for three more years, for a total of four years. Your deposit will look like this:

Year 1	110.00
Interest year 2	11.00
Year 2	121.00
Interest year 3	12.10
Year 3	133.10
Interest year 4	13.31
Year 4	146.41

This is called the compounding of interest. The interest paid to you by the bank earns interest itself, and this process is said to be compounding, or compound interest. Although the rate remains at 10 percent, the actual amount of interest paid increases each year, and in increasing amounts, because the amount on which interest is paid, including previously paid interest, increases each year. Theoretically, this can increase without limit.

Suppose the bank decides to continue paying 10 percent per year, but to pay interest semiannually instead of annually. Your deposit for the first year will look as follows:

Year 0 (now)	100.00
Interest—6 months	5.00
Amount—6 months	105.00
Interest—6 months	5.25
Amount—year 1	110.25

This is semiannual compounding, and we say that the rate paid by the bank is a nominal annual rate of 10.00 percent compounded semiannually. The actual rate of interest is 5.00 percent, and the period is six months. This works out to 10.25 percent annual return.

Quarterly compounding works in a similar manner. This example is for 10 percent nominal annual rate, compounded quarterly:

Amount (now)	100.00
Interest (Q1)	2.50
Amount	102.50
Interest (Q2)	2.56
Amount	105.06
Interest (Q3)	2.63
Amount	107.69

Interest (Q4)   2.69
Amount (Year 1)   110.38

We say that this is a nominal annual rate of 10.00 percent compounded quarterly. The annual equivalent is 10.38 percent, so we say that 10 percent per year, compounded quarterly, is the equivalent of 10.38 percent true annual rate.

Daily compounding is also possible. Daily compounding is used by many banks for computing interest on day-of-deposit to day-of-withdrawal savings accounts, or insured money market accounts. For daily compounding at a 10.00 percent nominal annual rate, the true annual interest is 10.52 percent.

Continuously compounded interest is mathematically possible. This is used by some life insurance companies in the calculation of net premiums, nonforfeiture values, and reserves.

The Equation for Compound Interest

Suppose your investment is 1 and the interest rate earned, expressed as a decimal, is i. Then the amount of interest earned on 1 at the end of a year is $1 + i$, and if you have a total amount P to invest, you will have $P(1 + i)$ at the end of a year.

In the case above, where the bank is paying 10 percent, $i = 0.1$, so that you will have $1 + 0.1$, or 1.1, at the end of the year. If you started with $1.00, you will have $1.10 at the end of the year.

If you leave your money on deposit, the total amount earns interest during the second year. You have $1 + i$ on deposit, and this will increase by $1 + i$ during the second year, so that at the end of the second year, you will have $(1 + i)^2$ on deposit. In the case above, this will be $(1 + 0.1)^2$ or $(1.1)^2$, which equals 1.21, as in the chart earlier in the chapter.

In general, for t years, where t is the number of years the amount will accumulate, the equation for the amount at compound interest is:

$$\text{Amount at compound interest} = (1 + i)^t$$

This is also sometimes called the future value of 1.

Suppose the bank states the interest at a nominal annual rate, but compounded more frequently. For example, in one of the cases above, the stated rate was 10 percent, but the bank compounded semiannually. In this case, the rate is divided in half, but the number of periods is doubled, so that the amount at compound interest at the end of one year equaled $[1 + (.1/2)]^2$

$$= (1.05)^2$$
$$= 1.1025,$$

which is 10.25 percent annual return, as shown in the tables earlier in the chapter.

In general, if the rate is compounded n times per year, for t years, the equation for the amount of compound interest is:

Amount at compound interest	=	$(1 + i/n)^{nt}$,
where:	i =	the nominal annual rate expressed as a decimal
	t =	the number of years
	n =	the number of compoundings per year

CALCULATING PRESENT VALUES

The previous section on compound interest answered the question: If I have a certain amount of money, say $1.00, now, how much will I have at some time in the future, assuming a particular interest rate and compounding period? But suppose I want a certain amount of money, say $1.00, sometime in the future. How much must I put aside now in order to have the desired amount of money?

For example, suppose I want $1.00 in one year, and the bank is paying 10 percent annual interest. How much must I put in the bank now to have $1.00 in one year?

Put X amount in the bank. At the end of the year, you will have:

Your original deposit	X
Interest paid at 10 percent	$.1\ X$

This total amount must equal 1, so

$$X + .1\,X \;=\; 1$$
$$(1 + .1)X \;=\; 1$$
$$X \;=\; 1/(1.1)$$
$$\;=\; .90909$$

Therefore, you put 90.9 cents in the bank. At the end of the year, you will have

Your original deposit	90.9
Interest at 10 percent	9.1 (rounded)
Total amount	100.0, or $1.00.

We say that the present value of $1.00 due in one year, at 10 percent annual interest, is $0.90909.

Suppose you want 1, but in two years instead of in one year, and that the bank still pays 10 percent per year. If you must have 1 in two years, you will need 0.90909 in one year, since this is required to increase to 1 in one year. To get 0.90909 in one year, you must put in the bank now the amount of (0.90909)(0.90909) or 0.8264.

The earnings and accrual will look like this:

Year 0 (now)	0.82645
Interest year 1	0.08264
End of year 1	0.90909
Interest year 2	0.09091
End of year 2	1.00000

Thus, your original amount of 0.82645 earns 10 percent or 0.08264 during the first year, and the total amount is 0.90909 at the end of year one. During the second year, it earns 10 percent on 0.90909, or 0.09091, which results in 1.0000 being on deposit at the end of the second year.

Similarly, for periods equal to three and four years, the present values of 1 are 0.7513 and 0.6830, respectively.

This operation is called finding the present value of a future payment.

The Equation for Present Value of a Future Payment

The present value of 1 to be received on one year is equal to $1/(1 + i)$, where i is the interest rate expressed as a decimal. For example, if the rate is 10 percent, as in the example earlier in this chapter, then $i = 0.1$, and the present value of 1 due in one year

$$= 1/(1 + 0.1)$$
$$= 1/(1.1)$$
$$= 0.90909$$

In general, for time equal to t years, the present value is the reciprocal of the amount at compound interest, and is expressed as v^t. Thus, for t years,

$$v^t = 1/(1 + i)^t$$

If the interest is compounded n times per year, the formula is

$$v^t = 1/(1 + i/n)^{nt}$$

Note that this is the reciprocal of the amount at compound interest.

CALCULATING AN ANNUITY CERTAIN

Suppose someone promises to give you $1.00 per year, starting in one year, and continuing for five years, for a total amount of $5.00. Thus the $5.00 would be paid at a rate of $1.00 per year, for five years, starting in one year. This is called an annuity certain.

An annuity certain is a series of equal payments, equally spaced in time, with a first payment date and a last payment date.

You might have a pension income, either Social Security, or from a previous employer, or you might have an annuity bought from an insurance company. This is a life annuity, so called because it stops or is reduced when the recipient dies. This is not an annuity certain. The annuity certain continues with its scheduled payments, no matter what happens to the person receiving the payments.

Suppose the person giving you the annuity asked you to pay for it, using an asssumed rate of interest. How would you calculate the amount due to that person?

You would calculate it in the following way. Each individual payment in the annuity has an individual present value. Add together the present values of all the individual payments and the result is the present value of the annuity certain.

For example, suppose you want to evaluate the five payment annuity certain, assuming an interest of 8 percent per year. You will receive five payments of $1.00, starting in one year. The value of the annuity is calculated as follows:

Time	Payment	Present value
1 year	1.000	0.92593
2 years	1.000	0.85734
3 years	1.000	0.79383
4 years	1.000	0.73503
5 years	1.000	0.68058
Total	5.000	3.99271

The present value of an annuity of 1 per year, at 8 percent per year interest, with five payments, is 3.99271. Thus the amount you should pay for the annuity in the example above is $3.99.

The Equation for the Annuity Certain

The value of the annuity certain is computed by adding together the present values of the individual payments. For example, in the above case, of an annuity of five annual payments at 8 percent annual interest, we add together the values of the five individual payments to compute the value of the annuity. The formula for the present value of an annuity certain is:

$$[1 - 1/(1 + i)^t]/i$$

HOW TO USE COMPOUND INTEREST AND ANNUITY TABLES

Few people use these tables now for calculations. Computers and calculators have replaced them. However, they are still useful for getting an idea of the operation of compound interest functions. You should have an idea of what they look like and how to use them.

We show six compound interest tables, as Figures 7.1 through 7.6. Figure 7.1 and Figure 7.2 show the amount at compound interest for an original amount of 1. The columns show various interest rates, from 2 percent to 3 percent, by 0.25-percent intervals, and from 3.5 percent to 8 percent by 0.5-percent intervals. The rows show periods, labeled years in the tables, from 1 to 100 in Figure 7.1, and from 1 to 50 in Figure 7.2. To find the amount at compound interest for an interest rate and time period, look in the column for the interest rate, and at the row for the time period to find the amount.

For example, in the case above, for 10 percent per year, compounded semiannually, the interest rate is 5 percent and the time period is 2. Looking in the column for interest rate 5 percent and time period 2 (Figure 7.2), the table shows the answer, 1.1025. For quarterly compounding, the interest rate is 2.5 percent and the time period is 4. Looking in the column for interest rate 2.5 percent and time period 4 (Figure 7.1), the table shows the answer, 1.10381289.

If you start with a certain amount of money, and want to know how much this will grow to, multiply the amount by the factor you find in the table. For example, suppose you start with $17.93, and want to know how much you will have after 4 periods, with interest at 2.5 percent per period. You multiply the amount you have now, $17.93, by the amount shown in the table, 1.10381289. You will have $19.79, computed as follows:

$$\$17.93 \times (1.10381289) = \$19.79$$

The amounts shown in the table increase as the number of periods increases, because the original money earns interest for a longer period of time. The amounts shown also increase as the interest rate increases, because the original money earns interest at a higher rate.

Present value tables work in the same way, except that they show the present value of 1 instead of the amount of 1 at compound interest. Figures 7.3 and 7.4 show present value tables. For example, the present value of 1, payable in 1 year, at 8-percent interest is 0.92592593. This is shown in Figure 7.4, in the column for 8-percent interest, and period (year) of 1. The other present values show in the calculation of an annuity certain above are shown directly below this number, because they are also at 8-percent interest rates, for years 2, 3, 4, and 5.

Figure 7.1

AMOUNT AT COMPOUND INTEREST $(1 + i)^n$
(Continued)

Years n	.02(2 %)	.0225(2¼ %)	.025(2½ %)	.0275(2¾ %)	.03(3 %)
			Rate i		
1	1.02000000	1.02250000	1.02500000	1.02750000	1.03000000
2	1.04040000	1.04550625	1.05062500	1.05575625	1.06090000
3	1.06120800	1.06903014	1.07689063	1.08478955	1.09272700
4	1.08243216	1.09308332	1.10381289	1.11462126	1.12550881
5	1.10408080	1.11767769	1.13140821	1.14527334	1.15927407
6	1.12616242	1.14282544	1.15969312	1.17676836	1.19405230
7	1.14868567	1.16853901	1.18868575	1.20912949	1.22987387
8	1.17165938	1.19483114	1.21840290	1.24238055	1.26677008
9	1.19509257	1.22171484	1.24886297	1.27654602	1.30477318
10	1.21899442	1.24920343	1.28008454	1.31165103	1.34391638
11	1.24337431	1.27731050	1.31208666	1.34772144	1.38423387
12	1.26824179	1.30604999	1.34488882	1.38478378	1.42576089
13	1.29360663	1.33543611	1.37851104	1.42286533	1.46853371
14	1.31947876	1.36548343	1.41297382	1.46199413	1.51258972
15	1.34586834	1.39620680	1.44829817	1.50219896	1.55796742
16	1.37278571	1.42762146	1.48450562	1.54350944	1.60470644
17	1.40024142	1.45974294	1.52161826	1.58595595	1.65284763
18	1.42824625	1.49258716	1.55965872	1.62956973	1.70243306
19	1.45681117	1.52617037	1.59865019	1.67438290	1.75350605
20	1.48594740	1.56050920	1.63861644	1.72042843	1.80611123
21	1.51566634	1.59562066	1.67958185	1.76774021	1.86029457
22	1.54597967	1.63152212	1.72157140	1.81635307	1.91610341
23	1.57689926	1.66823137	1.76461068	1.86630278	1.97358651
24	1.60843725	1.70576658	1.80872595	1.91762610	2.03279411
25	1.64060599	1.74414632	1.85394410	1.97036082	2.09377793
26	1.67341811	1.78338962	1.90029270	2.02454575	2.15659127
27	1.70688648	1.82351585	1.94780002	2.08022075	2.22128901
28	1.74102421	1.86454499	1.99649502	2.13742682	2.28792768
29	1.77584469	1.90649725	2.04640739	2.19620606	2.35656551
30	1.81136158	1.94939344	2.09756758	2.25660173	2.42726247
31	1.84758882	1.99325479	2.15000677	2.31865828	2.50008035
32	1.88454059	2.03810303	2.20375694	2.38242138	2.57508276
33	1.92223140	2.08396034	2.25885086	2.44793797	2.65233524
34	1.96067603	2.13084945	2.31532213	2.51525626	2.73190530
35	1.99988955	2.17879356	2.37320519	2.58442581	2.81386245
36	2.03988734	2.22781642	2.43253532	2.65549752	2.89827833
37	2.08068509	2.27794229	2.49334870	2.72852370	2.98522668
38	2.12229879	2.32919599	2.55568242	2.80355810	3.07478348
39	2.16474477	2.38160290	2.61957448	2.88065595	3.16702698
40	2.20803966	2.43518897	2.68506384	2.95987399	3.26203779
41	2.25220046	2.48998072	2.75219043	3.04127052	3.35989893
42	2.29724447	2.54600528	2.82099520	3.12490546	3.46069589
43	2.34318936	2.60329040	2.89152008	3.21084036	3.56451677
44	2.39005314	2.66186444	2.96380808	3.29913847	3.67145227
45	2.43785421	2.72175639	3.03790328	3.38986478	3.78159584
46	2.48661129	2.78299590	3.11385086	3.48308606	3.89504372
47	2.53634352	2.84561331	3.19169713	3.57887093	4.01189503
48	2.58707039	2.90963961	3.27148956	3.67728988	4.13225188
49	2.63881179	2.97510650	3.35327680	3.77841535	4.25621944
50	2.69158803	3.04204640	3.43710872	3.88232177	4.38390602

Source: Mathematical Tables from the Handbook of Chemistry and Physics, 10th Edition, Cleveland, OH, 1954. Used with permission.

Figure 7.1 (continued)

AMOUNT AT COMPOUND INTEREST $(1 + i)^n$
(Continued)

Years n	Rate i				
n	.02(2 %)	.0225(2¼ %)	.025(2½ %)	.0275(2¾ %)	.03(3 %)
50	2.69158803	3.04204640	3.43710872	3.88232177	4.38390602
51	2.74541979	3.11049244	3.52303644	3.98908562	4.51542320
52	2.80032819	3.18047852	3.61111235	4.09878547	4.65088590
53	2.85633475	3.25203929	3.70139016	4.21150208	4.79041247
54	2.91346144	3.32521017	3.79392491	4.32731838	4.93412485
55	2.97173067	3.40002740	3.88877303	4.44631964	5.08214859
56	3.03116529	3.47652802	3.98599236	4.56859343	5.23461305
57	3.09178859	3.55474990	4.08564217	4.69422975	5.39165144
58	3.15362436	3.63473177	4.18778322	4.82332107	5.55340098
59	3.21669685	3.71651324	4.29247780	4.95596239	5.72000301
60	3.28103079	3.80013479	4.39978975	5.09225136	5.89160310
61	3.34665140	3.88563782	4.50978449	5.23228827	6.06835120
62	3.41358443	3.97306467	4.62252910	5.37617620	6.25040173
63	3.48185612	4.06245862	4.73809233	5.52402105	6.43791379
64	3.55149324	4.15386394	4.85654464	5.67593162	6.63105120
65	3.62252311	4.24732588	4.97795826	5.83201974	6.82998273
66	3.69497357	4.34289071	5.10240721	5.99240029	7.03488222
67	3.76887304	4.44060576	5.22996739	6.15719130	7.24592868
68	3.84425050	4.54051939	5.36071658	6.32651406	7.46330654
69	3.92113551	4.64268107	5.49473449	6.50049319	7.68720574
70	3.99955822	4.74714140	5.63210286	6.67925676	7.91782191
71	4.07954939	4.85395208	5.77290543	6.86293632	8.15535657
72	4.16114038	4.96316600	5.91722806	7.05166706	8.40001727
73	4.24436318	5.07483723	6.06515876	7.24558791	8.65201778
74	4.32925045	5.18902107	6.21678773	7.44484158	8.91157832
75	4.41583546	5.30577405	6.37220743	7.64957472	9.17892567
76	4.50415216	5.42515396	6.53151261	7.85993802	9.45429344
77	4.59423521	5.54721993	6.69480043	8.07608632	9.73792224
78	4.68611991	5.67203237	6.86217044	8.29817869	10.0300599
79	4.77984231	5.79965310	7.03372470	8.52637861	10.3309617
80	4.87543916	5.93014530	7.20956782	8.76085402	10.6408906
81	4.97294794	6.06357357	7.38980701	9.00177751	10.9601173
82	5.07240690	6.20000397	7.57455219	9.24932639	11.2889208
83	5.17385504	6.33950406	7.76391599	9.50368286	11.6275884
84	5.27733214	6.48214290	7.95801389	9.76503414	11.9764161
85	5.38287878	6.62799112	8.15696424	10.0335726	12.3357085
86	5.49053636	6.77712092	8.36088834	10.3094958	12.7057798
87	5.60034708	6.92960614	8.56991055	10.5930070	13.0869532
88	5.71235402	7.08552228	8.78415832	10.8843147	13.4795618
89	5.82660110	7.24494653	9.00376228	11.1836333	13.8839487
90	5.94313313	7.40795782	9.22885633	11.4911832	14.3004671
91	6.06199579	7.57463688	9.45957774	11.8071908	14.7294811
92	6.18323570	7.74506621	9.69606718	12.1318885	15.1713656
93	6.30690042	7.91933020	9.93846886	12.4655154	15.6265065
94	6.43303843	8.09751512	10.1869306	12.8083171	16.0953017
95	6.56169920	8.27970921	10 4416038	13 1605458	16.5781608
96	6.69293318	8.46600267	10.7026439	13.5224608	17.0755056
97	6.82679184	8.65648773	10.9702100	13.8943285	17.5877708
98	6.96332768	8.85125871	11.2244653	14.2764226	18.1154039
99	7.10259423	9.05041203	11.5255769	14.6690242	18.6588660
100	7.24464612	9.25404630	11.8137164	15.0724223	19.2186320

Source: Mathematical Tables from the Handbook of Chemistry and Physics, 10th Edition, Cleveland, OH, 1954. Used with permission.

Figure 7.2

AMOUNT AT COMPOUND INTEREST $(1 + i)^n$
(Continued)

Years n	.035(3½ %)	.04(4 %)	.045(4½ %)	.05(5 %)	.055(5½ %)
			Rate i		
1	1.03500000	1.04000000	1.04500000	1.05000000	1.05500000
2	1.07122500	1.08160000	1.09202500	1.10250000	1.11302500
3	1.10871788	1.12486400	1.14116613	1.15762500	1.17424138
4	1.14752300	1.16985856	1.19251860	1.21550625	1.23882465
5	1.18768631	1.21665290	1.24618194	1.27628156	1.30696001
6	1.22925533	1.26531902	1.30226012	1.34009564	1.37884281
7	1.27227926	1.31593178	1.36086183	1.40710042	1.45467916
8	1.31680904	1.36856905	1.42210061	1.47745544	1.53468651
9	1.36289735	1.42331181	1.48609514	1.55132822	1.61909427
10	1.41059876	1.48024428	1.55296942	1.62889463	1.70814446
11	1.45996972	1.53945406	1.62285305	1.71033936	1.80209240
12	1.51106866	1.60103222	1.69588143	1.79585633	1.90120749
13	1.56395606	1.66507351	1.77219610	1.88564914	2.00577390
14	1.61869452	1.73167645	1.85194492	1.97993160	2.11609146
15	1.67534883	1.80094351	1.93528244	2.07892818	2.23247649
16	1.73398604	1.87298125	2.02237015	2.18287459	2.35526270
17	1.79467555	1.94790050	2.11337681	2.29201832	2.48480215
18	1.85748920	2.02581652	2.20847877	2.40661923	2.62146627
19	1.92250132	2.10684918	2.30786031	2.52695020	2.76564691
20	1.98978886	2.19112314	2.41171402	2.65329771	2.91775749
21	2.05943147	2.27876807	2.52024116	2.78596259	3.07823415
22	2.13151158	2.36991879	2.63365201	2.92526072	3.24753703
23	2.20611448	2.46471554	2.75216635	3.07152376	3.42615157
24	2.28332849	2.56330416	2.87601383	3.22509994	3.61458990
25	2.36324498	2.66583633	3.00543446	3.38635494	3.81339235
26	2.44595856	2.77246978	3.14067981	3.55567269	4.02312893
27	2.53156711	2.88336858	3.28200956	3.73345632	4.24440102
28	2.62017196	2.99870332	3.42969999	3.92012914	4.47784307
29	2.71187798	3.11865145	3.58403649	4.11613560	4.72412444
30	2.80679370	3.24339751	3.74531813	4.32194238	4.98395129
31	2.90503148	3.37313341	3.91385745	4.53803949	5.25806861
32	3.00670759	3.50805875	4.08998104	4.76494147	5.54726238
33	3.11194235	3.64838110	4.27403018	5.00318854	5.85236181
34	3.22086033	3.79431634	4.46636154	5.25334797	6.17424171
35	3.33359045	3.94608899	4.66734781	5.51601537	6.51382501
36	3.45026611	4.10393255	4.87737846	5.79181614	6.87208538
37	3.57102543	4.26808986	5.09686049	6.08140694	7.25005008
38	3.69601132	4.43881345	5.32621921	6.38547729	7.64880283
39	3.82537171	4.61636599	5.56589908	6.70475115	8.06948699
40	3.95925972	4.80102063	5.81636454	7.03998871	8.51330877
41	4.09783381	4.99306145	6.07810094	7.39198815	8.98154076
42	4.24125799	5.19278391	6.35161548	7.76158756	9.47552550
43	4.38970202	5.40049527	6.63743818	8.14966693	9.99667940
44	4.54334160	5.61651508	6.93612290	8.55715028	10.5464968
45	4.70235855	5.84117568	7.24824843	8.98500779	11.1265541
46	4.86694110	6.07482271	7.57441961	9.43425818	11.7385146
47	5.03728404	6.31781562	7.91526849	9.90597109	12.3841329
48	5.21358898	6.57052824	8.27145557	10.4012696	13.0652602
49	5.39606459	6.83334937	8.64367107	10.9213331	13.7838495
50	5.58492686	7.10668335	9.03263627	11.4673998	14.5419612

Source: Mathematical Tables from the Handbook of Chemistry and Physics, 10th Edition, Cleveland, OH, 1954. Used with permission.

Figure 7.2 (continued)

AMOUNT AT COMPOUND INTEREST $(1 + i)^n$
(Continued)

n	.06(6 %)	.065(6½ %)	.07(7 %)	.075(7½) %	.08(8 %)
1	1.06000000	1.06500000	1.07000000	1.07500000	1.08000000
2	1.12360000	1.13422500	1.14490000	1.15562500	1.16640000
3	1.19101600	1.20794963	1.22504300	1.24229688	1.25971200
4	1.26247696	1.28646635	1.31079601	1.33546914	1.36048896
5	1.33822558	1.37008666	1.40255173	1.43562933	1.46932808
6	1.41851911	1.45914230	1.50073035	1.54330153	1.58687432
7	1.50363026	1.55398655	1.60578148	1.65904914	1.71382427
8	1.59384807	1.65499567	1.71818618	1.78347783	1.85093021
9	1.68947896	1.76257039	1.83845921	1.91723866	1.99900463
10	1.79084770	1.87713747	1.96715136	2.06103156	2.15892500
11	1.89829856	1.99915140	2.10485195	2.21560893	2.33163900
12	2.01219647	2.12909624	2.25219159	2.38177960	2.51817012
13	2.13292826	2.26748750	2.40984500	2.56041307	2.71962373
14	2.26090396	2.41487418	2.57853415	2.75244405	2.93719362
15	2.39655819	2.57184101	2.75903154	2.95887735	3.17216911
16	2.54035168	2.73901067	2.95216375	3.18079315	3.42594264
17	2.69277279	2.91704637	3.15881521	3.41935264	3.70001805
18	2.85433915	3.10665438	3.37993228	3.67580409	3.99601950
19	3.02559950	3.30858691	3.61652754	3.95148940	4.31570106
20	3.20713547	3.52364506	3.86968446	4.24785110	4.66095714
21	3.39956360	3.75268199	4.14056237	4.56643993	5.03383372
22	3.60353742	3.99660632	4.43040174	4.90892293	5.43654041
23	3.81974966	4.25638573	4.74052986	5.27709215	5.8714636
24	4.04893464	4.53305081	5.07236695	5.67287406	6.34118070
25	4.29187072	4.82769911	5.42743264	6.09833961	6.84847520
26	4.54938296	5.14149955	5.80735292	6.55571508	7.39635321
27	4.82234594	5.47569702	6.21386763	7.04739371	7.98806147
28	5.11168670	5.83161733	6.64883836	7.57594824	8.62710639
29	5.41838790	6.21067245	7.11425705	8.14414436	9.31727490
30	5.74349117	6.61436616	7.61225504	8.75495519	10.0626569
31	6.08810064	7.04429996	8.14511290	9.41157683	10.8676694
32	6.45338668	7.50217946	8.71527080	10.1174451	11.7370830
33	6.84058988	7.98982113	9.32533975	10.8762535	12.6760496
34	7.25102528	8.50915950	9.97811354	11.6919725	13.6901336
35	7.68608679	9.06225487	10.6765815	12.5688704	14.7853443
36	8.14725200	9.65130143	11.4239422	13.5115357	15.9681718
37	8.63608712	10.2786360	12.2236181	14.5249009	17.2456256
38	9.15425235	10.9467474	13.0792714	15.6142684	18.6252756
39	9.70350749	11.6582859	13.9948204	16.7853386	20.1152977
40	10.2857179	12.4160745	14.9744578	18.0442390	21.7245215
41	10.9028610	13.2231194	16.0226699	19.3975569	23.4624832
42	11.5570327	14.0826221	17.1442568	20.8523737	25.3394819
43	12.2504546	14.9979926	18.3443548	22.4163017	27.3666404
44	12.9854819	15.9728621	19.6284596	24.0975243	29.5559717
45	13.7646108	17.0110981	21.0024518	25.9048386	31.9204494
46	14.5904875	18.1168195	22.4726234	27.8477015	34.4740853
47	15.4659167	19.2944128	24.0457070	29.9362791	37.2320122
48	16.3938717	20.5485496	25.7289065	32.1815001	40.2105731
49	17.3775040	21.8842053	27.5299300	34.5951126	43.4274190
50	18.4201543	23.3066787	29.4570251	37.1897460	46.9016125

Source: Mathematical Tables from the Handbook of Chemistry and Physics, 10th Edition, Cleveland, OH, 1954. Used with permission.

106

Figure 7.3

INTEREST TABLES (Continued)

PRESENT VALUE $1/(1 + i)^n$ (Continued)

Years n	.02(2 %)	.0225(2¼ %)	.025(2½ %)	.0275(2¾ %)	.03(3 %)
1	.98039216	.97799511	.97560976	.97323601	.97087379
2	.96116878	.95647444	.95181440	.94718833	.94259591
3	.94232233	.93542732	.92859941	.92183779	.91514166
4	.92384543	.91484335	.90595064	.89716573	.88848705
5	.90573081	.89471232	.88385429	.87315400	.86260878
6	.88797138	.87502427	.86229687	.84978491	.83748426
7	.87056018	.85576946	.84126524	.82704128	.81309151
8	.85349037	.83693835	.82074657	.80490635	.78940923
9	.83675527	.81852161	.80072836	.78336385	.76641673
10	.82034830	.80051013	.78119840	.76239791	.74409391
11	.80426304	.78289499	.76214478	.74199310	.72242128
12	.78849318	.76566748	.74355589	.72213440	.70137988
13	.77303253	.74881905	.72542038	.70280720	.68095134
14	.75787502	.73234137	.70772720	.68399728	.66111781
15	.74301473	.71622628	.69046556	.66569078	.64186195
16	.72844581	.70046580	.67362493	.64787424	.62316694
17	.71416256	.68505212	.65719506	.63053454	.60501645
18	.70015937	.66997763	.64116591	.61365892	.58739461
19	.68643076	.65523484	.62552772	.59723496	.57028603
20	.67297133	.64081647	.61027094	.58125057	.55367575
21	.65977582	.62671538	.59538629	.56569398	.53754928
22	.64683904	.61292457	.58086467	.55055375	.52189250
23	.63415592	.59943724	.56669724	.53581874	.50669175
24	.62172149	.58624668	.55287535	.52147809	.49193374
25	.60953087	.57334639	.53939059	.50752126	.47760557
26	.59757928	.56072997	.52623472	.49393796	.46369473
27	.58586204	.54839117	.51339973	.48071821	.45018906
28	.57437455	.53632388	.50087778	.46785227	.43707675
29	.56311231	.52452213	.48866125	.45533068	.42434636
30	.55207089	.51298008	.47674269	.44314421	.41198676
31	.54124597	.50169201	.46511481	.43128391	.39998715
32	.53063330	.49065233	.45377055	.41974103	.38833703
33	.52022873	.47985558	.44270298	.40850708	.37702625
34	.51002817	.46929641	.43190534	.39757380	.36604490
35	.50002761	.45896960	.42137107	.38693314	.35538340
36	.49022315	.44887002	.41109372	.37657727	.34503243
37	.48061093	.43899268	.40106705	.36649856	.33498294
38	.47118719	.42933270	.39128492	.35668959	.32522615
39	.46194822	.41988528	.38174139	.34714316	.31575355
40	.45289042	.41064575	.37243062	.33785222	.30655684
41	.44401021	.40160954	.36334695	.32880995	.29762800
42	.43530413	.39277216	.35448483	.32000968	.28895922
43	.42676875	.38412925	.34583886	.31144495	.28054294
44	.41840074	.37567653	.33740376	.30310944	.27237178
45	.41019680	.36740981	.32917440	.29499702	.26443862
46	.40215373	.35932500	.32114576	.28710172	.25673653
47	.39426836	.35141809	.31331294	.27941773	.24925876
48	.38653761	.34368518	.30567116	.27193940	.24199880
49	.37895844	.33612242	.29821576	.26466122	.23495029
50	.37152788	.32872608	.29094221	.25757783	.22810708

Source: Mathematical Tables from the Handbook of Chemistry and Physics, 10th Edition, Cleveland, OH, 1954. Used with permission.

Figure 7.3 (continued)

INTEREST TABLES (Continued)

PRESENT VALUE $1/(1+i)^n$ **(Continued)**

Years n	.02 (2 %)	.0225 (2¼ %)	.025 (2½ %)	.0275 (2¾ %)	.03 (3 %)
50	.37152788	.32872608	.29094221	.25757783	.22810708
51	.36424302	.32149250	.28384606	.25068402	.22146318
52	.35710100	.31441810	.27692298	.24397471	.21501280
53	.35009902	.30749936	.27016876	.23744497	.20875029
54	.34323433	.30073287	.26357928	.23109000	.20267019
55	.33650425	.29411528	.25715052	.22490511	.19676717
56	.32990613	.28764330	.25087855	.21888575	.19103609
57	.32343738	.28131374	.24475956	.21302749	.18547193
58	.31709547	.27512347	.23878982	.20732603	.18006984
59	.31087791	.26906940	.23296568	.20177716	.17482508
60	.30478227	.26314856	.22728359	.19637679	.16973309
61	.29880614	.25735801	.22174009	.19112097	.16478941
62	.29294720	.25169487	.21633179	.18600581	.15998972
63	.28720314	.24615635	.21105541	.18102755	.15532982
64	.28157170	.24073971	.20590771	.17618253	.15080565
65	.27605069	.23544226	.20088557	.17146718	.14641325
66	.27063793	.23026138	.19598593	.16687804	.14214879
67	.26533130	.22519450	.19120578	.16241172	.13800853
68	.26012873	.22023912	.18654223	.15806493	.13398887
69	.25502817	.21539278	.18199241	.15383448	.13008628
70	.25002761	.21065309	.17755358	.14971726	.12629736
71	.24512511	.20601769	.17322300	.14571023	.12261880
72	.24031874	.20148429	.16899805	.14181044	.11904737
73	.23560661	.19705065	.16487615	.13801503	.11557998
74	.23098687	.19271458	.16085478	.13432119	.11221357
75	.22645771	.18847391	.15693149	.13072622	.10894521
76	.22201737	.18432657	.15310389	.12722747	.10577205
77	.21766408	.18027048	.14936965	.12382235	.10269131
78	.21339616	.17630365	.14572649	.12050837	.09970030
79	.20921192	.17242411	.14217218	.11728309	.09679641
80	.20510973	.16862993	.13870457	.11414412	.09397710
81	.20108797	.16491925	.13532153	.11108917	.09123990
82	.19714507	.16129022	.13202101	.10811598	.08858243
83	.19327948	.15774105	.12880098	.10522237	.08600236
84	.18948968	.15426997	.12565949	.10240620	.08349743
85	.18577420	.15087528	.12259463	.09966540	.08106547
86	.18213157	.14755528	.11960452	.09699795	.07870434
87	.17856036	.14430835	.11668733	.09440190	.07641198
88	.17505918	.14113286	.11384130	.09187533	.07418639
89	.17162665	.13802724	.11106468	.08941638	.07202562
90	.16826142	.13498997	.10835579	.08702324	.06992779
91	.16496217	.13201953	.10571296	.08469415	.06789105
92	.16172762	.12911445	.10313460	.08242740	.06591364
93	.15855649	.12627331	.10061912	.08022131	.06399383
94	.15544754	.12349468	.09816500	.07807427	.06212993
95	.15239955	.12077719	.09577073	.07598469	.06032032
96	.14941132	.11811950	.09343486	.07395104	.05856342
97	.14648169	.11552029	.09115596	.07197181	.05685769
98	.14360950	.11297828	.08893264	.07004556	.05520164
99	.14079363	.11049221	.08676355	.06817086	.05359383
100	.13803297	.10806084	.08464737	.06634634	.05203284

Source: Mathematical Tables from the Handbook of Chemistry and Physics, 10th Edition, Cleveland, OH, 1954. Used with permission.

Figure 7.4

INTEREST TABLES (Continued)

PRESENT VALUE $1/(1 + i)^n$ (Continued)

n	.035(3½ %)	.04(4 %)	.045(4½ %)	.05(5 %)	.055(5½ %)
			Rate i		
1	.96618357	.96153846	.95693780	.95238095	.94786730
2	.93351070	.92455621	.91572995	.90702948	.89845242
3	.90194271	.88899636	.87629660	.86383760	.85161366
4	.87144223	.85480419	.83856134	.82270247	.80721674
5	.84197317	.82192711	.80245105	.78352617	.76513435
6	.81350064	.79031453	.76789574	.74621540	.72524583
7	.78599096	.75991781	.73482846	.71068133	.68743681
8	.75941156	.73069021	.70318513	.67683936	.65159887
9	.73373097	.70258674	.67290443	.64460892	.61762926
10	.70891881	.67556417	.64392768	.61391325	.58543058
11	.68494571	.64958093	.61619874	.58467929	.55491050
12	.66178330	.62459705	.58966386	.55683742	.52598152
13	.63940415	.60057409	.56427164	.53032135	.49856068
14	.61778179	.57747508	.53997286	.50506795	.47256937
15	.59689062	.55526450	.51672044	.48101710	.44793305
16	.57670591	.53390818	.49446932	.45811152	.42458109
17	.55720378	.51337325	.47317639	.43629669	.40244653
18	.53836114	.49362812	.45280037	.41552065	.38146590
19	.52015569	.47464242	.43330179	.39573396	.36157906
20	.50256588	.45638695	.41464286	.37688948	.34272896
21	.48557090	.43883360	.39678743	.35894236	.32486158
22	.46915063	.42195539	.37970089	.34184987	.30792567
23	.45328563	.40572633	.36335013	.32557131	.29187267
24	.43795713	.39012147	.34770347	.31006791	.27665656
25	.42314699	.37511680	.33273060	.29530277	.26223370
26	.40883767	.36068923	.31840248	.28124073	.24856275
27	.39501224	.34681657	.30469137	.26784832	.23560450
28	.38165434	.33347747	.29157069	.25509364	.22332181
29	.36874815	.32065141	.27901502	.24294632	.21167944
30	.35627841	.30831867	.26700002	.23137745	.20064402
31	.34423035	.29646026	.25550241	.22035947	.19018390
32	.33258071	.28505794	.24449991	.20986617	.18026910
33	.32134271	.27409417	.23397121	.19987254	.17087119
34	.31047605	.26355209	.22389589	.19035480	.16196321
35	.29997686	.25341547	.21425444	.18129029	.15351963
36	.28983272	.24366872	.20502817	.17265741	.14551624
37	.28003161	.23429685	.19619921	.16443563	.13793008
38	.27056194	.22528543	.18775044	.15660536	.13073941
39	.26141250	.21662061	.17966549	.14914797	.12392362
40	.25257247	.20828904	.17192870	.14204568	.11746314
41	.24403137	.20027793	.16452507	.13528160	.11133947
42	.23577910	.19257493	.15744026	.12883962	.10553504
43	.22780590	.18516820	.15066054	.12270440	.10003322
44	.22010231	.17804635	.14417276	.11636133	.09481822
45	.21265924	.17119841	.13796437	.11129651	.08987509
46	.20546787	.16461386	.13202332	.10599668	.08518965
47	.19851968	.15828256	.12633810	.10094921	.08074849
48	.19180645	.15219476	.12089771	.09614211	.07653885
49	.18532024	.14634112	.11569158	.09156391	.07254867
50	.17905337	.14071262	.11070965	.08720373	.06876652

Source: Mathematical Tables from the Handbook of Chemistry and Physics, 10th Edition, Cleveland, OH, 1954. Used with permission.

Figure 7.4 (continued)

INTEREST TABLES (Continued)

PRESENT VALUE $1/(1 + i)^n$ (Continued)

Years n	.06(6 %)	.065(6½ %)	.07(7 %)	.075(7½ %)	.08(8 %)
1	.94339623	.93896714	.93457944	.93023256	.92592593
2	.88999644	.88165928	.87343873	.86533261	.85733882
3	.83961928	.82784909	.81629788	.80496057	.79383224
4	.79209366	.77732309	.76289521	.74880053	.73502985
5	.74725817	.72988084	.71298618	.69655863	.68058320
6	.70496054	.68533412	.66634222	.64796152	.63016963
7	.66505711	.64350621	.62274974	.60275490	.58349040
8	.62741237	.60423119	.58200910	.56070223	.54026888
9	.59189846	.56735323	.54393374	.52158347	.50024897
10	.55839478	.53272604	.50834929	.48519393	.46319349
11	.52678753	.50021224	.47509280	.45134319	.42888286
12	.49696936	.46968285	.44401196	.41985413	.39711376
13	.46883902	.44101676	.41496445	.39056198	.36769792
14	.44230096	.41410025	.38781724	.36331347	.34046104
15	.41726506	.38882652	.36244602	.33796602	.31524170
16	.39364628	.36509533	.33873460	.31438699	.29189047
17	.37136442	.34281251	.31657439	.29245302	.27026895
18	.35034379	.32188969	.29586392	.27204932	.25024903
19	.33051301	.30224384	.27650833	.25306913	.23171206
20	.31180473	.28379703	.25841900	.23541315	.21454802
21	.29415540	.26647608	.24151309	.21898897	.19865575
22	.27750510	.25021228	.22571317	.20371067	.18394051
23	.26179726	.23494111	.21094688	.18949830	.17031528
24	.24697855	.22060198	.19714662	.17627749	.15769934
25	.23299863	.20713801	.18424918	.16397906	.14601790
26	.21981003	.19449579	.17219549	.15253866	.13520176
27	.20736795	.18262515	.16093037	.14189643	.12518682
28	.19563014	.17147902	.15040221	.13199668	.11591372
29	.18455674	.16101316	.14056282	.12278761	.10732752
30	.17411013	.15118607	.13136712	.11422103	.09937733
31	.16425484	.14195875	.12277301	.10625212	.09201605
32	.15495740	.13329460	.11474113	.09883918	.08520005
33	.14618622	.12515925	.10723470	.09194343	.07888893
34	.13791153	.11752042	.10021934	.08552877	.07304531
35	.13010522	.11034781	.09366294	.07956164	.06763454
36	.12274077	.10361297	.08753546	.07401083	.06262458
37	.11579318	.09728917	.08180884	.06884729	.05798572
38	.10923885	.09135134	.07645686	.06404399	.05369048
39	.10305552	.08577590	.07145501	.05957580	.04971341
40	.09722219	.08054075	.06678038	.05541935	.04603093
41	.09171905	.07562512	.06241157	.05155288	.04262123
42	.08652740	.07100950	.05832857	.04795617	.03946411
43	.08162962	.06667559	.05451268	.04461039	.03654084
44	.07700908	.06260619	.05094643	.04149804	.03383411
45	.07265007	.05878515	.04761349	.03860283	.03132788
46	.06853781	.05519733	.04449859	.03590961	.02900730
47	.06465831	.05182848	.04158747	.03340428	.02685861
48	.06099840	.04866524	.03886679	.03107375	.02486908
49	.05754566	.04569506	.03632410	.02890582	.02302693
50	.05428836	.04290616	.03394776	.02688913	.02132123

Source: Mathematical Tables from the Handbook of Chemistry and Physics, 10th Edition, Cleveland, OH, 1954. Used with permission.

Figure 7.5

INTEREST TABLES (Continued)

PRESENT VALUE OF ANNUITY $[1 - (1 + i)^{-n}]/i$
(Continued)

Years n	.02(2 %)	.0225(2¼ %)	.025(2½ %)	.0275(2¾ %)	.03(3 %)
1	0.98039216	0.97799511	0.97560976	0.97323601	0.97087379
2	1.94156094	1.93446955	1.92742415	1.92042434	1.91346970
3	2.88388327	2.86989687	2.85602356	2.84226213	2.82861135
4	3.80772870	3.78474021	3.76197421	3.73942787	3.71709840
5	4.71345951	4.67945253	4.64582850	4.61258186	4.57970719
6	5.60143089	5.55447680	5.50812536	5.46236678	5.41719144
7	6.47199107	6.41024626	6.34939060	6.28940806	6.23028296
8	7.32548144	7.24718461	7.17013717	7.09431441	7.01969219
9	8.16223671	8.06570622	7.97086553	7.87767826	7.78610892
10	8.98258501	8.86621635	8.75206393	8.64007616	8.53020284
11	9.78684805	9.64911134	9.51420871	9.38206926	9.25262411
12	10.5753412	10.4147788	10.2577646	10.1042037	9.95400399
13	11.3483737	11.1635979	10.9831850	10.8070109	10.6349553
14	12.1062488	11.8959392	11.6909122	11.4910081	11.2960731
15	12.8492635	12.6121655	12.3813777	12.1566989	11.9379351
16	13.5777093	13.3126313	13.0550027	12.8045732	12.5611020
17	14.2918719	13.9976834	13.7121977	13.4351077	13.1661185
18	14.9920313	14.6676611	14.3533636	14.0487666	13.7535131
19	15.6784620	15.3228959	14.9788913	14.6460016	14.3237991
20	16.3514333	15.9637124	15.5891623	15.2272521	14.8774749
21	17.0112092	16.5904277	16.1845486	15.7929461	15.4150241
22	17.6580482	17.2033523	16.7654132	16.3434999	15.9369166
23	18.2922041	17.8027896	17.3321105	16.8793186	16.4436084
24	18.9139256	18.3890362	17.8849858	17.4007967	16.9355421
25	19.5234565	18.9623826	18.4243764	17.9083180	17.4131477
26	20.1210358	19.5231126	18.9506111	18.4022559	17.8768424
27	20.7068978	20.0715038	19.4640109	18.8829741	18.3270315
28	21.2812724	20.6078276	19.9648887	19.3508264	18.7641082
29	21.8443847	21.1323498	20.4535499	19.8061571	19.1884546
30	22.3964556	21.6453298	20.9302926	20.2493013	19.6004413
31	22.9377015	22.1470219	21.3954074	20.6805852	20.0004285
32	23.4683348	22.6376742	21.8491780	21.1003262	20.3887655
33	23.9885636	23.1175298	22.2918809	21.5088333	20.7657918
34	24.4985917	23.5868262	22.7237863	21.9064071	21.1318367
35	24.9986193	24.0457958	23.1451573	22.2933403	21.4872201
36	25.4888425	24.4946658	23.5562521	22.6699175	21.8322525
37	25.9694534	24.9336585	23.9573181	23.0364161	22.1672354
38	26.4406406	25.3629912	24.3486030	23.3931057	22.4924616
39	26.9025888	25.7828765	24.7303444	23.7402488	22.8082151
40	27.3554792	26.1935222	25.1027751	24.0781011	23.1147720
41	27.7994895	26.5951317	25.4661220	24.4069110	23.4124000
42	28.2347936	26.9879039	25.8206068	24.7269207	23.7013592
43	28.6615623	27.3720332	26.1664457	25.0383656	23.9819021
44	29.0799631	27.7477097	26.5038495	25.3414751	24.2542739
45	29.4901599	28.1151195	26.8330239	25.6364721	24.5187125
46	29.8923136	28.4744445	27.1541696	25.9235738	24.7754491
47	30.2865820	28.8258626	27.4674826	26.2029915	25.0247078
48	30.6731196	29.1695478	27.7731537	26.4749309	25.2667066
49	31.0520780	29.5056702	28.0713695	26.7395922	25.5016569
50	31.4236059	29.8343963	28.3623117	26.9971700	25.7297640

Source: Mathematical Tables from the Handbook of Chemistry and Physics, 10th Edition, Cleveland, OH, 1954. Used with permission.

Figure 7.5 (continued)

INTEREST TABLES (Continued)

PRESENT VALUE OF ANNUITY $[1 - (1 + i)^{-n}]/i$
(Continued)

Years n	.02(2%)	.0225(2¼%)	.025(2½%)	.0275(2¾%)	.03(3%)
			Rate i		
50	31.4236059	29.8343963	28.3623117	26.9971700	25.7297640
51	31.7878489	30.1558888	28.6461577	27.2478540	25.9512272
52	32.1449499	30.4703069	28.9230807	27.4918287	26.1662400
53	32.4950489	30.7778062	29.1932495	27.7292737	26.3749903
54	32.8382833	31.0785391	29.4568288	27.9603637	26.5776605
55	33.1747875	31.3726544	29.7139793	28.1852688	26.7744276
56	33.5046936	31.6602977	29.9648578	28.4041545	26.9654637
57	33.8281310	31.9416114	30.2096174	28.6171820	27.1509357
58	34.1452265	32.2167349	30.4484072	28.8245081	27.3310055
59	34.4561044	32.4858043	30.6813729	29.0262852	27.5058306
60	34.7608867	32.7489529	30.9086565	29.2226620	27.6755637
61	35.0596928	33.0063109	31.1303966	29.4137830	27.8403531
62	35.3526400	33.2580057	31.3467284	29.5997888	28.0003428
63	35.6398432	33.5041621	31.5577838	29.7808163	28.1556726
64	35.9214149	33.7449018	31.7636915	29.9569989	28.3064783
65	36.1974655	33.9803440	31.9645771	30.1284661	28.4528915
66	36.4681035	34.2106054	32.1605630	30.2953441	28.5950403
67	36.7334348	34.4357999	32.3517688	30.4577558	28.7330488
68	36.9935635	34.6560391	32.5383110	30.6158207	28.8670377
69	37.2485917	34.8714318	32.7203034	30.7696552	28.9971240
70	37.4986193	35.0820849	32.8978570	30.9193725	29.1234214
71	37.7437444	35.2881026	33.0710800	31.0650827	29.2460401
72	37.9840631	35.4895869	33.2400780	31.2068931	29.3650875
73	38.2196697	35.6866376	33.4049542	31.3449082	29.4806675
74	38.4506566	35.8793521	33.5658089	31.4792294	29.5928811
75	38.6771143	36.0678261	33.7227404	31.6099556	29.7018263
76	38.8991317	36.2521526	33.8758443	31.7371830	29.8075983
77	39.1167958	36.4324231	34.0252140	31.8610054	29.9102896
78	39.3301919	36.6087267	34.1709405	31.9815138	30.0099899
79	39.5394039	36.7811509	34.3131127	32.0987969	30.1067863
80	39.7445136	36.9497808	34.4518172	32.2129410	30.2007634
81	39.9456016	37.1147000	34.5871388	32.3240301	30.2920033
82	40.1427466	37.2759903	34.7191598	32.4321461	30.3805858
83	40.3360261	37.4337313	34.8479607	32.5373685	30.4665881
84	40.5255158	37.5880013	34.9736202	32.6397747	30.5500856
85	40.7112900	37.7388765	35.0962149	32.7394401	30.6311510
86	40.8934216	37.8864318	35.2158194	32.8364380	30.7098554
87	41.0719819	38.0307402	35.3325067	32.9308399	30.7862673
88	41.2470411	38.1718730	35.4463480	33.0227153	30.8604537
89	41.4186677	38.3099003	35.5574127	33.1121317	30.9324794
90	41.5869292	38.4448902	35.6657685	33.1991549	31.0024071
91	41.7518913	38.5769098	35.7714814	33.2838490	31.0702982
92	41.9136190	38.7060242	35.8746160	33.3662764	31.1362118
93	42.0721754	38.8322975	35.9752352	33.4464978	31.2002057
94	42.2276230	38.9557922	36.0734002	33.5245720	31.2623356
95	42.3800225	39.0765694	36.1691709	33.6005567	31.3226559
96	42.5294339	39.1946889	36.2626057	33.6745078	31.3812193
97	42.6759155	39.3102092	36.3537617	33.7464796	31.4380770
98	42.8195250	39.4231875	36.4426943	33.8165251	31.4932787
99	42.9603187	39.5336797	36.5294579	33.8846960	31.5468725
100	43.0983516	39.6417405	36.6141053	33.9510423	31.5989053

Source: Mathematical Tables from the Handbook of Chemistry and Physics, 10th Edition, Cleveland, OH, 1954. Used with permission.

Figure 7.6

INTEREST TABLES (Continued)

PRESENT VALUE OF ANNUITY $[1 - (1 + i)^{-n}]/i$
(Continued)

Years n	Rate i				
	.035(3½ %)	.04(4 %)	.045(4½ %)	.05(5 %)	.055(5½ %)
1	0.96618357	0.96153846	0.95693780	0.95238095	0.94786730
2	1.89969428	1.88609467	1.87266775	1.85941043	1.84631971
3	2.80163698	2.77509103	2.74896435	2.72324803	2.69793338
4	3.67307921	3.62989522	3.58752570	3.54595050	3.50515012
5	4.51505238	4.45182233	4.38997674	4.32947667	4.27028448
6	5.32855302	5.24213686	5.15787248	5.07569207	4.99553031
7	6.11454398	6.00205467	5.89270094	5.78637340	5.68296712
8	6.87395554	6.73274487	6.59588607	6.46321276	6.33456599
9	7.60768651	7.43533161	7.26879050	7.10782168	6.95219525
10	8.31660532	8.11089578	7.91271818	7.72173493	7.53762583
11	9.00155104	8.76047671	8.52891692	8.30641422	8.09253633
12	9.66333433	9.38507376	9.11858078	8.86325164	8.61851785
13	10.3027385	9.98564785	9.68285242	9.39357299	9.11707853
14	10.9205203	10.5631229	10.2228253	9.89864094	9.58964790
15	11.5174109	11.1183874	10.7395457	10.3796580	10.0375809
16	12.0941168	11.6522956	11.2340150	10.8377696	10.4621620
17	12.6513206	12.1656689	11.7071914	11.2740662	10.8646086
18	13.1896817	12.6592970	12.1599918	11.6895869	11.2460745
19	13.7098374	13.1339394	12.5932936	12.0853209	11.6076535
20	14.2124033	13.5903263	13.0079365	12.4622103	11.9503825
21	14.6979742	14.0291599	13.4047239	12.8211527	12.2752441
22	15.1671248	14.4511153	13.7844248	13.1630026	12.5831697
23	15.6204105	14.8568417	14.1477749	13.4885739	12.8750424
24	16.0583676	15.2469631	14.4954784	13.7986418	13.1516990
25	16.4815146	15.6220799	14.8282090	14.0939446	13.4139327
26	16.8903523	15.9827692	15.1466114	14.3751853	13.6624954
27	17.2853645	16.3295857	15.4513028	14.6430336	13.8980999
28	17.6670188	16.6630632	15.7428735	14.8981273	14.1214217
29	18.0357670	16.9837146	16.0218885	15.1410736	14.3331012
30	18.3920454	17.2920333	16.2888885	15.3724510	14.5337452
31	18.7362758	17.5884936	16.5443910	15.5928105	14.7239291
32	19.0688655	17.8735515	16.7888909	15.8026767	14.9041982
33	19.3902082	18.1476457	17.0228621	16.0025492	15.0750694
34	19.7006842	18.4111978	17.2467580	16.1929040	15.2370326
35	20.0006611	18.6646132	17.4610124	16.3741943	15.3905522
36	20.2904938	18.9082820	17.6660406	16.5468517	15.5360684
37	20.5705254	19.1425788	17.8622398	16.7112873	15.6739985
38	20.8410874	19.3678642	18.0499902	16.8678927	15.8047379
39	21.1024999	19.5844848	18.2296557	17.0170407	15.9286615
40	21.3550723	19.7927739	18.4015844	17.1590864	16.0461247
41	21.5991037	19.9930518	18.5661095	17.2943680	16.1574642
42	21.8348828	20.1856267	18.7235498	17.4232076	16.2629992
43	22.0626887	20.3707949	18.8742103	17.5459120	16.3630324
44	22.2827910	20.5488413	19.0183831	17.6627733	16.4578506
45	22.4954503	20.7200397	19.1563474	17.7740698	16.5477257
46	22.7009181	20.8846536	19.2883707	17.8800665	16.6329154
47	22.8994378	21.0429361	19.4147088	17.9810157	16.7136639
48	23.0912443	21.1951309	19.5356065	18.0771578	16.7902027
49	23.2765645	21.3414720	19.6512981	18.1687217	16.8627514
50	23.4556179	21.4821846	19.7620078	18.2559255	16.9315179

Source: Mathematical Tables from the Handbook of Chemistry and Physics, 10th Edition, Cleveland, OH, 1954. Used with permission.

Figure 7.6 (continued)

INTEREST TABLES (Continued)

PRESENT VALUE OF ANNUITY $[1 - (1 + i)^{-n}]/i$
(Continued)

Years n	Rate i				
	.06(6 %)	.065(6½ %)	.07(7 %)	.075(7½ %)	.08(8 %)
1	0.94339623	0.93896714	0.93457944	0.93023256	0.92592593
2	1.83339267	1.82062642	1.80801817	1.79556517	1.78326475
3	2.67301195	2.64847551	2.62431604	2.60052574	2.57709699
4	3.46510561	3.42579860	3.38721126	3.34932627	3.31212684
5	4.21236379	4.15567944	4.10019744	4.04588490	3.99271004
6	4.91732433	4.84101356	4.76653966	4.69384642	4.62287966
7	5.58238144	5.48451977	5.38928940	5.29660132	5.20637006
8	6.20979381	6.08875096	5.97129851	5.85730355	5.74663894
9	6.80169227	6.65610419	6.51523225	6.37888703	6.24688791
10	7.36008705	7.18883022	7.02358154	6.86408096	6.71008140
11	7.88687458	7.68904246	7.49867434	7.31542415	7.13896426
12	8.38384394	8.15872532	7.94268630	7.73527827	7.53607802
13	8.85268296	8.59974208	8.35765074	8.12584026	7.90377594
14	9.29498393	9.01384233	8.74546799	8.48915373	8.24423698
15	9.71224899	9.40266885	9.10791401	8.82711975	8.55947869
16	10.1058953	9.76776418	9.44664860	9.14150674	8.85136916
17	10.4772597	10.1105767	9.76322299	9.43395976	9.12163811
18	10.8276035	10.4324664	10.0599869	9.70600908	9.37188714
19	11.1581165	10.7347102	10.3355952	9.95907821	9.60359920
20	11.4699212	11.0185072	10.5940142	10.1944914	9.81814741
21	11.7640766	11.2849833	10.8355273	10.4134803	10.0168032
22	12.0415817	11.5351956	11.0612405	10.6171910	10.2007437
23	12.3033790	11.7701367	11.2721874	10.8066893	10.3710589
24	12.5503575	11.9907387	11.4693340	10.9829668	10.5287583
25	12.7833562	12.1978767	11.6535832	11.1469459	10.6747762
26	13.0031662	12.3923725	11.8257787	11.2994845	10.8099780
27	13.2105341	12.5749977	11.9867090	11.4413810	10.9351648
28	13.4061643	12.7464767	12.1371113	11.5733776	11.0510785
29	13.5907210	12.9074898	12.2776741	11.6961652	11.1584060
30	13.7648312	13.0586759	12.4090412	11.8103863	11.2577833
31	13.9290860	13.2006347	12.5318142	11.9166384	11.3497994
32	14.0840434	13.3339293	12.6465553	12.0154776	11.4349994
33	14.2302296	13.4590885	12.7537900	12.1074210	11.5138884
34	14.3681411	13.5766089	12.8540094	12.1929498	11.5869337
35	14.4982464	13.6869567	12.9476723	12.2725114	11.6545682
36	14.6209871	13.7905697	13.0352078	12.3465222	11.7171928
37	14.7367803	13.8878589	13.1170166	12.4153695	11.7751785
38	14.8460192	13.9792102	13.1934735	12.4794135	11.8288690
39	14.9490747	14.0649861	13.2649285	12.5389893	11.8785824
40	15.0462969	14.1455269	13.3317088	12.5944087	11.9246133
41	15.1380159	14.2211520	13.3941204	12.6459615	11.9672346
42	15.2245433	14.2921615	13.4524490	12.6939177	12.0066987
43	15.3061729	14.3588371	13.5069617	12.7385281	12.0432395
44	15.3831820	14.4214433	13.5579081	12.7800261	12.0770736
45	15.4558321	14.4802284	13.6055216	12.8186290	12.1084015
46	15.5243699	14.5354257	13.6500202	12.8545386	12.1374088
47	15.5890282	14.5872542	13.6916076	12.8879429	12.1642674
48	15.6500266	14.6359195	13.7304744	12.9190166	12.1891365
49	15.7075723	14.6816145	13.7667985	12.9479224	12.2121634
50	15.7618606	14.7245207	13.8007463	12.9748116	12.2334846

Source: Mathematical Tables from the Handbook of Chemistry and Physics, 10th Edition, Cleveland, OH, 1954. Used with permission.

114

Present value amounts decrease as time increases because you need to put aside less money to achieve the final value of 1, since the original deposit has a longer time to earn interest. The present value also decreases as interest rates increase, because the original deposit grows at a greater rate.

Present value of annuity tables, shown in Figure 7.5 and Figure 7.6, also work in a similar way. For example, to find the present value of the annuity shown above, with five payments, at 8 percent interest, look at Figure 7.6, in the 8 percent column, for period (years) of 5. The amount shown is 3.99271004, as shown in the discussion above.

Many years ago, interest tables containing thousands of pages were published. Few people use them now, but smaller tables, for common interest rates and time period, are readily available at moderate cost. If you are active in bonds, perhaps you should have such a table.

HOW TO CALCULATE A MUNICIPAL BOND PRICE

A municipal bond pays semiannual interest until the maturity date, at which time it makes the last interest payment and repays the original principal as well. Thus the bond can be thought of as a stream of interest payments with a balloon payment at the end of the stream.

To compute the bond price, think of your bond as split into two parts: the coupon payments and the final maturity amount.

The coupon payments are an annuity certain. You are guaranteed to get a series of periodic payments, equally spaced in time, and all the payments are the same. To compute the value of this, use the present value of an annuity formula discussed earlier in the chapter.

The final maturity amount is an amount due at a specific time in the future. Compute the value of this by using the present value formula discussed earlier in the chapter.

Compute the price of the bond by adding together the value of the coupon stream and the value of the final maturity amount. Thus, we have the following:

bond price = value of coupon payments + value of final
maturity amount

Examples of Bond Price Calculation

For example, suppose we have a 2-percent bond due in 10 years at a 10-percent yield.

First, what does this mean? It means that the coupon rate on the bond is 2 percent of the par amount. A bond with a face or par amount of $1,000 will pay 2 percent of that amount per year, or $20.00 per year. This payment will be made in two semiannual portions of $10.00 each, with the last payment made on the maturity date of the bond.

The maturity date is ten years from now, so that ten years from now the owner of the bond will receive the face amount of the bond, or $1,000.

The yield basis, or yield, on which this calculation is based, is 10.00 percent. This is a nominal annual rate, compounded semiannually, so the true rate for calculation purposes is 5 percent every six months. Remember, this is not the same as 10 percent per year. When you look up values in the compound interest tables, the yield of 10 percent means that you look in the columns for 5-percent interest, because yields are nominal annual rates, compounded semiannually.

The yield basis, or yield, is mathematically the same as the interest rate *i* we have used previously in doing the computations of compound interest, present value, and present value of an annuity certain. It is not the same as the coupon rate of the bond.

The 2-percent coupon and the ten-year time to maturity are features of the original bond contract; the 10-percent yield is a statement about where the bond sells now in the market place. The 2-percent coupon and the ten-year time to maturity cannot change, although the time to maturity becomes shorter each day. The 10-percent yield can change each moment, as the market changes, and does change rapidly in fast-moving markets.

In the case of the 2-percent bond due in ten years at a 10 percent yield, the price is computed as follows:

Coupon payments of 1 every 6 months: 12.462
    This is found in Figure 7.6,
    in the column for 5 percent interest,
    and period of 20 (ten years is
    twenty half-years).

Final maturity of 100 in 10 years: 37.689
    This is found in Figure 7.4,
    in the column for 5 percent interest,
    and period of 20 (ten years is twenty
    half-years). Multiply for 100
    for the present value of the final
    maturity of 100.

Price of bond: 50.151

Bond prices are always stated as a percent of par, so the price of a $1,000 bond would be $501.51; the price of $10,000 of bonds would be $5,015.10.

Here is another example, this time of a bond selling at a premium over par (100.000).

Suppose the owner buys a bond with a 10-percent coupon, due in five years, at a 6-percent yield. The owner will pay a price of 117.0604, computed as follows:

Value of the coupons: 42.651
    (5 × 8.530203)
    (Found in the table for
    period = 10 and i = 3 percent)

Present value of final maturity: 74.409
    (100 × .7440939)
    (Found in the table for
    period = 10 and i = 3 percent)

Total amount (price of bond):   117.060

The investor will receive a payment of 5 every six months, equal to 10 percent per year, but made in two equal semiannual payments. The investor will also receive a final principal payment in five years of 100. Note that he will receive less in maturity amount (100) than he paid to buy the bond (117.060). The difference must be deducted from his coupon income to determine how much he actually earned from his investment.

HOW TO ACCRUE (OR ACCRETE) DISCOUNT

The return to the investor buying a bond at a discount comes from two sources: the coupon income, and a gain when the bond matures. The coupon income is paid every six months, but the gain at maturity only occurs upon maturity. If the bond is bought at a premium, the premium is deducted from the interest earnings to compute the net income.

For the first bond price calculation example shown above, this income and principal value accrual is shown, for each six-month period, in Figure 7.7.

Figure 7.7

THIS IS THE CHART FOR A BOND DISCOUNT ACCRETION

2 percent coupon
due in 10 years
at a 10 percent yield
value of coupons = 1 × (12.4622) = 12.462
value of maturity amount = 100 × (.376889) = 37.689
value of bond = 50.151

Year	Total Earned in Period	Coupon Payment	Book Value Increase in Period	Book Value at End of Period
0.0				50.151
0.5	2.508	1.0	1.508	51.659
1.0	2.583	1.0	1.583	53.242
1.5	2.662	1.0	1.662	54.904
2.0	2.745	1.0	1.745	56.649
2.5	2.832	1.0	1.832	58.481
3.0	2.924	1.0	1.924	60.405
3.5	3.020	1.0	2.020	62.426
4.0	3.121	1.0	2.121	64.547
4.5	3.227	1.0	2.227	66.774
5.0	3.339	1.0	2.339	69.113

Figure 7.7 (continued)

5.5	3.456	1.0	2.456	71.569
6.0	3.578	1.0	2.578	74.147
6.5	3.707	1.0	2.707	76.854
7.0	3.843	1.0	2.843	79.697
7.5	3.985	1.0	2.985	82.682
8.0	4.134	1.0	3.134	85.816
8.5	4.291	1.0	3.291	89.107
9.0	4.455	1.0	3.455	92.562
9.5	4.628	1.0	3.628	96.190
10.0	4.810	1.0	3.810	100.000

(Calculations may not quite conform, due to rounding.)

You start with a bond for which you paid 50.151. During the first six months, you earn at a rate of 10 percent per year on the 50.151. This is 5 percent of 50.151, or 2.508. Part of this is paid when you receive your coupon of 1; the rest is added to the book value of your bond, which is now, after six months, 51.659. Thus the 2.508 you receive is split in two parts. One part, the interest payment of 1, is paid immediately. The other part, equal to the total earned of 2.508, minus the amount paid as interest, equals 1.508. This is added to the book value at the start of the period, to equal the new book value of the bond. Let's look at this in the form of a chart:

Original investment:		50.151
Earnings: 5 percent of cost:	2.508	
Coupon payment (cash):	(1.000)	
Net increase in book value:		1.508
Book value after six months:		51.659

After six months, the book value of the bond has increased to 51.659. Note that the market value of the bond may or may not be 51.659; actually, it probably won't be. You may be able to sell your bond for more, or you may have to accept less if you sell it; the price depends on the market. For your internal accounting, however, the 51.659 is your book value.

Suppose you hold the bond for another six months. You earn another 5 percent on your investment (one-half of the annual 10 percent, remember?), but this time you earn it on the new increased book value. Here are the numbers for the second period:

Book value start of period:		51.659
Earnings (5 percent of book value):	2.583	
Coupon payment (cash):	(1.000)	
Net increase in book value:		1.583
Book value after one year:		53.242

Note that the earnings increase each six months. This happens because the book value is higher each six months. However, the coupon payment stays the same during the entire life of the bond. As a result, the change in book value increases during the life of the bond.

At the end of the next-to-last period, with just six months left until maturity, the bond has a book value of 96.1903. The values are:

Book value at start of period:		96.190
Earnings (5 percent of book value):	4.810	
Coupon payment (cash):	(1.000)	
Net increase in book value:		3.810
Book value at end of period (maturity):		100.000

At this time, the bond matures and you receive the par value. In the calculation, the book value is 100; this is 100 percent of par, regardless of the actual par value of the bond.

This process is called *accruing a discount*, or *accreting a discount*. The discount is accrued (or accreted) in a systematic way over the life of the bond. This particular method of accruing discount is called the yield basis, or scientific, method of accruing a discount.

Another method of accruing a discount is the straight-line method. This method accrues the discount in equal installments over the life of the bond. In our example, the discount of 49.8489 would be accrued in twenty equal semiannual installments of 2.4924. Before computers came along, this was the usual way of accruing discount; now, almost everybody uses the yield basis method, and it may even be required for income tax reporting purposes in determing the cost basis for the bonds. See the relevant Internal Revenue Service publication or your accountant for further details.

HOW TO AMORTIZE A PREMIUM

Amortization of a premium works in a comparable way, except that you reduce rather than increase the book value of the bond.

This reduction in turn reduces your actual earnings to an amount less than the coupon you receive every six months.

The income and principal amortization for the premium bond calculated above is shown in Figure 7.8.

Figure 7.8

BOND PREMIUM AMORTIZATION

10 percent coupon
due in 5 years
at a 6 percent yield

value of coupons	=	5 × (8.530203)
	=	42.651
value of maturity amount	=	100 × (.7440939)
	=	74.409
price of bond	=	117.060

Year	Total Earned in Period	Coupon Payment	Book Value Decrease in Period	Book Value at End of Period
0.0				117.060
0.5	3.512	5.0	1.488	115.572
1.0	3.467	5.0	1.533	114.039
1.5	3.421	5.0	1.579	112.461
2.0	3.374	5.0	1.626	110.834
2.5	3.325	5.0	1.675	109.159
3.0	3.275	5.0	1.725	107.434
3.5	3.223	5.0	1.777	105.657
4.0	3.170	5.0	1.830	103.827
4.5	3.115	5.0	1.885	101.942
5.0	3.058	5.0	1.942	100.000

For the first six-month period, the earnings and amortization are as follows:

Purchase price of the bond	117.060
Earnings (3 percent of price):	3.512
Coupon income (cash):	(5.000)
Net reduction in book value	(1.488)
Book value after six months	115.572

Thus, although you receive 5.00 in interest, your actual earnings are only 3.512; the remaining amount, 1.488, is a return of your original principal.

During the next semiannual period, you earn another 3 percent on your investment, but now the investment, or book value, is 115.572. Your earnings, therefore, are 3 percent of 115.572, or 3.467. Once more, you receive 5.000 in cash, with the excess over the earnings reducing your book value once more. The numbers are:

Book value:		115.572
Earnings (3 percent of book value):	3.467	
Coupon income (cash):	(5.000)	
Decrease in book value:		(1.533)
New book value:		114.039

Thus the book value after one year is 114.039.

After four and one-half years, the book value is 101.942, with just six months until the bond matures. The numbers are:

Book value:		101.942
Earnings (3 percent of book value):	3.058	
Coupon income (cash):	(5.000)	
Decrease in book value:		(1.942)
New book value:		100.000

The bond matures at 100.000. You have received 50.000 in coupon income over the five years of ownership, but 17.060 of this is actually a return of capital; only 32.940 is actual earnings from your investment.

This process is called premium amortization. The premium paid for the bond is written off against the interest income received during the life of the bond, reducing the actual interest earnings. This particular method of premium amortization is called the yield basis or scientific method of premium amortization.

The Straight-Line Method

Another method of premium amortization is the straight-line method. This method writes off the premium in equal installments over the life of the bond. In the example above, the premium would be written off in equal semiannual amounts of 1.706 (one-tenth of the total premium paid of 17.060), and earnings for each semiannual period would be 5.000 – 1.706, or 3.294. This method was a common method before computers, but now most premium amortization is done using the yield basis method, and this method may be required for income tax reporting purposes in some cases. See the relevant Internal Revenue Service publication or your accountant for further details.

Tax Consequences

Discount accrual and premium amortization have important tax consequences in determining reported interest income and calculating the cost basis of your bond. A discussion of this is beyond the scope of this book. You should consult with your accountant or the relevant Internal Revenue Service publications.

UNDERSTANDING THE MUNICIPAL SECURITIES RULEMAKING BOARD PRICE CALCULATION FORMULA (RULE G-33)

Figure 7.9 shows the formula for the calculation of municipal bond prices with more than six months to redemption, as required by the Municipal Securities Rulemaking Board, Rule G-33 as originally promulgated, and slightly modified by the author. It looks more fearsome than it actually is.

The formula contains three terms. The first term is the present value of the final maturity amount, or, as the MSRB calls it, the final redemption amount. This is the final maturity amount of the bond, or, if the bond has a call feature or has been called, the call price. The final redemption amount has been multiplied by a present value factor, shown in the denominator as an interest function raised to a power. This is just a present value.

The second term shows a sum, and the items being added are the present values of the series of coupon payments. This is the present value of the annuity certain of interest payments, each individual payment being multiplied by a present value to compute its present value, and the entire series of present values summed, indicated by the summation sign. Note that the interest terms are raised to the power of the time to payment of the coupon, redemption of the bond before maturity, or maturity at par. This is just the present value of an annuity.

Figure 7.9

MUNICIPAL SECURITIES RULEMAKING BOARD
RULE G-33

For securities with more than six months to redemption, the following formula is used:

Price =

$$\left[\frac{RV}{\left(1+\frac{Y}{2}\right)^{N-1+\frac{E-A}{E}}}\right] + \left[\sum_{K=1}^{N}\frac{100\left(\frac{R}{2}\right)}{\left(1+\frac{Y}{2}\right)^{K-1+\frac{E-A}{E}}}\right] - \left[100\left(\frac{A}{B}\right)(R)\right]$$

For purposes of this formula the symbols shall be defined as follows:

A is the number of accrued days from beginning of the interest payment period to the settlement date.

B is the number of days in the year. For most municipal bond transactions, this is 360.

E is the number of days in the interest payment period in which the settlement date falls. For most municipal bond transactions, this is 180.

N is the number of interest payments, expressed as a whole number, occurring between the settlement date and the redemption date, including the payment on the redemption date.

Price is the dollar price of the security for each $100 par value.

R is the annual interest rate expressed as a decimal. For example, if the coupon rate is 6 percent, *R* is 0.06.

RV is the redemption value of the security per $100 par value. If the bond matures at par, *RV* is 100. For calculating to the call, *RV* is the call price. For example, if the bond has been called at 102, *RV* is 102.

Y is the yield price of the transaction, expressed as a decimal. For example, if the yield is 5.75 percent, *Y* is .0575.

Source: Municipal Securities Rulemaking Board

The third term shows the accrued interest on the bond. Bonds not in default are sold at an agreed-upon price plus accrued interest. However, the first two terms in the MSRB formula calculate the total amount due, including accrued interest. To compute the price, the accrued interest must be deducted from the total amount calculation; it is then added in as accrued interest on the bond confirmation to compute the total amount due. Bonds in default are traded "flat," that is, without accrued interest. The bond calculations earlier in the chapter did not have accrued interest because they were calculated with an even number of payment periods to maturity, so that accrued interest was zero.

Rule G-33 contains other equations, including equations for notes and securities maturing in six months or less. These are beyond the scope of this book.

SOME GENERAL RULES FOR PRICES AND YIELDS

A few simple rules exist for the relationship between price and yield. You should have an understanding of these, especially that prices rise as yields fall, and that prices fall as yields rise.

1. Price moves inversely to yield:
   a. Increasing yield decreases price.

If you increase yield, you increase the earning power of the investment. Therefore, you need to invest less money to earn the bond payments you have bought, because the investment earns at a greater rate.

b. Decreasing yield increases price.

If you decrease yield, you decrease the earning power of the investment. Therefore, you need to invest more money to earn the bond payments you have bought, because the investment earns at a lower rate.

2. Increasing coupon increases price:

Increasing coupon income increases the total amount of money the investor will receive. Clearly this is worth more now, regardless of when the additional money will be received.

3. Increasing time to maturity:
    a. Decreases price if the bond is under par;
    b. Increases price if the bond is over par;
    c. Par bonds remain at par.

HOW TO UNDERSTAND A BOND BASIS BOOK

Bond investors, traders, and administrators used to use large books called bond basis books to look up and compute bond prices. Hardly anyone uses these now; this job is done by computers. But a look at a basis book shows how prices change as yields change. Figures 7.10 and 7.11 show pages from a basis book, over 2,800 pages long, published in 1962. The pages show monthly values for a 4-percent bond, at selected yields, for periods from three years even to three years eleven months. Values for periods other than even months were computed by day interpolation.

For example, suppose you want to find the price of a 4-percent bond, maturing in three years four months, at a 3.15-percent yield. You look at the column for three years four months and the row for 3.15 yield, and where the row and column meet, you find the price. In this case, the price is 102.67.

You can also use the tables to find an approximation of the yield, given the dollar price. For example, a 4-percent bond maturing in three years six months priced at 105 has a yield of 2.50. In most cases the yield won't be in the table, but you can use the table to get a good idea of the yield.

Note that price moves inversely to yield; as yield increases, price decreases. Note that for prices above par, moving to a longer maturity increases price for a given yield; for prices below par, the same process reduces price. Par bonds remain at par.

Many different basis books exist, and they are no longer used much. However, you may wish to obtain a small one which covers a wide variety of coupons, maturities, and yields, but not in great depth. It will give you an idea of the approximate price for your bonds at given yields. You can get them from Financial Publishing Company, in Boston, or perhaps your broker has some old ones he or she no longer needs.

A FINAL WORD

You should have some idea of how the concepts of financial mathematics work, at least for your bond investments. You should also know how to do elementary bond calculations, at least to have some idea of what will happen to bond prices, especially prices of bonds you own or might buy, as yields change. You don't need to know how to compute accrued interest, and we didn't discuss it in this chapter. You should, however, have some idea of how to compute discount accrual and premium amortization, if only to follow your accountant's explanations. With a little work, these calculations will become natural to you. You don't need to become an expert to use financial mathematics in meeting your investment needs.

Figure 7.10

3 YEARS

4%   4%

Yield	Even	1 mo	2 mo	3 mo	4 mo	5 mo	6 mo	7 mo	8 mo	9 mo	10 mo	11 mo
1.00	108.84	109.09	109.33	109.57	109.81	110.05	110.29	110.53	110.77	111.01	111.25	111.49
1.05	108.69	108.93	109.16	109.40	109.64	109.87	110.11	110.35	110.58	110.82	111.05	111.29
1.10	108.53	108.77	109.00	109.23	109.46	109.70	109.93	110.16	110.39	110.62	110.86	111.09
1.15	108.38	108.61	108.84	109.06	109.29	109.52	109.75	109.98	110.20	110.43	110.66	110.88
1.20	108.23	108.45	108.67	108.90	109.12	109.34	109.57	109.79	110.01	110.24	110.46	110.68
1.25	108.07	108.29	108.51	108.73	108.95	109.17	109.39	109.61	109.82	110.04	110.26	110.48
1.30	107.92	108.13	108.35	108.56	108.78	108.99	109.21	109.42	109.64	109.85	110.06	110.28
1.35	107.77	107.98	108.19	108.40	108.61	108.82	109.03	109.24	109.45	109.66	109.87	110.08
1.40	107.61	107.82	108.02	108.23	108.44	108.64	108.85	109.05	109.26	109.46	109.67	109.87
1.45	107.46	107.66	107.86	108.06	108.27	108.47	108.67	108.87	109.07	109.27	109.47	109.67
1.50	107.31	107.50	107.70	107.90	108.10	108.30	108.49	108.69	108.89	109.08	109.28	109.47
1.55	107.15	107.35	107.54	107.73	107.93	108.12	108.32	108.51	108.70	108.89	109.08	109.27
1.60	107.00	107.19	107.38	107.57	107.76	107.95	108.14	108.32	108.51	108.70	108.89	109.08
1.65	106.85	107.04	107.22	107.40	107.59	107.77	107.96	108.14	108.33	108.51	108.69	108.88
1.70	106.70	106.88	107.06	107.24	107.42	107.60	107.78	107.96	108.14	108.32	108.50	108.68
1.75	106.55	106.72	106.90	107.08	107.25	107.43	107.61	107.78	107.96	108.13	108.31	108.48
1.80	106.40	106.57	106.74	106.91	107.08	107.26	107.43	107.60	107.77	107.94	108.11	108.28
1.85	106.25	106.41	106.58	106.75	106.92	107.09	107.25	107.42	107.59	107.75	107.92	108.09
1.90	106.10	106.26	106.42	106.59	106.75	106.91	107.08	107.24	107.40	107.56	107.73	107.89
1.95	105.95	106.10	106.26	106.42	106.58	106.74	106.90	107.06	107.22	107.38	107.53	107.69
2.00	105.80	105.95	106.11	106.26	106.42	106.57	106.73	106.88	107.03	107.19	107.34	107.50
2.05	105.65	105.80	105.95	106.10	106.25	106.40	106.55	106.70	106.85	107.00	107.15	107.30
2.10	105.50	105.64	105.79	105.94	106.08	106.23	106.38	106.52	106.67	106.81	106.96	107.11
2.15	105.35	105.49	105.63	105.77	105.92	106.06	106.21	106.35	106.49	106.63	106.77	106.91
2.20	105.20	105.34	105.47	105.61	105.75	105.89	106.03	106.17	106.31	106.44	106.58	106.72
2.25	105.05	105.18	105.32	105.45	105.59	105.72	105.86	105.99	106.12	106.26	106.39	106.52
2.30	104.90	105.03	105.16	105.29	105.42	105.55	105.69	105.81	105.94	106.07	106.20	106.33
2.35	104.75	104.88	105.00	105.13	105.26	105.39	105.51	105.64	105.76	105.89	106.01	106.14
2.40	104.60	104.73	104.85	104.97	105.09	105.22	105.34	105.46	105.58	105.70	105.82	105.95
2.45	104.46	104.57	104.69	104.81	104.93	105.05	105.17	105.28	105.40	105.52	105.64	105.75
2.50	104.31	104.42	104.54	104.65	104.77	104.88	105.00	105.11	105.22	105.33	105.45	105.56
2.55	104.16	104.27	104.38	104.49	104.60	104.71	104.83	104.93	105.04	105.15	105.26	105.37
2.60	104.02	104.12	104.23	104.33	104.44	104.55	104.65	104.76	104.86	104.97	105.07	105.18
2.65	103.87	103.97	104.07	104.17	104.28	104.38	104.48	104.58	104.68	104.79	104.89	104.99
2.70	103.72	103.82	103.92	104.02	104.11	104.21	104.31	104.41	104.51	104.60	104.70	104.80

Source: Investors Bond Values Table, Financial Publishing Co., Boston, MA, 1962.

128

Figure 7.10 (continued)

Rate												
2.75	104.61	104.52	104.42	104.33	104.24	104.14	104.05	103.95	103.86	103.76	103.67	103.58
2.80	104.42	104.33	104.24	104.15	104.06	103.97	103.88	103.79	103.70	103.61	103.52	103.43
2.85	104.23	104.15	104.06	103.97	103.89	103.81	103.72	103.63	103.54	103.46	103.37	103.28
2.90	104.04	103.96	103.88	103.80	103.72	103.64	103.55	103.47	103.38	103.30	103.22	103.14
2.95	103.86	103.78	103.70	103.62	103.54	103.47	103.39	103.31	103.23	103.15	103.07	102.99
3.00	103.67	103.59	103.52	103.44	103.37	103.30	103.22	103.15	103.07	103.00	102.92	102.85
3.05	103.48	103.41	103.34	103.27	103.20	103.13	103.06	102.99	102.91	102.84	102.77	102.70
3.10	103.29	103.23	103.16	103.09	103.03	102.96	102.89	102.83	102.76	102.69	102.63	102.56
3.15	103.11	103.04	102.98	102.92	102.86	102.80	102.73	102.67	102.60	102.54	102.48	102.42
3.20	102.92	102.86	102.80	102.74	102.69	102.63	102.57	102.51	102.45	102.39	102.33	102.27
3.25	102.74	102.68	102.62	102.57	102.52	102.46	102.40	102.35	102.29	102.24	102.18	102.13
3.30	102.55	102.50	102.45	102.40	102.35	102.30	102.24	102.19	102.14	102.08	102.03	101.98
3.35	102.37	102.32	102.27	102.22	102.18	102.13	102.08	102.03	101.98	101.93	101.89	101.84
3.40	102.18	102.14	102.09	102.05	102.01	101.96	101.92	101.87	101.83	101.78	101.74	101.70
3.45	102.00	101.96	101.91	101.88	101.84	101.80	101.76	101.71	101.67	101.63	101.59	101.55
3.50	101.81	101.78	101.74	101.70	101.67	101.63	101.59	101.56	101.52	101.48	101.45	101.41
3.55	101.63	101.60	101.56	101.53	101.50	101.47	101.43	101.40	101.37	101.33	101.30	101.27
3.60	101.45	101.42	101.39	101.36	101.33	101.30	101.27	101.24	101.21	101.18	101.16	101.13
3.65	101.26	101.24	101.21	101.19	101.16	101.14	101.11	101.09	101.06	101.03	101.01	100.99
3.70	101.08	101.06	101.04	101.02	101.00	100.98	100.95	100.93	100.91	100.88	100.86	100.84
3.75	100.90	100.88	100.86	100.84	100.83	100.81	100.79	100.77	100.75	100.74	100.72	100.70
3.80	100.72	100.70	100.69	100.67	100.66	100.65	100.63	100.62	100.60	100.59	100.57	100.56
3.85	100.54	100.53	100.51	100.50	100.49	100.49	100.47	100.46	100.45	100.44	100.43	100.42
3.90	100.36	100.35	100.34	100.33	100.33	100.32	100.31	100.31	100.30	100.29	100.29	100.28
3.95	100.18	100.17	100.17	100.16	100.16	100.16	100.16	100.15	100.15	100.14	100.14	100.14
4.00	100.00	100.00	100.00	100.00	100.00	100.00	100.00	100.00	100.00	100.00	100.00	100.00
4.05	99.82	99.82	99.82	99.83	99.83	99.84	99.84	99.84	99.84	99.85	99.85	99.86
4.10	99.64	99.64	99.65	99.66	99.67	99.68	99.68	99.69	99.69	99.70	99.71	99.72
4.15	99.46	99.47	99.48	99.49	99.50	99.52	99.52	99.53	99.54	99.55	99.57	99.58
4.20	99.28	99.29	99.31	99.32	99.34	99.36	99.37	99.39	99.39	99.41	99.42	99.44
4.25	99.10	99.12	99.14	99.15	99.17	99.19	99.21	99.23	99.24	99.26	99.28	99.30
4.30	98.93	98.95	98.97	98.99	99.01	99.03	99.05	99.07	99.09	99.12	99.14	99.16
4.35	98.75	98.77	98.80	98.82	98.85	98.87	98.90	98.92	98.94	98.97	99.00	99.03
4.40	98.57	98.60	98.63	98.65	98.68	98.72	98.74	98.77	98.80	98.82	98.86	98.89
4.45	98.40	98.43	98.46	98.49	98.52	98.56	98.59	98.62	98.65	98.68	98.71	98.75
4.50	98.22	98.25	98.29	98.32	98.36	98.40	98.43	98.46	98.50	98.53	98.57	98.61
4.55	98.04	98.08	98.12	98.16	98.20	98.24	98.27	98.31	98.35	98.39	98.43	98.47
4.60	97.87	97.91	97.95	97.99	98.04	98.08	98.12	98.16	98.20	98.25	98.29	98.34
4.65	97.69	97.74	97.78	97.83	97.87	97.92	97.99	98.01	98.05	98.10	98.15	98.20
4.70	97.52	97.57	97.61	97.66	97.71	97.76	97.81	97.86	97.91	97.96	98.01	98.06

1308

Source: Investors Bond Values Table, Financial Publishing Co., Boston, MA, 1962.

Figure 7.11

3 YEARS

4% Yield	Even	1 mo	2 mo	3 mo	4 mo	5 mo	6 mo	7 mo	8 mo	9 mo	10 mo	11 mo — 4%
4.75	97.93	97.87	97.81	97.76	97.71	97.66	97.61	97.55	97.50	97.45	97.39	97.34
4.80	97.79	97.73	97.67	97.61	97.56	97.50	97.45	97.39	97.33	97.28	97.22	97.17
4.85	97.65	97.59	97.53	97.47	97.41	97.35	97.29	97.23	97.17	97.11	97.05	97.00
4.90	97.52	97.45	97.38	97.32	97.26	97.20	97.14	97.07	97.01	96.94	96.88	96.82
4.95	97.38	97.31	97.24	97.17	97.11	97.04	96.98	96.91	96.84	96.78	96.71	96.65
5.00	97.25	97.17	97.10	97.03	96.96	96.89	96.83	96.75	96.68	96.61	96.55	96.48
5.05	97.11	97.03	96.96	96.88	96.81	96.74	96.67	96.59	96.52	96.45	96.38	96.31
5.10	96.98	96.89	96.81	96.74	96.66	96.59	96.51	96.44	96.36	96.28	96.21	96.14
5.15	96.84	96.76	96.67	96.59	96.51	96.44	96.36	96.28	96.20	96.12	96.04	95.96
5.20	96.71	96.62	96.53	96.45	96.36	96.28	96.20	96.12	96.03	95.95	95.87	95.79
5.25	96.57	96.48	96.39	96.30	96.22	96.13	96.05	95.96	95.87	95.79	95.70	95.62
5.30	96.44	96.34	96.25	96.16	96.07	95.98	95.90	95.80	95.71	95.62	95.54	95.45
5.35	96.30	96.21	96.11	96.01	95.92	95.83	95.74	95.65	95.55	95.46	95.37	95.28
5.40	96.17	96.07	95.97	95.87	95.78	95.68	95.59	95.49	95.39	95.30	95.20	95.11
5.45	96.04	95.93	95.83	95.73	95.63	95.53	95.44	95.33	95.23	95.13	95.04	94.94
5.50	95.90	95.79	95.69	95.58	95.48	95.38	95.28	95.18	95.07	94.97	94.87	94.77
5.55	95.77	95.66	95.55	95.44	95.34	95.23	95.13	95.02	94.91	94.81	94.71	94.61
5.60	95.64	95.52	95.41	95.30	95.19	95.08	94.98	94.87	94.76	94.65	94.54	94.44
5.65	95.50	95.39	95.27	95.16	95.04	94.93	94.83	94.71	94.60	94.49	94.38	94.27
5.70	95.37	95.25	95.13	95.01	94.90	94.79	94.67	94.56	94.44	94.33	94.21	94.10
5.75	95.24	95.12	94.99	94.87	94.75	94.64	94.52	94.40	94.28	94.16	94.05	93.94
5.80	95.11	94.98	94.85	94.73	94.61	94.49	94.37	94.25	94.12	94.00	93.89	93.77
5.85	94.98	94.85	94.71	94.59	94.46	94.34	94.22	94.09	93.97	93.84	93.72	93.60
5.90	94.85	94.71	94.58	94.45	94.32	94.19	94.07	93.94	93.81	93.68	93.56	93.44
5.95	94.71	94.58	94.44	94.31	94.18	94.05	93.92	93.79	93.65	93.52	93.40	93.27
6.00	94.58	94.44	94.30	94.17	94.03	93.90	93.77	93.63	93.50	93.36	93.23	93.11
6.05	94.45	94.31	94.17	94.03	93.89	93.75	93.62	93.48	93.34	93.21	93.07	92.94
6.10	94.32	94.17	94.03	93.89	93.74	93.61	93.47	93.33	93.19	93.05	92.91	92.78
6.15	94.19	94.04	93.89	93.75	93.60	93.46	93.32	93.17	93.03	92.89	92.75	92.61
6.20	94.06	93.91	93.75	93.61	93.46	93.31	93.17	93.02	92.88	92.73	92.59	92.45
6.25	93.93	93.77	93.62	93.47	93.32	93.17	93.02	92.87	92.72	92.57	92.43	92.28
6.30	93.80	93.64	93.48	93.33	93.17	93.02	92.88	92.72	92.57	92.42	92.27	92.12
6.35	93.67	93.51	93.35	93.19	93.03	92.88	92.73	92.57	92.41	92.26	92.11	91.96
6.40	93.54	93.38	93.21	93.05	92.89	92.73	92.58	92.42	92.26	92.10	91.95	91.80
6.45	93.41	93.24	93.08	92.91	92.75	92.59	92.43	92.27	92.11	91.95	91.79	91.63

Source: Investors Bond Values Table, Financial Publishing Co., Boston, MA, 1962.

130

Figure 7.11 (continued)

Rate	1	2	3	4	5	6	7	8	9	10	11	12
6.50	91.47	91.63	91.79	91.95	92.12	92.29	92.44	92.61	92.77	92.94	93.11	93.28
6.55	91.31	91.47	91.63	91.80	91.97	92.14	92.30	92.47	92.63	92.81	92.98	93.16
6.60	91.15	91.31	91.48	91.65	91.82	91.99	92.16	92.33	92.50	92.67	92.85	93.03
6.65	90.99	91.15	91.32	91.49	91.67	91.85	92.01	92.19	92.36	92.54	92.72	92.90
6.70	90.83	91.00	91.17	91.34	91.52	91.70	91.87	92.05	92.22	92.40	92.59	92.77
6.75	90.67	90.84	91.01	91.19	91.37	91.55	91.73	91.91	92.09	92.27	92.45	92.64
6.80	90.51	90.68	90.86	91.04	91.22	91.41	91.59	91.77	91.95	92.13	92.32	92.52
6.85	90.35	90.53	90.71	90.89	91.07	91.26	91.44	91.63	91.81	92.00	92.19	92.39
6.90	90.19	90.37	90.55	90.74	90.93	91.12	91.30	91.49	91.68	91.87	92.06	92.26
6.95	90.03	90.21	90.40	90.59	90.78	90.97	91.16	91.35	91.54	91.73	91.93	92.13
7.00	89.87	90.06	90.25	90.44	90.63	90.83	91.02	91.21	91.40	91.60	91.80	92.01
7.05	89.71	89.90	90.09	90.29	90.48	90.68	90.88	91.07	91.27	91.47	91.67	91.88
7.10	89.56	89.75	89.94	90.14	90.34	90.54	90.73	90.93	91.13	91.34	91.54	91.75
7.15	89.40	89.59	89.79	89.99	90.19	90.40	90.59	90.79	91.00	91.20	91.41	91.63
7.20	89.24	89.44	89.64	89.84	90.04	90.25	90.45	90.66	90.86	91.07	91.29	91.50
7.25	89.08	89.28	89.48	89.69	89.90	90.11	90.31	90.52	90.73	90.94	91.16	91.38
7.30	88.93	89.13	89.33	89.54	89.75	89.97	90.17	90.38	90.59	90.81	91.03	91.25
7.35	88.77	88.98	89.18	89.39	89.61	89.82	90.03	90.25	90.46	90.68	90.90	91.13
7.40	88.61	88.82	89.03	89.25	89.46	89.68	89.89	90.11	90.33	90.55	90.77	91.00
7.45	88.46	88.67	88.88	89.10	89.32	89.54	89.75	89.97	90.19	90.42	90.64	90.88
7.50	88.30	88.52	88.73	88.95	89.17	89.40	89.62	89.84	90.06	90.29	90.52	90.75
7.55	88.15	88.36	88.58	88.80	89.03	89.26	89.48	89.70	89.93	90.16	90.39	90.63
7.60	87.99	88.21	88.43	88.66	88.88	89.12	89.34	89.56	89.79	90.03	90.26	90.50
7.65	87.84	88.06	88.28	88.51	88.74	88.98	89.20	89.43	89.66	89.90	90.14	90.38
7.70	87.69	87.91	88.13	88.36	88.60	88.83	89.06	89.29	89.53	89.77	90.01	90.25
7.75	87.53	87.76	87.99	88.22	88.45	88.69	88.92	89.16	89.40	89.64	89.88	90.13
7.80	87.38	87.61	87.84	88.07	88.31	88.55	88.79	89.02	89.26	89.51	89.76	90.01
7.85	87.23	87.46	87.69	87.93	88.17	88.41	88.65	88.89	89.13	89.38	89.63	89.88
7.90	87.07	87.31	87.54	87.78	88.03	88.27	88.51	88.75	89.00	89.25	89.50	89.76
7.95	86.92	87.16	87.40	87.64	87.88	88.13	88.38	88.62	88.87	89.12	89.38	89.64
8.00	86.77	87.01	87.25	87.49	87.74	88.00	88.24	88.49	88.74	88.99	89.25	89.52
8.05	86.62	86.86	87.10	87.35	87.60	87.86	88.10	88.35	88.61	88.87	89.13	89.39
8.10	86.47	86.71	86.96	87.21	87.46	87.72	87.97	88.22	88.48	88.74	89.00	89.27
8.15	86.31	86.56	86.81	87.06	87.32	87.58	87.83	88.09	88.35	88.61	88.88	89.15
8.20	86.16	86.41	86.66	86.92	87.18	87.44	87.70	87.95	88.22	88.48	88.75	89.03
8.25	86.01	86.26	86.52	86.78	87.04	87.30	87.56	87.82	88.09	88.36	88.63	88.91
8.30	85.86	86.12	86.37	86.63	86.90	87.17	87.43	87.69	87.96	88.23	88.50	88.78
8.35	85.71	85.97	86.23	86.49	86.76	87.03	87.29	87.56	87.83	88.10	88.38	88.66
8.40	85.56	85.82	86.08	86.35	86.62	86.89	87.16	87.43	87.70	87.98	88.26	88.54
8.45	85.41	85.67	85.94	86.21	86.48	86.76	87.02	87.29	87.57	87.85	88.13	88.42

1309

Source: Investors Bond Values Table, Financial Publishing Co., Boston, MA, 1962.

131

The Municipal Bond Marketplace

Many different institutions and individuals come together to make up the municipal bond market. Issuers sell the bonds in the first place; investors and others buy them; municipal bond persons underwrite, trade, research, sell, and perform other functions; rating agencies provide opinions on the relative merit of many bonds; bond insurers insure some of them; and others participate in this large market. This chapter discusses the major participants in the municipal market, what they do, and their place in the market.

WHO ISSUES MUNICIPAL BONDS?

Issuers of municipal bonds include state and local governments, their agencies, and their authorities. Usually, especially in the case of agencies and authorities, the power to issue bonds must be explicitly stated in the legislation that sets up the agency or authority in the first place. Sometimes limitations exist on the issuance of bonds. Usually, these are limits set by law, but in some cases the state constitution limits the amount of public debt that may be issued by an issuer, including the state itself.

A government may issue bonds for general government purposes or for specific purposes. General purposes may be any legitimate government spending. Frequently, bonds are issued for specific purposes, such as building a firehouse or a school. These are mentioned when the bonds are sold, and are frequently mentioned in the description of the bonds when they are traded.

Bonds may be secured by the general taxing power of the government. In this case, they are called general obligation (GO) bonds, because they become obligations of the issuer, payable out of tax revenues. Clearly, only a government with the power to tax can issue general obligation bonds.

If the taxes are levied on real estate, as is the case with the bonds of many cities, towns, and villages, the phrase "unlimited *ad valorem* taxes," or taxes on the value of the property without limit as to rate or amount, can be applied. In other cases, the issuer simply promises to levy enough taxes to pay the bonds. In the New York State bond shown in Figure 1.1, the State of New York promises to levy enough taxes to pay interest and principal on the bonds.

Bonds may be secured by the earnings of a governmental enterprise of some sort; these are called revenue bonds. Examples of these include water revenue bonds, paid from the earnings of a water supply system; electric revenue bonds, paid from the earnings of a municipal electric system; sewer revenue bonds, paid from the earnings of a sewer system; and swimming pool revenue bonds, paid from the earnings of a swimming pool.

An issuer need not be a government to issue revenue bonds. Government agencies and authorities also may have the power to issue revenue bonds. For example, The Port Authority of New York and New Jersey does not have the power to levy taxes, so the many bonds it has issued are all revenue bonds.

Sometimes, the same issuer will issue both revenue and general obligation bonds. For example, Houston, Texas, has issued general obligation bonds, and also a variety of revenue bonds. The revenue bonds include airport system revenue bonds, sewer system revenue bonds, water and sewer system revenue bonds, and water system revenue bonds. Interest and principal for each of the revenue bonds is paid only from revenues which Houston has pledged to pay the bond's interest and principal, but the general obligation bonds are paid from all the revenues, including tax revenues of the city.

Sometimes an issuer of bonds may be taken over by another government entity, which will assume responsibility for payment of the bonds. For example, Houston, Texas, has expanded, and in doing so has incorporated a number of previously independent utility districts, some of which had issued bonds (some of which were of dubious credit quality). These bonds are now all guaranteed by Houston, even though they may have been originally issued by a separate entity.

Authorities and Other Governmental Agencies

Authorities or governmental agencies may issue bonds in several different capacities. The agency may issue bonds to finance its own operations. For example, the Port Authority of New York and New Jersey issues revenue bonds to finance its own varied operations in the New York City metropolitan area.

However, the Allegheny County Industrial Development Authority, whose bond we displayed in Figure 1.2, does not issue bonds for its own activities, because it really has no activities of its own. It acts solely as a conduit to provide financing for other enterprises, usually private companies.

Usually, the companies use the proceeds for new construction of some sort. For example, the McDonald's company used the proceeds of the IDA bond to finance real estate. This real estate could be leased from the IDA, with the lease payments used to make the interest and principal payments on the bonds; or it could be bought from the authority, with a mortgage given to the authority to ensure payments. Payments on the mortgage are then used to make the interest and principal payments on the bonds. In either case, the authority itself assumes no responsibility whatever for payments on the bonds. It simply sends along to the bondholders the amounts due, provided it has already received these amounts from the actual entity obliged to make the payments. In this case, although the authority has its name on the bonds as issuer, and is in fact the legal issuer, the actual obligor on the bonds is the entity, usually a private firm, which is responsible for the payments.

The authority could issue different bonds for different projects, each of which might be guaranteed by a different company, and many authorities do just that. Each bond would have the same issuer (the authority), but each could be issued on behalf of a different company. Each would therefore have a different guaranty, because each would be issued on behalf of a different company.

For example, the Allegheny County Industrial Development Authority has issued bonds on behalf of Cyclops Corp., Colt Industries, Federated Department Stores, Kroger Company, US Air, and others, as well as additional issues for McDonalds Corporation. Payments for each bond issue came only from the company whose project was financed by the bond issue. The credit quality of these bonds varies considerably, depending on the credit quality of the company that guarantees payments for the bonds.

Other issuers may also issue bonds on behalf of different entities. A dormitory authority, such as New York State Dormitory Authority, could issue bonds to build different dormitories at different colleges and universities. Each bond issue would be paid from funds provided by the educational institution whose facility it financed, and no other educational institution would have any responsibility whatever for payment on the bonds. A dormitory authority might finance other projects as well.

For example, the New York State Dormitory Authority has financed a wide variety of educational and health projects for both public and private institutions ranging from Adelphi University to White Plains Hospital, including projects for Columbia University and the New York Public Library; for various facilities of the State University of New York; and for various projects of the City University of New York.

Hospital authorities provide financing means for a number of different hospitals, health care authorities for a variety of different nursing homes and hospitals, educational financing authorities for a variety of educational institutions. Others also issue bonds on behalf of other entities who are themselves responsible for the actual payments from which the bond payments are made. These may be both public and private agencies that use the authorities as a means to answer their financing needs.

For example, the Massachusetts Health and Educational Facilities Authority (Mass HEFA) has issued bonds for the Massachusetts Institute of Technology (for a utility plant); for Lesley College (for an academic and residential complex); for Harvard University (for two parking garages, a central refrigeration plant, and renovation of an apartment hotel); for Beth Israel Hospital (for repayment of loans for existing projects, construction of the Feldberg Building, and for renovations and purchase of equipment); for the Berklee College of Music (for refinancing of loans on the Administration Building and Berklee East, and for renovation of Berklee East and the Berklee Concert Hall); and for many other projects for institutions across the Commonwealth of Massachusetts. Each of these institutions makes payments for its own bonds, and the Authority can use the money from each institution only for those purposes. For example, Mass HEFA may not use money paid by MIT or Beth Israel (for their own projects) to make payments on Harvard's bonds.

Sometimes the same issuer issues bonds on behalf of both itself and another entity. Airports will sometimes issue bonds payable from the revenues of the entire airport, and other bonds payable only from the revenues of a particular airline. Only revenues from the airline responsible for payment may be applied towards the bond payments of the latter bonds.

For example, Memphis-Shelby County Airport Authority has issued both general revenue bonds and bonds for a project for Federal Express Company. The general revenue bonds are payable out of the general revenues of the airport, but the bonds for the Federal Express project are paid only out of lease revenues from Federal Express to pay for the project.

Another type of bond is a New Housing Authority (NHA), or Public Housing Authority (PHA) bond. These bonds were issued by local housing authorities, but were unconditionally guaranteed as to principal and interest by the United States Treasury, among the few municipal obligations to be so guaranteed. Although they have not been issued since 1974, they were issued in large amounts, they had an original final maturity of up to forty years, and they had level debt service, so that most of the bonds had relatively long periods to maturity. As a result, many are still outstanding and are frequently available. They all have the highest rating possible, since they all have a United States Treasury guaranty of payment. Coupon rates on these issues range from about 2 percent to 6 percent (the maximum), but most of them are in the 3 percent to 4 percent range.

Know Your Issuer

If you invest in municipals, you should know the issuer of the bonds and who is responsible for the actual payments from which the bonds themselves will be paid, if this is a different entity. You should certainly know whether your bonds are GO bonds or revenue bonds. Your salesperson should be able to tell you all of this, but in any case, you should carefully read the Official Statement, which contains all required information on a bond issue, when you receive it.

Arguments have raged for years about the relative merits of GO and revenue bonds and their relative safety. GOs have the advantage of resting on the power to tax, but revenue bonds may be secured by an essential service. Consider the following example. If a person had a house, with annual taxes of $5,000, and couldn't pay the taxes, a long period, perhaps years, would elapse before the taxing government could take the house for unpaid taxes, and the owner would have ample chance to pay up his taxes in arrears. But if the owner couldn't pay a water bill, of perhaps $20.00, his water could be promptly shut off. He couldn't take a shower, flush the toilet, or draw a drink of water. He would find it much easier to pay $20.00, with immediate benefits from an essential service, than to pay thousands of dollars in back taxes, for a house he wouldn't lose immediately in any case. Which bond would you prefer to own? The arguments continue because to many observers it is not clear which is better. Quality will depend on the individual issuer.

WHO BUYS MUNICIPAL BONDS?

Historically, three main types of investors have bought municipal bonds: banks, insurance companies, and individual investors (called "retail" by the municipal bond industry). Most sales during the last few years have been to retail investors. A chart showing ownership of municipal bonds, by major investor category, is shown in Figure 8.1.

Most municipal bonds are now bought by individual investors. They can buy them in a variety of ways.

How Individuals Can Buy Municipal Bonds

Individual investors can buy the individual bonds directly and own them directly, collecting the interest and principal as due. They can hold the actual bond certificates, if they exist, and clip the coupons for their bearer bonds and receive the interest directly on their registered bonds—and many investors do this. Most investors, though, keep their bonds in the name of their broker, who will credit their account for interest as it is paid and for principal as bonds mature or are called.

Investors can buy through a trust account. In this case, a bank or other trustee manages an account for the owner. Under instructions from the owner, the bank buys, sells, and manages a portfolio of bonds, collecting interest and forwarding interest and whatever principal payments are required or requested to the owner of the bonds. A common minimum requirement for a trust account might be in the $1,000,000 range for total security value.

An investor can buy bonds through a municipal investment trust or through an open or closed-end mutual fund. Most of the shareholders of these funds are individual investors.

Retail investors (individuals) including mutual funds, money market funds, closed-end funds, bank personal trusts, and direct holdings, now account for over 76 percent of all outstanding municipal holdings, according to the Federal Reserve System and the Public Securities Association.

If you are an individual investor in municipals, you belong to a group that now represents the vast bulk of municipal bond pur-

Figure 8.1

Public Securities Association
Trends in the Holdings of Municipal Securities
1970 - 1994:Q1

	Total Amount Outstanding	Retail*		Commercial Banks		Property & Casualty Insurance Companies		Other	
		Amount	% of Total	Amount	% of Total	Amount	% of Total	Amount	% of Total
1970	144.4	46.0	31.9%	70.2	48.6%	17.0	11.8%	11.1	7.7%
1971	161.8	46.1	28.5%	82.8	51.2%	20.5	12.7%	12.4	7.7%
1972	176.5	48.4	27.4%	90.0	51.0%	24.8	14.1%	13.4	7.6%
1973	191.2	53.7	28.1%	96.7	50.5%	28.5	14.9%	12.4	6.5%
1974	208.0	62.2	29.9%	101.1	48.6%	30.7	14.7%	14.0	6.7%
1975	223.0	67.2	30.1%	102.9	46.2%	33.3	14.9%	19.6	8.8%
1976	243.9	74.2	30.4%	106.0	43.5%	38.7	15.9%	25.0	10.3%
1977	273.6	82.0	30.0%	115.2	42.1%	49.4	18.1%	27.1	9.9%
1978	313.5	96.7	30.8%	126.2	40.3%	62.9	20.1%	27.7	8.8%
1979	341.5	106.0	31.1%	135.6	39.7%	72.8	21.3%	27.1	7.9%
1980	365.4	108.8	29.8%	148.8	40.7%	80.5	22.0%	27.3	7.5%
1981	398.3	132.0	33.1%	154.0	38.7%	83.9	21.1%	28.4	7.1%
1982	451.3	174.5	38.7%	158.3	35.1%	87.0	19.3%	31.5	7.0%
1983	505.7	222.7	44.0%	162.1	32.1%	86.7	17.1%	34.2	6.8%
1984	564.4	267.1	47.3%	174.6	30.9%	84.7	15.0%	38.0	6.7%
1985	743.0	374.6	50.4%	231.7	31.2%	88.2	11.9%	48.5	6.5%
1986	789.6	433.1	54.9%	203.4	25.8%	101.9	12.9%	51.2	6.5%
1987	873.1	531.7	60.9%	174.3	20.0%	124.8	14.3%	42.3	4.8%
1988	939.4	611.1	65.1%	151.6	16.1%	134.1	14.3%	42.6	4.5%
1989	1,004.7	692.5	68.9%	133.8	13.3%	134.8	13.4%	43.6	4.3%
1990	1,062.1	758.1	71.4%	117.4	11.1%	136.9	12.9%	49.7	4.7%
1991	1,131.6	850.5	75.2%	103.2	9.1%	126.8 **	11.2%	51.1	4.5%
1992	1,197.3	914.6	76.4%	97.5	8.1%	134.3	11.2%	50.9	4.3%
1993	1,257.8	963.3	76.6%	99.4	7.9%	138.3	11.0%	56.8	4.5%
1994:Q1	$1,270.0	$981.5	77.3%	$99.8	7.9%	$139.4	11.0%	$49.3	3.9%

* Includes mutual, money market, closed-end funds, bank personal trusts and direct holdings by individuals.
** A series break in 1991 distorts comparisons to prior-year figures of property & casualty insurance companies.

Source: Federal Reserve System, Public Securities Association
All Amounts in Billions

MUNIT094.XLS· 8/6/94

chases. As a result, you now have a wide range of resources available to you. More firms with more salespeople are available to serve you, more materials are available in public libraries, and more financial information is reported on municipals and on bonds generally. Stock market reports now frequently include bond reports as well; a few years ago, this was rare. Don't be afraid to use the resources available to you.

How Banks Buy Municipal Bonds

In the past, a major market for municipal bonds was commercial banks. Large commercial banks also brought large amounts of municipal new issue to market. Recently, this market has declined, and in fact commercial banks have been net sellers of municipal bonds for the past few years. One reason for this was a change in the tax law for banks, that no longer allowed banks to deduct the interest cost of carrying municipal bonds with a few exceptions. This made municipal bond investments much less attractive to banks; they haven't continued to buy them, but in fact have been selling bonds they owned. Another reason was the availability of other tax shelters to banks, such as leases, that had important tax advantages. Finally, a change in the general features of new municipal issues from general obligation to revenue bonds resulted in lower bank underwriting of municipal new issue and probably also less bank buying of municipal bonds.

The result is a substantial decline in the position of banks as holders of outstanding municipal debt. Banks now account for just under 8 percent of outstanding municipal debt ownership and have been net sellers of municipal bonds for the last few years.

How Property and Casualty Insurance Companies Buy Municipal Bonds

The third major owner of municipal bonds is composed of property and casualty insurance companies. They now own about 11 percent of outstanding municipal debt.

The insurance companies' need of tax-exempt income changes as their insurance fortunes change. In years of poor underwriting results, the insurance companies don't need tax-exemption and therefore don't buy municipal bonds. As a result, insurance company ownership of municipals fluctuates somewhat over the years, and has been as high as 20 percent or more of outstanding municipals.

HOW MUNICIPAL DEALERS, DEALER BANKS, AND BROKERS FUNCTION

A broker acts as an agent for someone else in carrying out (executing) the transaction desired by the customer. In doing this, the broker receives as compensation a commission, which is charged to the customer in addition to the cost of the purchase, or which is deducted from the proceeds of the sale. For example, if you buy or sell common stock executed on the New York Stock Exchange, you will pay a commission on the sale. Your broker acted as your agent in executing your order to buy or sell the stock, and you were charged an explicit commission for executing the order.

A dealer buys and sells for his or her own account and risk, directly from or to the customer. The customer does not pay an explicit commission; rather, the dealer makes a profit from the buying and the selling. Dealers expect to charge more for the bonds they sell than they pay for the bonds they buy. Dealers do not charge a commission.

For example, a dealer may offer to buy a particular bond at 99, and offer to sell the bond at 100. If the dealer buys $100,000 par amount at 99, and sells the $100,000 par amount at 100, there is a $1,000 gross profit on the transaction. The dealer must pay the expenses of operating the firm, compensation to the salesperson who made the sale, fees and taxes, and other expenses out of this gross profit.

Almost all municipal bond transactions and most transactions in United States Treasury securities are dealer transactions.

Sometimes banks engage in the municipal bond business. When they do this, they usually set up a special department to act as a municipal bond dealer. They are then known as a dealer bank. They function as a municipal bond dealer, although they are regulated by the bank regulatory authorities.

Almost all municipal bond transactions with municipal bond buyers and sellers are dealer transactions. A very few broker transactions are done by dealers, but these are almost all bonds that the dealer does not want to own and resell to his or her own customers. They might be bonds in default, bonds with questionable payment prospects, bonds with hardly any buyers, or simply bonds that the dealer is not comfortable with in selling to his or her own customers.

A few municipal bond brokers exist, but they act as brokers only to municipal bond dealers and dealer banks. In the early 1980s, in the New York City area there were about eighteen municipal bond brokers; in 1993, there were only about six.

You should understand that when you buy a municipal bond, you are almost always buying it from a dealer who is the owner of the bond; when you sell a municipal bond you are selling it to a firm who is actually buying it. Usually, the firm hopes to resell the bond to another one of its customers.

Bonds sold by a firm's customers to the firm are one source of the supply of bonds that the firm sells to its own customers. The other two main sources are new issue, discussed in Chapter 9, and bonds bought from other dealers and from municipal bond brokers.

WHO WORKS IN THE MUNICIPAL BOND INDUSTRY?

What do underwriters, traders, sales representatives, researchers, and others do all day long in the municipal bond business? We will attempt to answer this question, in some detail. Remember that all the activities of these persons are dedicated to doing their part in bringing municipal bonds to market, selling them, and trading them once they are issued. In one large firm, this is called "bringing product to the system." The product is municipal bonds; the system is the sales force to sell the bonds.

What Traders Do

A trader makes bids for bonds in an effort to buy them to reoffer to his or her customers and makes offerings of bonds to customers, and to traders at other firms. Only a trader can perform this activity. Sales representatives generally are not allowed to make bids and offerings to their customers, but may only pass on to their customers the bids and offerings from the traders and the underwriters. Traders are constantly in touch with the municipal bond market and convey market information to others in their firm and to the firm's customers. Traders will also suggest bond swaps (sales of bonds owned to purchase other bonds) to the firm's customers and to the marketing representatives who serve these customers.

What Underwriters Do

Underwriters work with new issues of municipal bonds, and set the structure, terms, and prices for these new issues. They develop syndicates to bid for and market new issues of bonds. They work with investment bankers to develop negotiated new-issue municipal business for their firm, and they work with the marketing departments to market these new issues of bonds when they get them.

This activity of underwriting and selling of new issues of municipal bonds is called the primary market. Underwriters work in the primary market. The secondary market is the trading and sale of issues that were previously issued. Some of these might have been issued years earlier and are now being resold, perhaps for the first time since their original issue. Other bonds might have been issued just a month or two previously.

Theoretically, a gray area might exist between primary and secondary markets. In practice, it is pretty clear when a bond is no longer a new issue and is traded in the secondary market.

In larger firms, separate departments do underwriting and trading, but in small firms, and in some regional offices of large firms, the same individuals may perform both functions.

What Investment Bankers Do

Investment bankers work to bring negotiated new-issue business to their firm. They call on issuers and prospective issuers of bonds, in an effort to persuade the issuers to employ the investment banker's firm to underwrite the bonds. Investment banking involves large amounts of travel and long hours of work. If successful, the firm (and the banker) will be paid a management fee for the underwriting. Investment bankers work hard to develop business, sometimes for many years, before the issuer finally awards them a share, or all, of a new issue to underwrite. In doing so, the banker and other members of his firm, will advise the issuer about the issue and its features.

Investment bankers will also occasionally act as financial advisors to governments, on a fee basis, even though no new issue of bonds is forthcoming, or, as advisors they may not be able to underwrite it. Usually, however, this work is done by financial advisory firms, which specialize in this work.

What Institutional Sales Representatives Do

Institutional sales representatives sell municipal bonds, and possibly other securities as well, to institutional customers. Institutional customers include banks, insurance companies, mutual funds, municipal investment trusts, and other business firms. Other municipal dealers, who are also customers of the firm, are frequently serviced from the institutional sales desk, but usually by sales representatives who specialize in that kind of business. Institutional accounts are generally assigned, especially larger accounts.

In the large firms, institutional sales representatives sell only one kind of security. Municipal institutional sales representatives would sell only municipal bonds. In smaller firms, and in some branches of some large firms, institutional sales representatives may sell other kinds of securities as well.

Institutional salespeople propose swaps to their customers and keep them informed about changes in the municipal market and about new municipal issues coming to market.

Most institutional sales representatives service relatively few accounts, possibly as few as five or six. However, these are large and active accounts, and the sales representative speaks on the phone with them many times each day. A good institutional salesperson, with good accounts, with a good firm, in a good year, can make a very large amount of money.

What Marketing Personnel Do

Marketing personnel, also called liaison personnel, act as an interface between sales representatives and traders and underwriters. They provide new issue and market information to sales representatives. They relay bids and offers to salespeople from the traders and underwriters, propose swaps and answer questions from sales representatives about new issues and about the market. Institutional marketing personnel work with institutional sales representatives. Retail marketing persons work with retail sales representatives.

What Municipal Research People Do

Municipal researchers analyze issuers, sometimes with special reference to new issues coming to market. They analyze both the financial and economic aspects of issuers and new issues. Frequently they assign quality ratings, comparable to the ratings assigned by the rating agencies. They also usually inform their clients about prospective rating or quality changes.

Many top-level municipal researchers work for firms other than municipal bond dealers. Some work for the rating agencies, and some work for the municipal bond insurers. At the rating agencies, researchers analyze municipal bond issuers and new issues and assign quality ratings to both the issuers and the issues. At the municipal bond insurance companies they decide whether to qualify the issue for bond insurance and how much premium the insurer should charge for issues that are insured.

How the Retail Broker Works in Municipal Bonds

If you are the usual retail customer, your salesperson will be a retail salesperson who offers to sell you many different securities. The firm will operate as a dealer rather than as a broker for your municipal bond transactions, although it will probably act as a broker for your transactions in listed stocks. Therefore, the firm will not usually charge you an explicit commission on your purchase or sale of municipal bonds, but expects to make money on a business which is overall profitable. Your salesperson will be given what is called a "sales credit," which represents a portion of what the firm might expect to earn on its trade with you. He or she will be given this credit, even if the firm loses money on the sale because of a declining bond market. The salesforce will actually be paid a percentage of the sales credit, the payout percentage. Typical payout for retail sales are in the range of 30 percent to 40 percent, although extremely successful salespeople, the "big producers," or "heavy hitters" may be paid higher rates. Institutional salespeople receive a much lower percentage, possibly 8 percent to 12 percent, but they presumably sell a much larger volume of bonds. They also usually receive somewhat lower sales credits.

You should understand that even though you pay no explicit commission, the firm still expects to make money on its transactions with you, and your personal securities broker will be paid for selling you municipal bonds.

How a Municipal Bond Department Is Organized

Municipal bond departments can conceivably be organized in a number of different ways, but, depending on the size of the firm, only a few ways are typical.

The investment banking function is almost always separated from the underwriting, trading, sales, marketing, and research functions into a separate department. This is usually called the Public Finance Department, the Municipal Investment Banking Department, or something similar. The department might itself be divided into geographic regions, such as Northeast, Southeast, and South Central. These regions would have headquarters in a large city in the region, such as Boston, Atlanta, Dallas, Chicago, Los Angeles, or San Francisco. The investment banking function might alternatively be separated into areas of specialty according to type of issuer, such as housing, public power, and health care.

The trading and underwriting functions are usually put in the same department. This department might be called Municipal Trading and Underwriting. Large brokerage firms with many branches (called wire houses) frequently have regional departments for trading and underwriting as well. For example, one large wire house has municipal bond department headquarters in New York City, with the trading and underwriting functions for the major municipal bond issues, which have nationwide interest. These include issues such as issues of states, large cities, and large agencies and authorities. This department also has municipal regions in Chicago, Dallas, Clearwater, and San Francisco. The municipal regions underwrite and trade issues in which there is usually only local or regional interest. For example, issues of the States of New York, Illinois, and California, the cities of New York, Chicago, and San Francisco, and agencies such as The Port Authority of New York and New Jersey and the Municipal Electric Authority of Georgia would all be underwritten and traded in the national trading and underwriting department. The municipal regions would trade and underwrite local or regional names, such as Portchester, New York, Freeport, Illinois, or Macon, Georgia.

The institutional sales function may be part of the municipal bond department, but frequently it is part of the company's sales department instead. This means that individuals who work closely together may actually have quite different reporting chains of command.

The marketing or sales liaison function may also be part of the municipal bond department, but frequently it is part of another company department, either the company's sales department or a separate marketing department. Once more, this means that persons who work closely together may have quite different reporting chains of command.

The municipal research function is usually part of the company's research department, although sometimes it is part of the municipal bond department.

As a result, investors or their sales representatives could find themselves dealing with individuals in different parts of the company and located in different parts of the country. For example, an investor might find his salesperson talking with persons in New York, in several different regions, and possibly also buying bonds directly off a computer system.

Smaller firms, of course, will have smaller and simpler organizations, owing to their smaller size. However, many smaller firms have several different branches, each able to make municipal commitments. In that case, the investor dealing with these firms might often talk with different people in different parts of the country.

REGULATING MUNICIPAL BONDS

The Securities Exchange Act of 1934 regulated the securities markets but left the municipal bond markets mostly untouched, and these are still generally exempt from much security regulation. After New York City defaulted on its notes in 1975, however, Congress set up the Municipal Securities Rulemaking Board (MSRB), which has some general oversight on municipal bond regulation. Other federal agencies also have a part in municipal bond regulation.

The MSRB proposes regulations and asks for comments from the municipal bond industry and other interested parties. After the comment period, the MSRB adopts the proposed regulations, if it wishes to, possibly with changes responding to the comments made on the proposed regulations during the comment period. However, the MSRB cannot give final approval to the proposed regulation; that is done by the Securities and Exchange Commission (SEC). Neither the MSRB nor the SEC actually performs the regulatory control which enforces the regulation. That is done by the relevant regulatory authority: the National Association of Securities Dealers (NASD) for municipal bond dealers, and the appropriate bank regulatory authority for dealer banks. A municipal bond dealer is a securities dealer who deals in municipal bonds as all or part of a securities business. A dealer bank, or bank dealer, is a bank or a separately identifiable part or division of a bank which deals in municipal bonds.

Although municipal securities are generally exempt from the 1934 Act, they are not exempt from its anti-fraud provisions. You may not cheat someone with a municipal bond any more than you may not cheat with any other security. Section 10b-5 is the applicable SEC regulation.

The MSRB rules are divided into three parts. Administrative Rules concern the management of the MSRB. There are Definitional Rules that define the meaning of widely used terms. General Rules govern the behavior of municipal bond dealers and dealer banks and their relationships with issuers, customers, and each other.

If you invest in municipals, most of these rules are relevant to you in some way, but you should be particularly aware of two of them. Rule G-15 covers confirmations, clearance, and settlement of transactions with customers. Rule G-17 covers conduct of the municipal securities business. If you are active in municipals, you should have some awareness of the MSRB, some familiarity with all of its regulations, and access to them if required. You should understand that municipal bonds are generally exempt from SEC registration requirements and have their own regulatory system, except for cases of fraud.

These rules can go into considerable detail. For example, Rule G-15 lists at least twenty-four (count 'em) items of information that may be required to appear on a municipal bond confirmation. Consideration of this level of detail is beyond the scope of this book.

The MSRB publishes the *MSRB Manual*. The *Manual* contains all the MSRB Rules, as well as interpretative comments on them. The comments arise from questions submitted to the MSRB; they contain the questions, and the MSRB's reply. The *Manual* also contains information about the MSRB, the law text of the Securities Exchange Act of 1934, the law text of the Securities Investor Protection Act of 1970, and other applicable rules and regulations.

The MSRB publishes the *Manual* semiannually and makes it generally available at moderate cost; the most recent edition costs $5.00. The MSRB also publishes *MSRB Reports* several times per year, which contain information on changes and developments of interest to persons in municipal bonds. These publications are available free of charge. The MSRB also publishes the *Glossary of Municipal Securities Terms*. This was first published in January, 1983, by the Division of Bond Finance of the State of Florida, and a revised version has been published by the MSRB since 1985. It badly needs updating, but is still quite handy and useful to municipal bond persons. It is available for $1.50 from the MSRB.

If you are active in municipals, you should probably have a reasonably current copy of the *MSRB Manual*, if only for reference. You should also have a copy of the *MSRB Glossary*. You should consider subscribing to *MSRB Reports*. They don't cost anything and will keep you updated on changes in municipal bond regulation and other developments of interest.

HOW MUNICIPAL RESEARCH IS DONE

A large number of municipal bond researchers analyze the various municipal issues using a variety of techniques. There are two main techniques used, depending on whether the bonds are general obligation or revenue bonds. These techniques are quite different, and you should understand the difference and how the techniques are applied. A detailed discussion of these techniques is beyond the scope of this book, but it is important for you to have some understanding of the basic principles of municipal research.

General obligation bonds depend on the taxes raised by the issuer, so the bond analyst looks at the issuer's tax-paying ability and at the issuer's overall debt. The analyst develops measures of tax burden and debt burden. These include taxes per capita, debt per capita, debt service cost per capita, and other similar measures. The analyst may apply these measures to both the issuer and all the other debt-issuing entities which apply to the issuer's geographic area. The analyst also examines the financial and economic status of the issuer to determine whether the overall status is improving.

A revenue bond depends on the earnings of a municipal enterprise of some sort, so the analysis focuses on the earning power of the enterprise. A wide variety of enterprises exists. Examples include public power, hospitals, nursing homes, colleges and universities, dormitories, toll roads, toll bridges, airports, seaports, single family housing, multifamily housing, and refuse disposal, as well as the more traditional water, sewer, and electric revenue issues. Probably no one person can become expert in all these fields. Most municipal researchers develop a specialty and become expert in the specialty.

One measure applied to most revenue bonds is debt service coverage. This is the ratio of net earnings to total debt service requirements, including both interest and principal. For example, if a public enterprise had debt service requirements of $1,000,000 (interest and principal) and net earning, after expenses, of $2,000,000, it would have coverage of 2.0. Generally, higher coverage indicates better security for the bonds. Coverage is frequently measured using the highest prospective debt service requirement, which could be some years in the future.

Researchers also analyze the adequacy of reserves set aside for future debt service payments and whether the issuer is making the payments to fund accounts, as required in the indenture. The analyst will also estimate the future prospects of the enterprise.

Researchers particularly examine whether the issuer has complied with the requirements of the indenture of the bonds it has issued, whether all payments required under the indenture have been made and whether any funds remain after all the payments have been made.

UNDERSTANDING MUNICIPAL BOND RATINGS AND RATING AGENCIES

Many municipal bonds have a quality rating, which is assigned to them by one or more of the rating agencies. Ratings are a simple system of gradation of relative investment merit. They are opinions based on the ability and willingness of the issuer to repay his obligations.

Ratings are issued by organizations called rating agencies; four such agencies exist. The two largest and best known are Moody's Investors' Service, part of Dun & Bradstreet Corporation, and Standard & Poor's Corporation, part of McGraw-Hill. The other two are Fitch Investors' Service and Duff and Phelps, both privately owned.

An issuer who wishes to receive a rating must apply for the rating to the bond rating agency or agencies that he wishes to rate his bonds. Frequently this means that issuers will apply to several bond rating agencies for ratings. Rating agencies charge a fee for their ratings, which is paid by the issuer. If a rating is not applied for, it usually will not be assigned. In particular, bonds that have been escrowed, either to call or to maturity, and that would otherwise be rated AAA, are sometimes not rated because the issuer did not apply for a new rating when the bonds were escrowed. The rating agency will not automatically assign a new rating in such cases.

Figure 8.2 shows the ratings of each agency, in decreasing order of quality.

Figure 8.2

Moody's	S&P	Fitch	Duff & Phelps	Meaning of rating
Aaa	AAA	AAA	AAA	Highest rating
Aa	AA	AA	AA	High
A	A	A	A	Adequate
Baa	BBB	BBB	BBB	Below average
Ba	BB	BB	BB	Uncertain
B	B	B	B	Risk
Caa	CCC	CCC	CCC	High risk
Ca	CC	CC		
C	C	C		
	D	DDD, DD, D	DD	Default or liquidation

Sources for Figure 8.2

Moody's Investors Service
Standard & Poor's, A Division of McGraw-Hill, Inc.
Fitch Investors Service, Inc.
Duff & Phelps Credit Rating Co.

Within a rating level, adjustments can be made by adding plus and minus signs. For example, AA+, AA, and AA– are all separate ratings within the AA category. Moody's sometimes adds a 1 to its Aa, A, Baa, and Ba ratings. Figure 8.3 shows a complete description of Moody's ratings. The other rating agencies have comparable descriptions.

The top four major ratings are called "investment grade." Achieving an investment-grade rating is considered very desirable by issuers. Sometimes investment managers are required by law, or by trust agreements, to invest only in investment-grade obligations. Achieving an investment-grade rating would considerably expand the market for the rated bonds. Sometimes an investment banker will believe that one particular rating agency will give an investment-grade rating to an issuer, while another agency will not rate the issuer investment-grade, or is doubtful. In such a case, the banker might apply only to the first agency for a rating.

Figure 8.3

The Bond Rating

The purpose of Moody's ratings is to provide investors with a simple system of gradation by which the relative investment qualities of bonds may be noted. It is important to remember that the ratings express our opinion on the relative creditworthiness of specific debt obligations; they are not an opinion on the issuer itself but on its ability and willingness to repay its debt obligations.

Definitions of Bond Ratings

Aaa

Bonds which are rated **Aaa** are judged to be of the best quality. They carry the smallest degree of investment risk and are generally referred to as "gilt edge." Interest payments are protected by a large or by an exceptionally stable margin and principal is secure. While the various protective elements are likely to change, such changes as can be visualized are most unlikely to impair the fundamentally strong position of such issues.

Aa

Bonds which are rated **Aa** are judged to be of high quality by all standards. Together with the **Aaa** group they comprise what are generally known as high grade bonds. They are rated lower than the best bonds because margins of protection may not be as large as in **Aaa** securities or fluctuation of protective elements may be of greater amplitude or there may be other elements present which make the long-term risks appear somewhat larger than in **Aaa** securities.

A

Bonds which are rated **A** possess many favorable investment attributes and are to be considered as upper medium grade obligations. Factors giving security to principal and interest are considered adequate, but elements may be present which suggest a susceptibility to impairment some time in the future.

Baa

Bonds which are rated **Baa** are considered as medium grade obligations; *i.e.*, they are neither highly protected nor poorly secured. Interest payments

Figure 8.3 (continued)

and principal security appear adequate for the present but certain protective elements may be lacking or may be characteristically unreliable over any great length of time. Such bonds lack outstanding investment characteristics and in fact have speculative characteristics as well.

Ba

Bonds which are rated **Ba** are judged to have speculative elements; their future cannot be considered as well assured. Often the protection of interest and principal payments may be very moderate, and thereby not well safeguarded during both good and bad times over the future. Uncertainty of position characterizes bonds in this class.

B

Bonds which are rated **B** generally lack characteristics of the desirable investment. Assurance of interest and principal payments or maintenance of other terms of the contract over any long period of time may be small.

Caa

Bonds which are rated **Caa** are of poor standing. Such issues may be in default or there may be present elements of danger with respect to principal or interest.

Ca

Bonds which are rated **Ca** represent obligations which are speculative in a high degree. Such issues are often in default or have other marked shortcomings.

C

Bonds which are rated **C** are the lowest rated class of bonds, and issues so rated can be regarded as having extremely poor prospects of ever attaining any real investment standing.

Con.(...)

Bonds for which the security depends upon the completion of some act or the fulfillment of some condition are rated conditionally. These are bonds secured by: (a) earnings of projects under construction, (b) earnings of projects unseasoned in operating experience, (c) rentals which begin when facilities are completed, or (d) payments to which some other limiting condition attaches. Parenthetical rating denotes probable credit stature upon completion of construction or elimination of basis of condition.

The bonds in the **Aa, A, Baa, Ba,** and **B,** groups which Moody's believes possesses the strongest investment attributes are designated by the symbols **Aa1, A1, Baa1, Ba1,** and **B1**.

Source: Moody's Investors Service

Conditional (Con) means that a rating has been applied for and assigned, but the rating is conditioned upon receiving additional information from the issuer or on the issuer meeting certain requirements.

Not rated (N/R) means that the bonds have not been rated. This does not necessarily mean that the bonds are of low quality; it only means that no one applied to the rating agency for a rating, so the rating agency did not assign a rating or the agency does not rate these bonds as a matter of policy. Many fine bonds exist which do not have a rating, such as the escrowed bonds discussed earlier. Sometimes, as mentioned above, an investment banker or underwriter deliberately will apply to only one agency for a rating, so the other agencies will not rate that bond. In such cases, the bond will be rated by one agency, but not by others.

However, usually a N/R bond should be subjected to especially careful scrutiny by the prospective investor. Most issuers whose bonds would get good ratings apply for them, because the improved marketability and lower interest costs more than offset the cost of the rating.

Sometimes different rating agencies will give different levels of rating to the same bond. For example, one agency might rate the bond A and another, BBB. These are called split ratings, and reflect a difference of opinion between the agencies about the relative investment merit of the bonds. Almost always, split ratings differ by one level. Very rarely they differ by more than that; in the late 1970s, Moody's and S&P gave Municipal Assistance Corporation for the City of New York (MAC) bonds ratings which differed by two levels (S&P was higher). Such situations are rare and don't usually last very long. Usually, experts will have the same opinion, or close to it.

Why Ratings Are Important

Ratings are important to municipal bond buyers, issuers, underwriters, and traders for several reasons.

The ratings are published and readily available. Most individual investors will find that their local public library has at least one report by a rating agency, and many have several such reports.

Investors can also subscribe to rating agency reports on their own at moderate cost. These reports also contain rating changes.

The ratings are prepared by experts in the business. The experts are impartial and detached, well trained and with solid experience. Rating bonds is their full-time job. Their opinions are a valuable addition to the municipal bond industry.

Issuers also receive advantages from their purchase of a rating. They receive the quality recognition at the level they are entitled to. As a result, their bonds will have improved market acceptance and lower borrowing costs. The bond buyer receives an expert opinion, and can choose bond quality to meet his investment objectives.

If you are a municipal bond investor, you should know the ratings of your bonds and be aware of rating changes if and when they occur. You should always remember that a rating is an opinion. It is an opinion of experts, but it is still an opinion. Sometimes people have the idea that there is a golden rating out there, similar to the Platonic ideal. No such rating exists. All ratings are opinions.

Don't discount the output of the two smaller rating agencies (Fitch and Duff & Phelps) just because they are smaller. They have excellent staffs and produce excellent work within their areas.

Very occasionally, rating agencies give high ratings to bonds which later have problems. For example, for many years, Washington Public Power Supply System #4 and #5 bonds were rated A, an investment-grade rating, by both Moody's and S&P. The rating was eventually reduced to Baa (Moody's) and BBB (S&P), a lower rating, but still investment grade. The bonds later defaulted. The 2.25 billion dollar default was one of the largest municipal defaults of all time, and one of the largest defaults of any kind.

HOW MUNICIPAL BOND INVESTMENT TRUSTS AND MUTUAL FUNDS WORK

Many, perhaps even most, investors have some knowledge of or personal experience with mutual funds; usually, this experience is with common stock mutual funds. But the mutual fund form of investment is also important for municipal bonds. Not all readers will have knowledge of these important investment vehicles, so this book will give an introductory description of mutual funds in general. But we won't discuss the various kinds of loads (sales commissions) and fees that may be charged investors in mutual funds; these are beyond the scope of this book.

Frequently an investor does not have enough money to make his own investments, or does not have the time or the inclination to do so, but does have the funds and the desire to make some investment. In such a case, the investor might combine his or her investment with investments of others into a pool of funds for investment. This offers several advantages. The larger size of the pool allows both diversification among a variety of securities and more efficient execution of trades due to the larger trade sizes. The pool may also generate sufficient income to employ a professional investment manager for the investment fund.

Historical Background

Mutual funds themselves do not pay any federal income tax provided that they pay out to the shareholders almost all their investment income. Almost all mutual funds pay out all their investment income, except for the costs of running the fund, to avoid payment of federal income taxes.

Early on, the question arose whether dividends paid from tax-exempt interest would themselves be exempt from federal income tax. For years, the Internal Revenue Service said that it would not be so exempt; in other words, even though the original interest was exempt from federal income tax, the resulting dividends would be fully taxable to the fund shareholders who received them. This effectively stopped anyone from setting up a tax-exempt bond mutual fund. Why would anyone accept lower tax-free yields, only to pay a tax on the interest income?

Municipal Investment Trusts (Unit Investment Trusts)

In 1961, several firms started up a tax-exempt investment trust, called a municipal investment trust (MIT). This new vehicle was not an investment company, but rather a trust.

Such a trust has transferable shares, so that investors can sell and otherwise transfer their ownership interests in the trust. All payments to the trust, both interest and principal payments, are distributed *pro rata* to the trust shareholders. However, because the investment is a trust and not an investment company, all distributions of tax-exempt interest are exempt from federal income tax, while distributions of principal payments, from bonds maturing, called, or sold, are returns of principal.

The bonds to be owned by the trust are assembled, and when the trust is complete, but not before, the trust is offered for sale to investors. Thus, the buyer of shares in the trust knows what bonds he or she is buying. The investment portfolio is not managed, but simply held until the bonds mature or are called, although the trust supervisor might sell bonds if it seems wise to do so; this has rarely been done. The portfolio is said to be supervised, not managed, and it remains unchanged during the life of the trust, except for maturities, calls, and very occasional sales.

As bonds mature, are called, or are sold, the trust decreases in size, until finally it becomes so small that it is discontinued, the bonds sold, and the proceeds distributed *pro rata* to the trust shareholders.

Each trust is of fixed size, usually from about $5,000,000 to about $15,000,000. Once a trust is assembled and the shares sold, the trust cannot be changed. Therefore, a new trust must be set up if the bond firm wishes to continue with this kind of offering. For that reason, a large number of municipal investment trusts have been established since their inception in 1961. Municipal Investment Trusts are also called Unit Investment Trusts (UITs).

The new MITs meet an important investment need for municipal investors. They allow investment in relatively small amounts ($1,000 minimum, usually), with diversification and professional selection and supervision, although not active management. They allow sale of the investment easily and at reasonable prices. They are sold with a sales commission of about 4 percent to 5 percent. Income is usually distributed monthly.

Income reinvestment is also possible, although difficult, because the trusts are closed-end. If the investor wants dividends reinvested, the income is placed in a special accumulation fund and invested in a new trust when a new trust is formed that meets the investor's requirements. This system therefore requires the investor to own small amounts of large numbers of funds.

The investor is not able to purchase additional shares in his or her trusts unless such shares happen to be offered on the market. Fund sponsors maintain secondary market trading in previously issued funds, but not all funds have shares available at all times. Therefore, an investor who wants to invest additional funds might have to buy shares in trusts other than the ones already invested in.

The trust form allows trust sponsors to form trusts which specialize in certain types of bonds. For example, special MITs have been formed owning only bonds issued by a specific state, such as New York State, or the Commonwealth of Massachusetts. An investor could purchase a fund specializing in bonds of his or her state of residence, and thereby usually avoid state income taxes as well as federal income taxes on the interest income. Some funds specialize in bonds of a specific maturity range, so that an investor can invest in a maturity closer to personal needs, and some funds specialize in bonds of a particular quality, or insured bonds. Some trusts may specialize in bonds insured by a particular insurer.

Target funds also exist. These are funds which own bonds having the same maturity year. The fund could be thought of as having a maturity date of the year in which the bonds mature. These funds appeal to investors who want to make an investment with a particular specific maturity.

Redemption of MIT shares is possible. The funds are periodically evaluated by one of the bond evaluation firms, usually daily. The fund will usually redeem any shares offered at the redemption price. Frequently, however, the sponsor of the fund will maintain a market in the funds shares, purchase any shares offered, and reoffer them to the firm's other customers.

Quotations of bid and asked prices are not usually readily available in daily newspapers. The firms that sponsor and sell the MIT will provide bids and offers.

Municipal Bond Mutual Funds

In the autumn of 1976, the Internal Revenue Service allowed the tax-exempt feature to flow through to investors in municipal bond mutual funds. A number of such funds were promptly created. Many such investment companies now exist, both closed-end and open-end. Many closed-end municipal funds are listed on the New York Stock Exchange, and active markets are maintained in others.

Reinvestment of dividends from open-end municipal mutual funds is easy; the money is simply used to buy additional shares. Target funds are possible and exist.

The funds are evaluated daily by a municipal bond evaluation firm, and, like most mutual funds, municipal bond mutual funds will usually redeem shares offered at the net asset value. Quotations of bid and ask prices are usually available in many daily newspapers. Many no-load municipal mutual funds exist, in addition to load funds. Most mutual fund families offer at least one municipal mutual fund.

Comparing Municipal Investment Trusts and Municipal Bond Mutual Funds

Arguments have raged for years about whether municipal investment trusts or municipal mutual funds were better investment vehicles. Not all the persons engaged in these arguments have been entirely disinterested. Both forms have been around for years, so clearly both must meet investment needs to some extent; otherwise, one form or the other would not survive. Perhaps neither form is clearly superior to the other in all respects.

Both municipal investment trusts and municipal mutual funds can be satisfactory ways to invest in municipal bonds. Both will accept relatively small investments, and both provide some degree of diversification. Nonetheless, investors should understand the differences between them and how they might answer different investment needs.

If you buy an MIT, you know precisely the bonds you will own, and you know that they will never be changed. You know that as the issuer makes payments, you will receive your *pro rata* share in these payments. You know that your investment has a final maturity date and an average life, and you can compute the average life. Management fees will be modest, probably a little lower than the management fees of a municipal mutual fund. You will almost certainly pay a commission when you buy the trust shares. You can sell your shares if you want. You know exactly what you have bought and that it won't be changed except by sale, call, or maturity. However, you should understand that if you have more funds to invest later, you may not be able to buy additional shares in the fund you already own and you will find reinvestment of income difficult.

If you own shares in a municipal mutual fund, you own shares in a portfolio of municipal bonds which may change, in some cases quite rapidly and extensively. The portfolio manager should still make sure that any newly bought bonds conform to the original objectives of the portfolio. However, your portfolio will change without you being aware of the changes until later, possibly much later. Your fund will never have a maturity date which gets closer, unless you own one of the target funds; additional investments will usually extend the life of the mutual fund. You may, however, make additional investments easily and reinvest dividends easily in the same fund. Many large and well-managed municipal mutual funds have no load charges, so you can invest without paying a sales commission. Municipal mutual funds do have management fees. The management fees are usually higher than the supervisory fees charged by the municipal investment trusts.

Which is better for you? Only you can decide. And remember, you can still buy municipal bonds directly if you want to.

HOW MUNICIPAL BOND INSURANCE WORKS

The Bond Insurance Contract

Municipal bond insurance guarantees payment of interest and principal that the issuer is obligated to pay, but does not in fact pay. The reason the issuer does not pay doesn't matter; it only matters that he does not pay.

The insurer promises to make payment of interest and principal, including mandatory sinking fund payments which are due and payable. These are the only payments that the insurer guarantees and will make. The promise to pay does not include payments to other fund accounts (such as our bridge painting fund, discussed earlier in the book), or other bond payments, such as calls and possible other redemptions which are not required. Even if the underlying bonds are accelerated (paid in full ahead of time), the original insured bondholder has continued to receive his scheduled payments. A sample bond insurance contract from a major bond insurer is shown as Figure 8.4.

Understanding the Benefits of Municipal Bond Insurance

Municipal bond insurance gives the buyer three important benefits: (1) additional security for the bond payments; (2) a higher rating from rating agencies than the issuer would command on his own; and (3) market homogeneity with other insured issues, which improves the salability of the bondholder's own bonds.

How bond insurers provide additional security

Bond insurers, like insurers of any kind, provide additional security in the form of large policy reserves, which they hold to ensure payment of any claims made against them. All claims made so far against any municipal bond insurer have been paid promptly and in full. Sometimes these claims have involved making full payment on the face amount of the bonds, but usually they have involved making continued payment of interest when due and principal when the bonds mature. For example, AMBAC Indemnity Corporation, one of the major municipal bond insurance companies, insured some of the Washington Public Power Supply District #4 and #5 bonds, in the secondary market, as part of a portfolio insurance policy. When these bonds defaulted, AMBAC continued to make interest payments on the insured bonds. Frequently, the insurer will work out receiving salvage payments from the issuer, or foreclosing on a property as final settlement. The insurer may also receive settlement if payment of the bonds is accelerated under the terms of the indenture. This is not the concern of the insured bondholder; who only expects to receive the promised payments as scheduled.

Figure 8.4

FINANCIAL GUARANTY INSURANCE POLICY

Municipal Bond Investors Assurance Corporation
Armonk, New York 10504

Policy No. [NUMBER]

Municipal Bond Investors Assurance Corporation (the "Insurer"), in consideration of the payment of the premium and subject to the terms of this policy, hereby unconditionally and irrevocably guarantees to any owner, as hereinafter defined, of the following described obligations, the full and complete payment required to be made by or on behalf of the Issuer to [INSERT NAME OF PAYING AGENT] or its successor (the "Paying Agent") of an amount equal to (i) the principal of (either at the stated maturity or by any advancement of maturity pursuant to a mandatory sinking fund payment) and interest on, the Obligations (as that term is defined below) as such payments shall become due but shall not be so paid (except that in the event of any acceleration of the due date of such principal by reason of mandatory or optional redemption or acceleration resulting from default or otherwise, other than any advancement of maturity pursuant to a mandatory sinking fund payment, the payments guaranteed hereby shall be made in such amounts and at such times as such payments of principal would have been due had there not been any such acceleration); and (ii) the reimbursement of any such payment which is subsequently recovered from any owner pursuant to a final judgment by a court of competent jurisdiction that such payment constitutes an avoidable preference to such owner within the meaning of any applicable bankruptcy law. The amounts referred to in clauses (i) and (ii) of the preceding sentence shall be referred to herein collectively as the "Insured Amounts." "Obligations" shall mean:

[PAR]
[LEGAL NAME OF ISSUE]

Upon receipt of telephonic or telegraphic notice, such notice subsequently confirmed in writing by registered or certified mail, or upon receipt of written notice by registered or certified mail, by the Insurer from the Paying Agent or any owner of an Obligation the payment of an Insured Amount for which is then due, that such required payment has not been made, the Insurer on the due date of such payment or within one business day after receipt of notice of such nonpayment, whichever is later, will make a deposit of funds, in an account with State Street Bank and Trust Company, N.A., in New York, New York, or its successor, sufficient for the payment of any such Insured Amounts which are then due. Upon presentment and surrender of such Obligations or presentment of such other proof of ownership of the Obligations, together with any appropriate instruments of assignment to evidence the assignment of the Insured Amounts due on the Obligations as are paid by the Insurer, and appropriate instruments to effect the appointment of the Insurer as agent for such owners of the Obligations in any legal proceeding related to payment of Insured Amounts on the Obligations, such instruments being in a form satisfactory to State Street Bank and Trust Company, N.A., State Street Bank and Trust Company, N.A. shall disburse to such owners, or the Paying Agent payment of the Insured Amounts due on such Obligations, less any amount held by the Paying Agent for the payment of such Insured Amounts and legally available therefor. This policy does not insure against loss of any prepayment premium which may at any time be payable with respect to any Obligation.

As used herein, the term "owner" shall mean the registered owner of any Obligation as indicated in the books maintained by the Paying Agent, the Issuer, or any designee of the Issuer for such purpose. The term owner shall not include the Issuer or any party whose agreement with the Issuer constitutes the underlying security for the Obligations.

Any service of process on the Insurer may be made to the Insurer at its offices located at 113 King Street, Armonk, New York 10504 and such service of process shall be valid and binding.

This policy is non-cancellable for any reason. The premium on this policy is not refundable for any reason including the payment prior to maturity of the Obligations.

This policy is not covered by the Property/Casualty Insurance Security Fund specified in Article 76 of the New York Insurance Law.

IN WITNESS WHEREOF, the Insurer has caused this policy to be executed in facsimile on its behalf by its duly authorized officers, this [DAY] day of [MONTH, YEAR].

MUNICIPAL BOND INVESTORS
ASSURANCE CORPORATION

_____
President

Attest: _____
Assistant Secretary

STD-R-NY-5
1/1/94

Source: Municipal Bond Investors Assurance Corp.

How bond insurers provide a higher rating

Most municipal bond insurers have an AAA rating, the highest, from Moody's and Standard & Poor's (the major rating agencies); one has an AA, and several have AAA ratings from Fitch and Duff and Phelps. These high ratings improve the salability of the issuer's insured bonds and are one main reason for the purchase of bond insurance in the first place. The high ratings of bond insurance companies give each bond insured by the company the rating of the company; therefore, almost all insured bonds have an AAA rating.

The need of the bond insurance companies to keep a high rating gives the rating agencies considerable power over the activities, investments, and underwriting policies of the companies.

How bond insurance provides improved bond salability

Buyers of insured municipal bonds tend only to ask that the bonds they buy be insured; they usually don't really care very much which of the bond insurance firms insures their bonds, especially if their bonds are insured by one of the three largest insurers. Bonds insured by different bond insurance companies all tend to trade at close to the same levels. This market homogeneity provides the bond owner with an advantage when he or she wants to sell them. The owner is selling what the municipal bond marketplace calls "insured paper," with much less attention paid to the actual bond issuer and bond insurer. Instead, the buyer responds to the bond insurance in placing a value on the bond. This market homogeneity, which tends to apply to all bond insurance companies, adds a great value to the bond insurance. Some municipal bond observers think that the municipal bond insurance industry has not paid enough attention to this feature of bond insurance; in any case, it is of great value to the investor in insured bonds. The homogeneity provided by bond insurance puts the investor's bond into a much larger set of bonds of interest to prospective bond buyers.

Understanding the Place of Bond Insurance in the Municipal Bond Market

About 37 percent of total municipal new issue was insured in 1993. Since a portion of new issue is of such high quality as not to require bond insurance, and more was of such low quality as to be uninsurable, the percentage of eligible new issue that was insured is even higher.

Bond insurance clearly meets an investor need. Since most insured bonds are purchased by individual investors, clearly individual investors see value added by the insurance. The bond insurance industry estimates that about 80 percent of insured new issue is bought by individual investors; nobody knows for sure exactly what the percentage is.

If you buy insured bonds, you should understand that you are implicitly paying a premium for this insurance, and that you are receiving in exchange a better guarantee of payment, a better rating, and better marketability.

Regulating Bond Insurance Companies

Bond insurance has a totally different regulatory environment than municipal bond regulation. Insurance companies of all sorts are regulated by the states in which they do business, and they must be licensed by a state to do business in that state. For example, for several years a major bond insurance firm was not licensed in several states and could not do business directly in those states. The regulatory agency is the state Department of Insurance. State departments of insurance periodically examine the books of all insurance companies licensed to do business in their state. The purpose of state insurance regulation is to assure prompt, full payment of claims by the companies.

Securities regulation, by contrast, is largely done by the federal government, and the important agency is the Securities and Exchange Commission. The purpose of federal securities regulation, generally, is full disclosure of information on securities and fair, efficient, and honest securities markets.

For the person insured, disclosure has no real place in state insurance regulation. However, all insurance companies file extensive reports with the insurance departments of the states in which they operate. If you want to find out information about any particular bond insurance company, one way is to examine the company's reports on file with the state insurance department. These reports are usually open to public inspection.

The question of the extent of federal government interest in disclosure about bond insurance companies in official statements of insured new issues remains unexamined. In 1994, the only statement made in official statements about insured bonds is that they are insured. No information is provided about the insurance companies.

How Bonds Can Be Insured

Bonds can be insured in three ways. The most important way is insuring new-issue bonds at the time they are underwritten. The bonds are insured at inception, sold as insured bonds, the bond insurance contract is printed on the bond certificate, the official statement describes the bonds as insured, and the CUSIP description indicates that the bonds are insured. Most insured bonds are insured in this way.

A second method is to insure bonds after they have been issued. This is called secondary market insurance. It works in the following way. A municipal bond trader buys a block of uninsured bonds, usually at least several million dollars worth. The trader then buys bond insurance on that block of bonds from one of the bond insurance companies. The newly insured bonds are thereafter insured. They receive a new CUSIP number, a new rating as insured bonds, and a new description as insured bonds. Presumably they will sell at a higher price; that is why the trader made this transaction in the first place. Secondary market insurance is offered by most bond insurance firms, but it is a minor part of their overall business; estimates range from about 5 percent to about 20 percent.

A third way of insuring bonds is as part of a municipal investment trust or municipal mutual fund portfolio. Frequently MITs or mutual funds will be offered which consist only of insured bonds. The fund can obtain insured bonds by buying bonds insured at issue, or by buying bonds and buying secondary market insurance for them. A third method is to buy an insurance policy for the fund which insures bonds while they are held by the fund. The fund pays a monthly premium to the insurance company. When and if the bonds are sold, are called, or mature, the premium is no longer paid, and the bonds are no longer insured. The bonds are insured only as long as they are in the fund. The fund frequently may buy permanent insurance on the bonds before it sells them. This business is also a small part of the total bond insurance business.

How Municipal Bond Reinsurance Works

Most insurance companies, no matter what risks they insure, transfer part of their insurance risks to another insurance company. This procedure is called reinsurance, and the company that provides the reinsurance is called the reinsurer. The company providing the original insurance is called the primary insurer. Reinsurance allows the primary insurance company to reduce its liability on any particular risk. The primary company can thereby offer larger insurance coverage, insure risks that it might not otherwise be able to insure, and reduce its potential liability on any particular large risk.

Bond insurance companies frequently reinsure a portion of their insured bonds. Reinsurance allows them to sell additional insurance. Bond insurers have limits on the amount of insurance they can sell on bonds of any one particular issuer. Reinsurance allows them to sell additional insurance on these issuers, and in fact to sell additional insurance of all sorts. It also allows them to transfer or lay off the risk onto another insurance company. A variety of reinsurance techniques exist.

Who Insures Municipal Bonds?

Eight companies insure municipal bonds, but three of them provide about 90 percent of the insurance coverage, and the fourth provides most of the rest. The companies with their abbreviations and share of 1993 insured municipal market are shown in Figure 8.5.

Figure 8.5

Municipal Bond Investors Assurance Corp. (MBIA)	36.7 %
AMBAC Indemnity Corp. (AMBAC)	28.2
Financial Guaranty Insurance Co. (FGIC)	25.7
Financial Security Assurance, Inc. (FSA)	6.3
Capital Guaranty Insurance Co. (Capital Guaranty)	2.0
Connie Lee Insurance Co. (Connie Lee)	0.8
Asset Guaranty Insurance Co. (Asset Guaranty)	0.2
Capital Markets Assurance Corp. (CapMac)	0.2

Source: Fitch Investors Source, Inc. Company Reports

MBIA is about 89 percent owned by the public and is traded on the New York Stock Exchange. Small amounts are held by Aetna Life & Casualty Co. and by Credit Local de France. AMBAC is entirely publicly owned and is traded on the New York Stock Exchange. FGIC is 99 percent owned by GE Capital Corporation, part of General Electric. The others have a combination of public and institutional holders, or entirely institutional owners.

Insuring a New Bond Issue

A prospective new issue for insurance may come to a bond insurer in several ways. The bond should be of investment grade, however, if it is to qualify for insurance at all.

If the bond is to be offered at competitive bid, one of the bond insurer's underwriters will automatically review it for possible insurance. If the bond insurer decides that the new issue qualifies for insurance, it will publish that fact and state the premium for insuring the issue. The bond underwriter at the time of sale will compare offering the issue with and without insurance and make the decision based on which choice results in the most attractive offering to his customers and which has the lowest interest cost to the issuer.

Frequently the new issue is negotiated, and comes to the insurer as a result of the insurer's own sales efforts, or from the investment banker working on the new issue. In either case, an insurance underwriter will review the issue for possible insurance. The insurance underwriter may work with the investment banker to provide special clauses in the bond indenture to make sure that the interests of the insurance company are protected. An offer to insure the bonds is made, which may be accepted by the issuer. If the insurance company is working with the issuer and the issuer's investment banker, usually the offer will be acceptable to the issuer. The insurer delivers the policy and receives his premiums at the time the bonds are delivered to the bond underwriter for payment.

HOW RETAIL INVESTORS BUY AND SELL MUNICIPAL BONDS

Investors buy and sell municipal bonds in a different way from the usual trades of common stocks, especially common stocks listed on the New York Stock Exchange. Almost all investor purchases and sales of municipal bonds are done with their broker acting as a municipal bond dealer. Investors don't usually give buy and sell orders to their broker. They obtain offerings and bids from their broker or dealer. They may accept or decline, or, on rare occasions, make a counteroffer.

This is quite different from the usual procedure for buying stocks listed on the New York Stock Exchange. In the case of the normal retail common stock transaction, the broker acts as the customer's agent and carries out the customer's order to buy or sell at the auction market known as the New York Stock Exchange.

Investors should clearly understand the difference. The investor usually buys a municipal bond from a dealer who has the bond in an inventory of bonds available for sale. It might make a big difference to the dealer's profit, and to the salesperson's commission, which bond the investor buys. The investor should fully understand this.

Over one and one-half million different municipal bonds exist (no one knows for sure how many), with over fifty thousand different issuers and possible issuers and approximately ten thousand different new issues of bonds each year. These numbers dwarf the numbers of common stocks available, even including all the penny stocks.

The broker has an incentive to sell municipal bonds his firm owns. The investor should understand that this might restrict the bonds made available for sale.

Some firms specialize in certain types of bonds and will be especially knowledgeable about these bonds and their markets; they might easily be able to provide the investor with better prices, both buying and selling. Also, a firm might temporarily have too much of a particular issue or kind of bond. This could lead to special sales efforts and possible lower prices.

Rarely, the bond dealer will act as an agent. This usually happens with bonds that the dealer does not want to reoffer to other customers. They might be bonds of such low credit quality that the dealer considers them unsuitable investments for his or her customers, or they might be bonds that are not the usual type of bond handled by the dealer. In such cases, the dealer will offer them to other dealers or put them out with one of the municipal bond brokers. In either case, the dealer will transmit the bids to the bond owner. The bond owner will consider the bids and decide whether to sell.

The firm and the firm's sales representative who is serving the individual investor have several sources for municipal offerings. The main source is the firm's inventory of municipal bonds. These could be the firm's participations in new issue underwritings, or they could be secondary market bonds which the firm has obtained either by purchase from other customers of the firm who wished to sell them or from other municipal bond dealers. These bonds are then offered to the firm's customers. These secondary market purchases and offerings are made by the firm's municipal bond traders.

Other sources of municipal bonds for firms to offer to their customers are *The Blue List of Current Municipal Offerings*, and offerings over *Munifacts* and other news wires serving the municipal bond industry.

Often, these offerings are made available to the sales representatives by means of an online computer system run by the firm. The salesperson has only to refer to the computer system to determine the offerings being made. Frequently, the salesperson can search the entire range of the company's offerings for bonds which meet the particular requirements of his customer.

The firm might have many bond offerings, only some of which meet the customer's needs. By using the computer system, the salesperson can select only those bonds which meet the customer's requirements. For example, the customer might want only bonds within a certain maturity range, or bonds issued only within a particular state, or bonds with coupons within a particular range.

Sometimes, the salesperson can even sell bonds to a customer directly from the computer system, with the trades going automatically into the firm's trades processing system. These automated systems don't replace the concept of the salesperson making an offering of bonds to the customer, with the customer agreeing (or not agreeing) to buy them. The offerings and the offering prices have been set by the trader or underwriter, not by the salesperson or the computer. The offerings were then entered into the system by the trader, underwriter, or an assistant. The salesperson only relays them to the customer; the computer system is only a help in this relay.

Frequently, the salesperson will call his or her marketing liaison person, the municipal trading desk, or a particular regional office to obtain additional offerings which might interest customers.

Investors considering buying municipal bonds should examine the offerings of several municipal bond dealers. They might find worthwhile differences in prices for comparable bonds.

A customer sells work in the opposite way, but using the same system. The customer's salesperson obtains a bid for the customer's bonds from the trader responsible for trading that particular bond; sometimes some bids may be already available through the computer system, and sometimes the computer system may be used to send the bid request to the trader. The salesperson receives the bid from the trader and then informs the customer. The customer then accepts or rejects the bid. If the customer rejects the bid, nothing is done, but if the customer accepts the bid, the bonds are sold to the firm, and are then usually reoffered to the firm's other customers.

Investors who are selling bonds should consider getting bids from several firms. Sometimes there are large enough differences between bids from different firms to justify the extra effort required to obtain the additional bids.

UNDERSTANDING BOND SWAPPING

A bond swap is an exchange of bonds presently owned for new bonds. The investor does this by selling bonds presently owned and buying new ones. In most swaps, the investor plans and expects that the value of the bonds sold will approximately equal the value of the bonds bought, but both the buy and the sell are separate transactions.

Why should an investor ever want to swap at all? If the securities were well selected in the first place, why would anyone want to change them? Other purchases we make, such as clothing or household goods, are made with the expectation of use until worn out, obsolete, or otherwise unusable. Why should a municipal bond investment be any different?

Reasons for Swapping Bonds

There are four main reasons for swapping bonds:

- change in market levels;
- change in investor requirements;
- change in bond characteristics; and
- portfolio improvement.

Change in market levels

A large change in market level, either up or down, could cause an investor to swap his or her bonds to take advantage of this change. The most important change, from the point of view of large-scale, publicized swaps, is the large market decline, especially late in the calendar year. This leads to tax-loss selling, or tax swapping.

The investor sells bonds, taking a loss for federal income tax purposes, and replaces them with similar bonds, but not so similar as to disallow taking the loss for income tax purposes. The investor thus has capital loss for income tax purposes, but has not changed his or her portfolio in any important respect. If the investor has swapped for the same par amount, there will be a capital gain later on, but this could be years off, and not something to worry about now. The new bonds must differ from the old bonds in issuer, coupon rate, or maturity date. The investor should consult with a tax advisor to make sure that the swap will result in a loss for income tax purposes.

In times of very low bond prices, many municipal bond deal-ers actively seek to swap their customers' bonds. They can provide their customers with tax losses, and offer the swaps without any risk of the dealer owning the bonds; they simply try to persuade their customers to exchange bonds they own for bonds owned by other customers of the firm.

For example, suppose an investor bought $100,000 face amount of long-term municipal bonds in January, 1994. In July, 1994, the investor could easily have a 15-percent loss if he or she bought long-term bonds. If the bonds were sold for $85,000, the investor would have a $15,000 capital loss for income tax purposes and could possibly deduct it from capital gains. This loss could pos-sibly give the investor a tax saving of about $5,000. If the sold bonds were replaced with similar bonds, the portfolio would be essential-ly unchanged.

A large market rise could also cause an investor to swap, this time to take advantage of the increase in the market value of the holdings. For example, some United States Treasury bonds sold dur-ing the early 1980s were selling in early 1994 for prices of about 150. An investor could decide to sell these bonds, take a profit, and place the proceeds in another investment, especially if he thinks that inter-est rates are about to rise again.

Change in investor requirements

The investor's requirements may change, resulting in a possible desire to swap. For example, an individual investor may no longer need tax-exempt income; he or she may have business or other loss-es or may simply retire, with somewhat lower income.

The investor may move to another state, resulting in a desire to sell bonds issued in the former state of residence and buy bonds issued in the new state of residence, to avoid state income taxes. For example, an investor living in New York State could have a portfolio consisting of New York State municipal bonds to avoid the New York State income tax. If the investor moves to Massachusetts, he or she might want to sell his New York State bonds and buy bonds issued by the Commonwealth of Massachusetts or one of its political subdivisions. The investor would avoid Massachusetts state income taxes on income from the New York State bonds and would receive income exempt from both federal and Massachusetts income taxes.

Changes in portfolio policy could cause the investor to consider bond swaps. For example, the investor may decide, based on personal analysis, to sell one market segment and buy another; for example, the investor may decide to sell public power bonds and buy hospital bonds. This could result in portfolio swaps.

Legal changes could result in bond swaps. For example, a few years ago, some insurance companies were required by the laws of their states to possess the actual certificates for securities owned by them; this law kept them from owning book-entry bonds. When the laws were changed, the insurance companies could own book-entry bonds and may have made some swaps to add bonds they considered desirable but could not previously own. Also, bonds that were desirable under one set of tax laws might become less desirable under a new set of tax laws.

Change in bond characteristics

Sometimes the investor's requirements don't change, but the bond characteristics do change, resulting in a bond that no longer meets the investor's requirements. Two important changes are advance refundings and shorter time to final maturity date.

Advance refunding usually both shortens the time to maturity and improves the quality of the bond. The maturity date is now frequently the call date rather than the final maturity date. Since the bonds are escrowed to either call date or final maturity date, they usually have an improved rating as well; usually, this rating is AAA.

The investor now owns a bond possibly quite different from the one owned before the refunding, and the new bond may not suit the investment objectives. The investor should consider a swap.

For example, in late 1982, Municipal Assistance Corporation for the City of New York (MAC) sold some 9 $7/_8$ percent bonds due July 1, 2003. Early in 1983, the bonds traded as low as 93. Then, in December, 1986, interest rates had fallen, and MAC refunded the bonds to the call on July 1, 1993 at 102. The bonds traded close to 120, with an AAA rating due to the escrow by United States Treasury securities. The owners of these bonds had bought a medium-grade long-term revenue bond, and now owned a very high grade, relatively short-term bond which was secured by United States Treasury bonds placed in escrow. If the investors' requirements had remained unchanged, this bond would have been a suitable candidate for a swap. The investor would have sold the escrowed bond and bought revenue bonds with a similar rating and maturity, and almost certainly increased income in doing so. However, many very competent bond portfolio managers prefer to simply hold prerefunded bonds to their call date and price.

A second characteristic that changes is time to maturity. Each day, each bond is one day closer to final maturity. If an investor has owned the same bonds for a considerable period of time, their time to maturity has shortened and may no longer meet his or her investment requirements.

For example, an investor may wish to have a medium-term portfolio, composed of bonds with a maturity of seven to twelve years. If he or she buys some ten-year bonds, after more than three years, these bonds no longer meet the time-to-maturity requirements; they now have less than seven years to maturity. The bonds would be candidates for a swap.

Bonds can, of course, decline in quality. If a bond's quality declines, it may no longer meet the investor's requirements. Many trustees who manage bond investment accounts are required by law to invest only in bonds which meet certain requirements. Frequently, the laws require that the bonds be of investment grade, or the highest four ratings. Decline in quality rating may mean that the bonds no longer meet these requirements. They would become candidates for a swap.

For example, some states require that investment funds be placed only in bonds of investment grade. If a bond's rating is reduced so that it is no longer in the top four rating grades, these investors would sell it in order to comply with the law.

Portfolio improvement

Sometimes an investor is offered a swap which improves quality or yield, or both. This portfolio improvement swap may take advantage of a market imperfection, or simply a special opportunity in the market. This occurs with some frequency for institutional investors in municipal bonds. It doesn't happen very often for individual municipal bond holders because the spreads required to trade the bonds are generally too high, but it does occasionally happen.

Computer programs have existed since the 1960s which analyze proposed swaps and tell the investor the advantages of particular swaps. Some of these programs are quite elaborate. They will show the investor what he or she gives up and gains from a particular proposed swap as well as the overall advantage of the swap.

For most individual investors, judicious swapping can improve the portfolio, and they should analyze all reasonable swaps. However, aside from tax swaps or swaps of bonds escrowed to maturity, most swaps involve accepting longer-term bonds. Most longer-term bonds will have higher yields caused by the normal yield curve, and this is what makes the bond swap attractive to the investor after paying the expense of the spread in making the swap. This increase in maturity period may not conform to the investor's requirements; the investor should always keep these needs in mind when making swaps.

The investor should also be prepared to propose his or her own swaps. As needs change, perhaps his or her portfolio should change also; the broker needs to be made aware of these changes.

Formerly, bond investors rarely traded. Those times have changed. An investor in municipal bonds should always be prepared to swap if it is advantageous and should always be thinking about possible swaps to improve his or her portfolio. If any bonds in the portfolio are advance refunded, he or she should consider a swap.

As an investor's bonds approach maturity, he or she should also consider a swap to extend maturity. In a normal investment environment, extending maturity almost always results in a yield increase. The investor might obtain a worthwhile income increase and still remain within the original investment requirements.

FINDING INFORMATION IN THE MUNICIPAL MARKETPLACE

If you invest in municipal bonds, you should have some idea of what information you need and where to get it. The following organizations all provide information to the municipal marketplace, and might be helpful to you. The author has always found them very cooperative in answering questions. You might also find it worthwhile to subscribe to some of their publications.

These organizations frequently offer services through one or more subsidiaries, sometimes with different names. Here, their service is placed under the main name of the organization. They should be able to help you with any of the services offered by any part of their organization.

Nationally Recognized Municipal Securities Information Repositories offer information on municipal securities. At present, this is almost entirely copies of official statements, which are available for a modest fee, usually about $10.00.

The organizations are printed in alphabetical order. A New York City address is provided whenever available.

When you try to find information, start with your local public library. They frequently will have some of the publications listed here. Local college and university libraries may also be helpful.

Organizations Providing Municipal Information Services

Bloomberg provides municipal bond information to subscribers to their various services, through terminals in the offices of the subscribers. A wide variety of online information on municipal bonds is provided, including call features, sinking fund payments, and much else. You must be a subscriber to have access to the information. If your dealer subscribes, he may be able to give you information. Bloomberg is also one of the three Nationally Recognized Municipal Securities Information Repositories (NRMSIRs).

Bloomberg Financial Markets
499 Park Avenue
New York, New York 10022
1-800-448-5678

The Bond Buyer prints the daily newspaper, *The Bond Buyer*, which almost everyone in the municipal business reads. It also offers a news wire, called Munifacts, and does bond evaluations for mutual funds and others. It offers a list of municipal bond dealers, and providers of information and other services to the municipal bond industry. It also has a variety of other publications. The Bond Buyer is one of the Nationally Recognized Municipal Securities Information Repositories.

The Bond Buyer
One State Street Plaza
New York, New York 10004
212-803-8200

The Chicago Board of Trade has information about the Municipal Future.

The Chicago Board of Trade
Publications Department
141 West Jackson Blvd., Suite 2210
Chicago, Illinois 60604-2994
1-800-THE-CBOT (312-435-3558)

Duff & Phelps offers ratings and other credit analysis and reporting services. They have a background in corporate ratings and are now entering municipal ratings as well.

Duff & Phelps
17 State Street
New York, New York 10004
212-908-0200

Financial Publishing Company offers a variety of interest tables and bond value tables. Municipal bond investors might find some of these useful for reference.

Financial Publishing Company
82 Brookline Avenue
Boston, Massachusetts 02215
617-262-4040
1-800-247-3214

Fitch Investors Service offers ratings and other credit analysis
and reporting services, including some excellent reports on municipal bond insurance companies.

Fitch Investors Service
One State Street Plaza
New York, New York 10004
212-908-0500
1-800-75FITCH (1-800-753-4824)

J.J. Kenny Co., Inc., part of McGraw-Hill, offers a variety of
information services, including a municipal database service; notification of bond calls and refundings; and the Blue List, a daily list
of municipal bond offerings by dealers. A subsidiary offers bond
evaluation services, including municipal bond evaluations.
Another subsidiary is a leading municipal bond broker. J. J. Kenny
Co. is a Nationally Recognized Municipal Securities Information
Repository.

J. J. Kenny Co., Inc.
65 Broadway
New York, New York 10006
212-770-4000

Moody's Investors Service, part of Dun and Bradstreet, is one
of the leading sources of municipal bond information and has many
publications on municipal bonds. These include *Moody's Municipal
and Government Manual,* a blue-bound three-volume annual publication containing information on almost every bond issue known,
and *Moody's Bond Survey,* a weekly publication. Moody's publishes
well-known ratings of many bonds, including municipals. A subsidiary offers bond evaluation services, including municipal bond
evaluations.

Moody's Investors Service
99 Church Street
New York, New York 10007
212-553-0300

The Municipal Securities Rulemaking Board publishes its *Manual* semiannually, offers the *Glossary of Municipal Bond Terms,* and publishes *MSRB Reports* about four times per year. These are useful sources of information about municipal bond regulations.

Municipal Securities Rulemaking Board
1150 18th Street, N.W. Suite 400
Washington, D.C. 20036-3816
202-223-9347
FAX: 202-872-0347

The Public Securities Association is an association of firms in the business or interested in the business of underwriting and trading public securities. This includes United States Treasury securities and associated securities as well as municipal securities. They offer a variety of industry training programs and other research and information services. They frequently represent the municipal bond industry in Washington.

Public Securities Association
40 Broad Street
New York, New York 10004-2373
212-809-7000

Standard & Poor's Corporation, part of McGraw-Hill, offers bond ratings, a variety of information services, and publications. The CUSIP Service Bureau assigns CUSIP numbers to securities under contract with the American Bankers Association.

Standard & Poor's Corporation
25 Broadway
New York, New York 10004
212-248-2525

HEDGING AND SPECULATING USING MUNICIPAL FUTURES

If you heat your house with oil, your oil company might offer you the chance to buy oil in August for delivery in the following February, at the price set in August. If you accept, you have just made a forward contract. You promise to buy fuel oil at some time in the future (February) at a price set now (in August). In general terms, a forward is a contract to buy or sell something (commodity, security, or anything else) at some specified future time at some specified price. A wide variety of such contracts exist. We will look at only one contract, the municipal index future and its options. A future is a special kind of forward, traded on an exchange, with a standardized contract. A more extensive discussion of futures is far beyond the scope of this book. Many fine books exist on futures contracts and futures trading.

The futures contracts of greatest interest to most investors are those traded on organized exchanges, such as the Chicago Board of Trade. Organized trading exists in futures for various grains and other foodstuffs, metals (including precious metals), oil, lumber, and other commodities. Organized trading also exists in futures for United States Treasury securities, various stock market indices, and the Municipal Bond Index.

The Municipal Bond Index is constructed in the following way. Forty recently issued bonds are selected, which must meet specific requirements. The requirements are as follows:

- The bond must have an A or better rating from Moody's, or an A– or better rating from Standard & Poor's.

- The issue size must be at least $50 million ($75 million if it is a housing issue).

- The bond must have at least nineteen years until maturity date.

- The bond must be callable before maturity with the first call between seven and sixteen years from the date it is included in the index.

- The bond must have a fixed coupon with semiannual payments of interest.

- The bond must have been reoffered, must be out of syndicate, and must have a market price from 95 to 105.

Private placement bonds may not be included, nor may bonds with unusual redemption features.

Each month, on the fifteenth and on the last day of the month, new issues are added and the same number of older issues are dropped from the Index. This ensures that the Index includes current and actively traded bonds. As a result, the list always contains forty recently issued bonds.

These bonds are appraised twice per day, at 11:00 A.M. and 2:00 P.M., by six leading municipal bond brokers, and the appraisal prices are reported to *The Bond Buyer*. The person managing the calculation process deletes the lowest and the highest prices for each bond and takes the average of the four remaining prices. The average is then divided by a conversion factor that equates the bond's price to that of an 8-percent coupon bond. The forty numbers resulting from this are then averaged, and the average is multiplied by a coefficient that determines the value of the Index.

The future for the Index is traded on the Chicago Board of Trade. Delivery months are March, June, September, and December.

Because the Index is based on appraisals of bonds, and because the bonds used in the Index change frequently, no delivery of a security under the future is possible. Therefore, any contracts outstanding on settlement day are settled in cash at the value of the Index on the settlement day.

Activity in the municipal index future is much lower than activity in the United States Treasury bond future. Trading might be about 2 percent of the level of the U.S. Bond trading, and the open interest less than 10 percent of the open interest in the bonds. However, it is an actively traded index. Trading rose immediately after the Index was introduced in 1985, and reached a peak in 1987. It then declined until 1991, and has been rising since, reaching a projected peak in 1994 a little higher than the peak of 1987.

If you are active in municipals, you should know about the existence of a municipal bond index future contract, and the options on the Index future. You should realize that it is based on appraisals of recently issued bonds, not on publicly reported trades of these bonds. In fact, the bonds need not have actually traded at all, although they probably have, since they are large, recent issues. The appraisals are based on trades done by or known to the reporting broker. You should understand that you cannot buy or sell actual bonds using the municipal future, but that it can only be used for hedging or speculation and that your position must be settled on settlement day unless you close it out earlier. If you trade the Index, you should understand that the market is not nearly as active as that for United States Treasury security futures.

You can use the Index as an indication of the interest rate levels of municipal bonds comparable to the bonds used to make up the Index; these are long-term, investment-grade bonds, mostly revenue bonds, but with some general obligation bonds.

Another index widely used for trading is the Municipals Over Bonds (MOB) spread. This is the relation between the Municipal Index and the Treasury Bond future. Many people follow this spread and use it for hedging or speculation. You should know about the spread and its uses.

Both call and put options on the municipal future are also traded on the Chicago Board of Trade. You can use these as you would any other call or put option.

SHORT SELLING OF MUNICIPAL BONDS

In real life, if you sell something you don't own, you could be in serious trouble. In Wall Street, if you do this in the right way you can make a lot of money. This procedure is called the short sale.

A short sale of a security occurs when the seller sells a security which he or she does not own, or, if he or she does own it, does not intend actually to deliver the security. The seller makes a profit if the price falls and he can buy back the security, called "covering the short," at a lower price than he sold at. For example, if a seller sells $100,000 of bonds at 100, he receives $100,000 from the sale.

If he can buy back the bonds later on at a price of 95, he pays $95,000 to buy them back. He has made $5,000 ($100,000 − $95,000) on the trade. In order to make delivery of the security, the seller must obtain it from somewhere. The usual procedure is to borrow the security and deliver it to the buyer. The short seller then owes the security to the person he or she borrowed it from (the lender), and must return it, either upon demand, or at the completion of a particular, specified time period. Usually, the borrower also posts some collateral with the lender. Meanwhile, the borrower of the security must pay to the lender all interest and dividend payments paid on the security by the issuer. Thus, in the case of municipal bonds, all interest payments made by the issuer to the bondholder, which in this case is the buyer, must be also made by the borrower to the lender of the bonds.

This leads to a concern of the Internal Revenue Service. The interest payment made to the bondholder by the issuer is a payment of tax-exempt interest, usually. But the payment made by the borrower of the bonds to the lender of the bonds is not tax-exempt interest. In fact, it is not even interest, it is only a payment. The Internal Revenue Service will not allow additional tax-exempt interest to be created by the short sale of the bonds.

But if the payment received by the lender is not tax-exempt, the lender is substituting taxable income for tax-exempt income. The lender would do this only if the taxability of the income makes no difference to him or her. This can occur only if the lender pays no income taxes anyway.

This in turn raises questions about the lender's credit rating. If the lender pays no taxes, he or she may not have any income to pay taxes on. If the lender defaults, the borrower would still have the obligation to return the securities borrowed, but would remain only a creditor as far as the security he or she posted for the loan. This could be unsound from the borrower's point of view.

As a result, short sales of municipals by actually borrowing the securities are rare. However, other short sales are possible and frequently occur. For example, during the underwriting period, underwriters will frequently trade the new bonds on a when-issued basis, and they will frequently go short. Since the bonds are not yet issued, and the entire position will be settled up when they are issued, the short sales do not result in additional tax-exempt income and cause no problem from that standpoint. These short sales are quite common in cases of a large issue of term bonds.

These transactions, long and short, can become quite complicated. Years ago, one particularly large issue was traded, when-issued, so widely and so actively that no one could settle the accounts by simple reconciliation. The industry tradition is that all the participants had to sit in a large room and actually deliver the certificates against payment until all the trades were settled.

A third kind of short sale is called the *de minimus* short sale. It usually occurs when, by mistake, the underwriter sells more bonds than he or she owns. Usually, these are small, and no one worries about them, although the underwriter tries to cover the short by buying back the bonds from one of the owners.

An amusing example of this situation happened to the author in 1978. His employer at the time had accidentally shorted $5,000 Wallingford, Connecticut, 6-percent bonds due March 1, 1994, MBIA insured. For months he checked *The Blue List* every day for offerings, to no avail. Finally one day, sure enough, there was a listing! Who owned the bonds? His own firm's Northeast Region! The Regional Manager wanted to sell the entire block of 25M, but was willing to sell 5M at cost in this situation. The short was finally covered.

HOW MUNICIPAL BOND INDUSTRY TRENDS WILL AFFECT YOU

Since the late 1970s, several changes throughout the United States have reshaped the municipal bond market, with results affecting almost every issuer of and investor in municipal bonds. This chapter discusses the effects on municipal issuers, municipal investors, the municipal marketplace, the municipal regulators, and the resulting industry changes.

How Issuers Have Changed

Governments throughout the United States have moved to keep taxes under control. As a result, a strong trend has developed to remove activities, to the greatest extent possible, from being tax-supported to being supported by users of the government service. This includes raising user fees and imposing of user fees where none previously existed. For example, one large state recently raised both its driver's license and car registration fees. On a local level, one village runs a municipal pool, which is one of its most popular village recreation activities. Gradually, over several years, the salary of the head of the Village Recreation Department has been increasingly paid from the swimming pool operating fund, with the result that now about one-tenth the salary of the recreation department head is paid from pool user fees, and no longer from tax revenues. Other Recreation Department expenses are now paid from the pool operating fund as well. Libraries have raised overdue book fines and instituted charges for other services.

Governments have also set up new enterprises and new kinds of enterprises. For example, New York City set up a Water Authority, which will allow separate funding of improvements to the New York City water supply. The State of New York set up the Municipal Assistance Corporation for the City of New York (MAC), to take over and finance New York City's debt after the default on the notes in 1975. Westchester County, New York, set up a Refuse Disposal District to handle the refuse collected by most, but not all, of the cities, villages, and towns in Westchester County. The Refuse Disposal District issued Industrial Revenue Bonds to finance the construction of a resource recovery plant; a few years earlier, this type of financing would more likely have been done by Westchester County itself.

Results of this include creation of new governmental agencies and authorities, many of which have the authorization to issue bonds and have used this to issue bonds to finance their activities. One result has been a relative increase in revenue bond issuance. A second result has been increased complexity in these bonds, with increased analysis required to understand their features, their security, and their relative value in the municipal marketplace. In the opinion of many observers, this has also resulted in a general decline in overall quality of municipal bond new issuance.

How Bond Buyers Have Changed

Changes have also taken place in the market for municipal bonds. Banks and insurance companies have declined in their importance relative to individual investors, or retail.

Banks have been net sellers of municipal bonds for many years now. The 1986 changes in the tax laws made ownership of most municipal bonds much less attractive to banks, and other income sheltering devices, such as leasing techniques, have become available to them. As a result, banks are no longer the major factor they once were in the municipal market, and in fact, are not much of a factor at all.

According to Federal Reserve System reports, as shown in Figure 8.1, bank ownership of municipal bonds as a percent of total amount outstanding has fallen from about 41 percent in 1980 to about 8 percent in 1993, a decline of about 33 percentage points, and about 80 percent in percentage. The total amount of municipal bonds owned by banks has declined from about 149 billion dollars in 1980 to about 100 billion dollars in 1993, a net actual decline of about one-third, during a time when total municipals outstanding increased from 365 billion dollars to about 1,257 billion dollars.

Insurance companies have not had the relative decline that banks have had, but their position has declined compared to that of the mid-1970s. Percentage share of ownership of municipal bonds by insurance companies appears to have stabilized.

Retail has made up the difference. Retail includes municipal money market funds, mutual funds, closed-end funds, bank personal trusts, and direct holdings by individuals. Retail's share of municipal bond ownership has increased, to the point where it now accounts for about 75 percent of all municipal bond ownership.

How Municipal Regulation Has Changed

Municipal bonds traditionally had hardly any regulation. In 1975, New York City defaulted on four issues of notes, totaling about 2 billion dollars in face value. This default provided part of the impetus to start regulation of municipal bonds. In addition, official statements were not usual on new issues of bonds, except for larger revenue bond isssues, such as toll roads. As a result, Congress set up a regulatory mechanism for municipal bonds, which is still in effect.

The 1975 changes to the Securities Exchange Act of 1934 set up the Municipal Securities Rulemaking Board (MSRB). The MSRB first concerned itself with disclosure, standards, and procedures with customers. Municipal sales representatives and municipal principals, including municipal financial principals, were required to pass examinations proving they had a required level of proficiency. Standards were set for procedures with customers, including disclosure to the customer of important features of the bonds he or she was buying. Then regulatory concerns shifted to the areas of operations, delivery, and registration. In early 1994, attention once more shifted, focusing again on disclosure, but this time continuing ongoing disclosure by issuers of their financial results, and other issuer changes important to investors as well as municipal bond traders. Regulators are also concerned about political campaign contributions by municipal bond professionals to candidates for public office.

How These Changes Affect You, the Municipal Investor

These changes, and those affecting all fixed-income securities, have almost totally changed the municipal bond industry from what it was during the mid-1970s, as shown in Figure 8.6. New issue volume has increased enormously. Revenue bonds have increased in percentage of new-issue volume, from about 44 percent of new issue in 1974 to about 69 percent of new issue in 1993. General obligation bonds decreased from about 56 percent of new issue to about 35 percent of new issue during the same time. Revenue bonds reached a peak of about 75 percent of new issue in the early 1980s, but have since come down somewhat.

Competitive new issue, where issuers invite competitive bids for their bonds, has given way to negotiated new issue, in which issuers select the underwriter they wish to do business with. In 1974, about 70 percent of new issue was sold competitively, with about 29 percent sold by negotiation. In 1993, only about 19 percent of new issue was sold competitively, with about 80 percent sold by negotiation.

These two changes together mean that the typical municipal bond has changed from being a general obligation bond, sold by competitive bid, underwritten by a bank, and sold to a bank, to being a revenue bond, sold by negotiation, underwritten by a municipal bond dealer, and sold to retail.

Figure 8.6

MUNICIPAL BOND STATISTICS

	New Issue Volume (Billions)	GO %	Rev %	Comp %	Nego %	Other %
1974	23.6	56	44	70	29	0
1975	30.7	52	48	63	35	2
1976	35.4	51	49	58	37	6
1977	46.7	39	61	50	46	5
1978	48.2	37	63	44	50	5
1979	43.3	28	72	43	53	4
1980	48.4	29	70	40	58	2
1981	47.7	26	74	32	61	4
1982	78.3	27	73	31	68	1
1983	85.8	25	75	25	73	2
1984	101.9	27	73	21	77	2
1985	222.2	24	76	16	82	2
1986	148.5	29	71	22	76	2
1987	105.5	29	71	23	73	4
1988	117.8	27	73	23	75	2
1989	124.2	31	69	24	74	2
1990	127.9	31	69	24	74	2
1991	171.2	35	66	24	74	2
1992	235.0	35	65	19	80	1
1993	292.0	31	69	19	80	1

Source: The Bond Buyer

The complexity of many municipal bonds has increased. Yields have increased compared to U.S. Treasury yields. Households (retail municipal bond buyers) hold an increasing percentage of outstanding municipal bonds. Responding to this increased retail demand, municipal bond insurance has increased its share of insured new issue. Most municipal bonds which are insured are bought by retail customers. Finally, regulation and control have increased and will probably continue to do so.

These changes are important to all investors. They have radically changed the nature of municipal bond investment of today from what it was in 1974.

The bond you are likely to buy will not be paid out of taxes, but will instead be paid from the earnings of a governmental or other enterprise. For example, in the case of the bonds previously mentioned which were issued by Mass HEFA for Harvard, to build two garages and other construction, if Harvard cannot make its payments, Mass HEFA—and you—cannot look to the funds from MIT or Beth Israel Hospital or anyone else to pay Harvard's bonds; their funds can only be used to pay their own bonds. Likewise, the Commonwealth of Massachusetts is not obligated to make payments on the Harvard bonds. About two-thirds of municipal new issue now depends on the earnings of such enterprises.

Similarly, the Industrial Development Authority bonds shown in Chapter 1 depend on payments from McDonald's Corporation. If McDonald's doesn't pay, the bondholder cannot look to the Allegheny County Industrial Development Authority, the Common-wealth of Pennsylvania, or any other source for payment on his bonds.

Not many individual investors have the resources to investigate thoroughly all the prospective investments in municipal securities. This would involve an investigation into a wide variety of enterprises, requiring enormous competence in a variety of financial reporting techniques, and business activities. This requirement is so great that it is one reason why this book does not discuss municipal bond analysis; the activity is simply too large to fit into a book of this size. Probably no one person could attain expert capabilities in all these areas.

What Individual Investors Can Do

Individual investors can pool their funds and hire professional bond selection and portfolio management. Many have done this, and it is one reason for the enormous growth in municipal bond mutual funds, both open- and closed-end, and in municipal investment trusts.

Retail investors can buy bond insurance. Many bonds, especially of the lower investment grades, have been insured, and many individual investors have benefited from the insurance. The growth in retail municipal bond ownership is one reason for the enormous growth in bond insurance during the last fifteen years.

Investors can develop a relationship with a retail broker who, backed by a firm, will help them in their selection of municipal securities. Many investors have done that, and some brokers have developed a large clientele for their municipal bond business.

Investors can hire a professional portfolio manager to run their own personal investments, if they have enough money to do this. Many fine banks and investment advisory firms manage municipal bond portfolios of wealthy investors.

Investors can restrict their municipal investments to the very highest quality of general obligation bonds, as some have done.

Investors can develop investment competence in one area of municipal bond investment and restrict themselves to that one area. Some investors have done that.

You should understand the changed nature of the municipal bond business and take whatever action is required for you to make good municipal bond investments.

Whatever you do requires a policy decision for you on your municipal investments. You can hire someone to manage your investments for you, as is done with mutual funds and municipal investment trusts. This requires the expense of management. You can insure your bonds; this requires the expense of insurance. You can develop relationships with experts in the municipal investment field. This will require expense, at least in the form of sales commissions or management expense. You can develop competence in an area and invest in that particular area. This will require time and effort and will restrict your area of investment.

You can no longer lock up your municipal bonds and forget about them until they mature.

Understanding the New Issue Process for Municipal Bonds

This chapter covers the new issue process, from its very beginning as a need of the issuer until the bonds have been underwritten and offered, sold, and delivered to the public. It provides a complete overview of this important process.

WHY THE NEW ISSUE PROCESS IS IMPORTANT

The new issue process constitutes a major part of the municipal bond business. It determines municipal bond activity and overall profitability. In times of high new issue volume, such as during the year 1993, municipal bond business profits tend to be much higher than in times of lower new issue volume, such as the first half of 1994. In times of relatively low volume, municipal bond business profits fall off to much lower levels.

The new issue process also allows underwriters and investment bankers to respond directly to issuer and bond buyer needs and

193

desires. They can do this in the areas of pricing, contractual provisions, and maturity structure, adjusting these provisions in the newly issued bonds to meet the joint needs of buyer and issuer. Most new municipal bond features of the last few years, such as put options, variable-rate bonds, bond insurance, and various municipal derivatives were first introduced to the municipal bond market in the new issue process. Only later were they added to secondary market bonds, if at all.

Municipal new issue dominates the secondary market, and even drives it to an important extent. Finally, many municipal bond jobs apply only to the new issue process.

You should have at least some understanding of the new issue process because any municipal bonds you buy have a high probability of being municipal new issue. You should understand both the competitive underwriting and the negotiated underwriting, how they work, and, at least in general terms, how they bring bonds to market.

Conventional investment wisdom on the new issue of common stock states that the investor should subject these new issues to unusual scrutiny. In the case of municipal bonds, this is true in a different way.

Each year, many municipal bond issuers of the highest quality issue new bonds, and many knowledgeable municipal bond investors buy them. An investor should not be afraid to buy municipal new issue just because it is new.

But it is also true that most new features in municipal finance have been tried out on new issue. Not all of these features have worked out well for the investors, and some, such as step-rate coupon bonds, are no longer offered. If you are a municipal investor, you should subject each new feature to particularly close scrutiny, to make sure it will meet your needs over the time you expect to own the bond. Of course, you should subject any proposed municipal bond investment to the same level of scrutiny as any other investment.

HOW AN ISSUER COMES TO MARKET

In order to justify any financing at all, an issuer must first establish a need for funds. Several such needs might exist:

1. A new project, otherwise called a capital project, might be required. Examples of capital projects include a new road, new school, new town hall, new fire engine, and the like. All of these usually are of such large size as to require financing over a few years, rather than payment in full in one year.

2. Financing might be required for repair and maintenance on property owned by the issuer. For example, one school district neglected to keep the roofs and windows of its schools in good repair. This neglect later required borrowing to repair both roofs and windows.

3. Borrowing to refinance outstanding obligations might be advisable. Borrowing to reduce interest obligations was done frequently in 1993. This process is called refunding, and it accounted for almost half of new municipal issue in 1993.

4. Refinancing might also be useful to revise an indenture for bonds now outstanding. As discussed earlier, this is done by calling for redemption of the outstanding bonds, or defeasing them if they cannot be called now.

5. Paying current expenses by borrowing is sometimes done. There is nothing theoretically wrong with this, but still it is not usually considered a wise reason to finance. This was one of the conditions that got New York City into financial trouble in the early 1970s and caused eventual default on New York City's notes. Some current expenses, such as extraordinary expenses due to a natural disaster, like an earthquake, hurricane, or unexpectedly heavy snow, could be repaid over time. Normal expenses should be paid from normal revenues, not from borrowing. Borrowing to pay current expenses is a possible warning; investors should be alert to this.

A new issue frequently will have more than one of these purposes, and could conceivably have all five purposes. For example, the North Carolina Municipal Power Agency No. 1 issue, discussed later in the chapter, had two reasons for their refinancing: reducing interest costs and changing the indenture. The changes involved security provisions currently applicable to the agency's debt. The changes would allow issuance of variable rate securities, use a letter of credit for debt service reserves, and allow more flexibility in reinvestment. The investor should know the purpose of the bonds, and this purpose should be reasonable, considering the issuer and his needs.

If the bonds are issued to finance a project, the investor should also make sure that the project is likely to be completed, regardless of any other security for payment. For example, the ill-fated Washington Public Power Supply System bonds, for projects 4 and 5, were secured by a "take or pay" contract, which guaranteed that the public power districts that contracted for the power would pay the costs of the project, even if no power was actually delivered. When the bonds defaulted, the Supreme Court of the State of Washington held that the districts were not legally empowered to enter into those contracts, and did not have to pay. Just the same, it seems unlikely that, if the plants had been constructed and were actually delivering electric power as planned, the default would have occurred. In this case, the purpose was reasonable, but the project was so large and complicated that eventual completion was doubtful.

When the issuer has determined a need for financing, he next decides how to raise the money. He could decide to sell bonds, but other actions might be possible. Assets owned by the issuer might be sold. Other types of borrowings might be done. A bank could possibly be a better source of funds for the issuer. The issuer might have reserve funds which could be used for the needed purpose. All of these are possible ways to obtain funds for the needed purpose or purposes, and all of them have been used by issuers at various times.

The Role of the Financial Advisor

In making the decision on how to finance, the prospective issuer may call upon the services of a financial advisor. Financial advisors advise issuers on the process of issuing bonds, but usually do not themselves participate in the underwriting of the issue; they receive a fee for their advice. Frequently these are independent firms, whose main business activity is providing this advice. Some commercial banks also perform financial advisory services for their municipal customers. Sometimes an investment banking firm acts as financial advisor, although usually these firms hope to obtain investment banking business, and pure financial advisory work is not their main line of business.

MSRB Rule G-23 governs the activities of financial advisors. If a financial advisor wishes to participate in the underwriting, he must, in the case of a competitive underwriting, receive the consent of the issuer. In the case of a negotiated underwriting, he must withdraw as financial advisor, obtain the consent of the issuer, and disclose the possibility of a conflict of interest, as well as the source and amount of his remuneration.

The issuer then decides whether to sell the new issue by receiving competitive bids (a competitive underwriting) or by choosing an investment banker and hiring the banker to do the underwriting (a negotiated underwriting). The financial advisor will usually advise the issuer in this process.

In competitive underwriting, the issuer sets the terms of the sale, working with the financial advisor. The issuer publishes the offering in an Official Notice of Sale and subsequently receives competitive bids. The issuer awards the bonds to the best bid, and delivers the bonds and receives payment, about one month later.

If the issuer uses a negotiated underwriting, he selects a lead underwriter to manage the underwriting, and selects joint underwriters and possibly the syndicate account members as well. The lead underwriter or manager negotiates the issue's terms and timing with the issuer, and the account markets the bonds. The terms and timing may change, based on the market's acceptance of the new issue. The managers receive a management fee for their efforts.

The issuer must also comply with other laws to make sure that the bonds will be legally offered. These laws vary from state to state. Frequently, the bond issue must be approved by the voters in the jurisdiction that will offer the bonds. This approval is usually voted on, along with candidates for public office, at election time, although occasionally special elections may be held. The issue must also be formally awarded to the underwriter before he actually owns the bonds.

The issuer then gets on to the calendar of new issues.

Comparing Competitive and Negotiated Bids

Much has been written about the relative advantages of competitive and negotiated deals, and many of the writers have themselves not been entirely disinterested. Both systems have been around for years, so clearly each must have something to offer issuer, underwriter, and bond buyer.

With a competitive deal, the underwriter bidding on the deal does not know he will win it, so he cannot devote much effort to bid preparation and presale selling effort. The issuer, on the other hand, will receive competitive bids, and will be able choose the highest bid, which will have the lowest interest cost to him. The competition should result in a lower interest cost. Once the issue has been advertised with an official notice of sale, it is highly unusual for the sale to be withdrawn or postponed.

In the case of a negotiated deal, the underwriter knows that he will have the deal to sell. He can therefore devote as much time as necessary to presale selling effort, and can even design the deal to meet the needs of his bond-buying clientele, as well as the needs of the issuer. He can expect to be paid for these efforts, and the issuer can expect to receive a more effective marketing job, with possibly resulting lower interest cost. The underwriter can also advise the issuer on the best time to sell the issue, which should also result in interest savings to the issuer.

Both methods have positive and negative features. Many observers believe that competitive sales are best when the issue is of high quality, simple and straightforward in nature, has no features that require special information or selling efforts, and is not especially sensitive to market changes. They think that negotiated sales are best when the issue requires extra efforts to sell, has special features that require explanations, requires time to bring to market, and is particularly sensitive to interest rate levels.

UNDERSTANDING COMPETITIVE BIDS AND SALES

If the issuer has chosen to offer his bonds competitively, he must first set the terms of the issue and the offering. His financial advisor will help him with this. These terms include, but are not limited to, the size of the issue; the schedule of bond maturities, also called the maturity schedule; the time, place, and date of sale; the size of the good faith check; and the method for selecting the winning bid. The issuer then advertises the bonds for sale; this advertisement is called an official notice of sale. He may advertise in local newspapers, and issuers frequently do this; for example, the State of New York and the Port Authority of New York and New Jersey usually advertise their new competitive bond offerings in *The New York Times*. However, if the issuer wants to obtain the widest attention possible for his issue, he will advertise it in the municipal bond trade publication, *The Bond Buyer*. *The Bond Buyer* will also enter a notice in the "Sealed Bids Invited" section of the paper.

All underwriters, and almost all municipal bond persons, check the Sealed Bids Invited section. Any underwriter interested in bidding on the prospective new issue will see the Official Notice of Sale in *The Bond Buyer* and the notice in the Sealed Bids Invited section. He will check his files for each new issue to determine, if he does not already know, whether or not he already bids on new issues of this issuer and whether he is a member of a syndicate that will bid on the deal. If he is a member of a syndicate, he calls the lead manager to verify that the syndicate will function on the newly announced deal; if he is the lead manager, he sets up the account to bid on the issue. Usually, syndicates on competitive deals are long established, although changes occasionally occur as old members drop out and new members join.

A municipal syndicate or account is a short-term partnership set up to bid for and underwrite a new issue of municipal bonds. After the new issue has been sold, and after all the bonds have been sold if the syndicate wins the deal, the syndicate is disbanded and no longer exists. Syndicates exist for both competitive and negotiated new issues. The partners in the syndicate are municipal bond dealers and dealer banks. They sign a partnership agreement, called a syndicate letter or agreement among underwriters.

A syndicate will have a lead manager. The lead manager manages the account and presides over syndicate meetings, if any are held. A syndicate may have joint managers, and the joint managers may rotate in the lead manager position; quite elaborate rotation systems have been devised.

The share of a manager or member in the syndicate is called *participation* and is usually measured in number of bonds. Occasionally, participation may be measured in a fraction or percentage of the syndicate. Different managers or members may have different participations; they are said to be in different brackets. Account members in the same bracket will have the same participation. A syndicate may have two or three brackets, usually no more.

The managers and the members together agree on coupons, reoffering yields and prices (the prices and yields at which the syndicate will offer the bonds to the public), concessions (a small reduction in price given to municipal bond dealers not in the syndicate), spread (the planned gross operating profit), and the order period (the time period during which all orders to buy bonds will receive equal treatment). This can be done at a formal syndicate meeting, but recently, and especially for small syndicates, telephone conferences have frequently replaced the formal meeting.

The lead manager is responsible for bid calculations, for bid submission, and for making sure that the bid complies with the bidding requirements.

After sale time, the syndicates compare bids, and determine the apparent winning syndicate, which then goes ahead to offer the bonds. The issuer or his financial advisor always checks the financial calculations for accuracy. The winner does not own the bonds until the issuer has actually awarded the bonds to him; this is done by a vote of the governing body of the issuer.

Very occasionally the apparent winner turns out not to be the actual winner after the calculations are checked. This is very embarrassing to the apparent winner, and is due to an error in bid submission, usually an error in interest cost calculation or a clerical error in writing down the terms on the issue on the bid submission form, or a late bid. The mistake might even be legally binding on the syndicate, and they may have to accept a money-losing bid.

UNDERSTANDING A NEGOTIATED new issue UNDERWRITING

In a negotiated underwriting, the issuer chooses the lead manager, the joint managers, and sometimes even the members of the syndicate. The issuer invites a number of prospective underwriters to make presentations on their underwriting and sales capabilities. Investment bankers, frequently joined by underwriters and others, from each of the invited firms will give presentations and answer questions, explaining why their firm should be chosen to be the lead underwriter or lead manager. They will discuss their experience in underwriting and selling bonds, especially bonds similar to the ones being competed for. They may compare their skills and experience to the skills and experience of the competition. The issuer usually subjects prospective underwriters to close questioning about their skills in selling bonds, especially bonds comparable to those proposed to be issued by the prospective issuer, and frequently other questions as well.

Sometimes considerations other than investment banking will govern membership in an account. For example, at one time when Ed Koch was Mayor of New York, Merrill Lynch was named manager of the New York City underwriting account. In a totally unrelated move, Merrill Lynch shortly thereafter announced that part of its organizaton would move from New York to New Jersey, in a cost-cutting action. Mayor Koch promptly removed Merrill Lynch from the New York City underwriting account.

After the lead manager, the joint managers, and sometimes even the members, have been selected by the issuer, the underwriters form a syndicate account, with an agreement among underwriters.

The issuer works with the lead manager and the joint managers in structuring, timing, the pricing, placement and spread of the deal.

Structuring the deal means setting up maturity schedules and choosing serial bonds or term bonds, with or without mandatory sinking funds, to suit the needs of the issuer and the bond buyers. Timing means selling the issue at a time relatively favorable to the issuer, rather than relatively unfavorable to the issuer, considering a variety of factors, including the issuer's need for money. Pricing means setting the reoffering prices (or reoffering yields) at a level that will attract buyers for the issue. Placement means selling the bonds to the types of customers, possibly including even individual customers, desired by the issuer. Many issuers prefer to have their bonds owned by certain types of investors. Some prefer to have their bonds widely owned by individual investors in the issuer's community or area of service. Other issuers prefer to have their bonds owned in relatively large amounts by institutional investors. The spread of a new issue is the hoped for gross operating margin for the issue. Out of the spread the underwriter pays the sales commissions to the salespeople and other operating expenses of the underwriter, and hopes to obtain a profit as well.

After the issuer and the lead managers have agreed to these, the account offers the bonds. Based on the market's response to the offering, the managers, with approval from the issuer, may reprice the offering. This could mean changes in any or all of structuring, timing, pricing, placement and spread to sell the bonds. The changes could be either price increases or price decreases, depending on the market. Underwriters rarely reprice a negotiated deal more than once, fearing that it will reflect unfavorably on their underwriting and marketing competence. This could adversely affect future negotiated underwriting business.

After the bonds have been sold, to the satisfaction of the underwriter at least, the underwriter and issuer make an informal agreement, called a "handshake," that the issuer has agreed to sell the bonds to the account on the terms arranged so far, and that the issuer will award the bonds to the underwriters. The handshake is not binding. The account does not actually own the bonds until the issuer actually awards them. This is done by a vote of the governing board of the issuer within a short time, usually a day or two.

Closing, with the actual delivery of the bonds and payment from the underwriters to the issuer, usually occurs about a month after the sale.

UNDERSTANDING NEW ISSUE BIDDING SCALES

This section concerns itself with understanding new issue bidding scales.

Figure 9.1

NEW ISSUE BID SCALE CALCULATION

Dated Date:	08/01/94			Total Amount:	300,000		
Delivery Date:	08/03/94						

DUE	MAT AMT	ACC BOND YEARS	COUPON	YIELD BASIS OR PRICE	CONC	ADD'L TD	PRICE
8/1/95	100	100	8.00	5.50	1/4	1/4	102.400
8/1/96	100	300	6.00	100.00	3/8	3/8	100.000
8/1/97	100	600	6.00	99.00	1/2	1/2	99.000

GROSS PRODUCTION	301,400	100.4667
PROFIT (SPREAD)	4,200	1.4000
BID	297,200	99.0667

TOTAL INTEREST COST:	38,000
ADD DISCOUNT:	2,800
NET INTEREST COST:	40,800

NIC (%)	6.80
TIC (%)	6.86

DATE OF SALE:	07/06/94
TIME OF SALE:	11:00 A.M. EDST
ORDER PERIOD:	1 HOUR

Figure 9.1 shows a sample scale. This particular example shows a $300,000 total amount of the issue, consisting of three maturities of $100,000 each, on August 1, 1995, August 1, 1996, and August 1, 1997. This is called a serial issue. Another way of having annual principal payments would be to have the whole $300,000 maturing on August 1, 1997, with mandatory sinking fund payments of $100,000 each on August 1, 1995 and August 1, 1996. This would be called a term issue with a mandatory sinking fund.

The dated date of the issue is August 1, 1994. Interest will start to accrue on this date. The delivery date is August 3, 1994. On this date, the issuer will deliver the bonds to the underwriter and receive payment for them. Usually the dated date and delivery date are different dates, although theoretically they could be the same date. For most zero-coupon bonds, the delivery date is also the dated date.

The third column from the left shows accumulated bond years. A bond year is one bond ($1,000) for one year. Bond years are used in the calculation of net interest cost. Thus, the 100 bond maturity in one year (August 1, 1995) provides 100 bond years, as shown. The next maturity of 100 bonds is in two years, providing 200 bond years; accumulating from the first maturity gives a total of 300 accumulated bond years. The third maturity adds 100 bonds for three years, or 300 additional bond years, for a total of 600 accumulated bond years.

The underwriter gave an 8-percent coupon to the first maturity and 6-percent coupons to the second and third maturities. This is called a high-low coupon arrangement. Underwriters frequently used this arrangement because it provides an advantage in the calculation of net interest cost. Another arrangement would be to have all coupons the same, called a level coupon arrangement, or have later coupons higher than earlier coupons, called ascending coupons.

The underwriter is offering the first maturity at a 5.50 yield to maturity, which gives a dollar price of about 102.400. The second and third maturities are offered at dollar prices of 100 and 99 respectively.

If the underwriter sells all the bonds at his offering prices, he will receive $301,400, as follows:

$100,000 due 8/1/95 @ 102.400	$102,400
$100,000 due 8/1/96 @ 100	100,000
$100,000 due 8/1/97 @ 99	99,000
Total amount received	$301,400

This is called the gross production of the scale. The gross production can also be expressed as a unit, as a percentage of par. In this case, the unit gross production would be 100.4667, and the scale is said to produce 100.4667. Unit gross production is calculated by dividing the gross production in dollars by the par amount of the issue.

The underwriter then deducts his hoped-for operating profit from the underwriting. In our example, this is $4,200, or 1.400. The underwriter pays the sales commissions, advertising, computer expenses, and other syndicate expenses from this amount, and hopes to keep a profit.

The result after deducting the spread from the gross production is the bid. In this case, the bid is $297,200, and the unit bid is 99.0667. This is the amount the underwriter offers to pay the issuer for the bonds.

In this case, the underwriter is bidding under par. He is bidding a discount, and the bid is said to be a discount bid. If the underwriter bid par, it would be a par bid; if the underwriter bid above par, he would be bidding a premium, and the bid would be said to be a premium bid.

The example shows concessions of 1/4, 3/8, and 1/2 on the three maturities, respectively. A concession is a reduction in price offered to dealers who are not members of the syndicate. The additional takedowns were also 1/4, 3/8, and 1/2 respectively. The additional takedown is an additional reduction in price offered to the account member when he buys bonds from the account for resale to a customer or for his own inventory; this is called taking down the bonds.

In our example, the bonds were sold on July 6, 1994, at 11:00 A.M. EDST.

After the time of sale, 11:00 A.M., one hour was set aside as an order period. In most security transactions, orders to buy or sell are executed in the sequence in which they are received by the broker. In the case of an order period, all orders received during the order period receive the same priority, and need not be executed in the sequence in which they are received by the dealer. For example, in this case, orders received at 11:01 A.M. and at 11:59 A.M. will receive exactly equal treatment in execution.

COMPUTING NET INTEREST COST

A single new issue could receive a wide variety of different bids with different coupon arrangements and bid prices. Some way is needed to compare the different bids to select the best one. The best bid is the bid which offers the issuer the lowest cost of borrowing the funds. There are two ways of measuring this cost: net interest cost (NIC) and true interest cost (TIC), also called Canadian interest cost (CIC).

Net interest cost in total dollars is computed by taking the total amount of interest paid on the issue over the life of the issue and deducting the premium, in the case of a premium bid, or adding the discount, in the case of a discount bid. The percent NIC is computed by dividing this result by the accumulated bond years for the total issue. In our example, the total and net interest costs are computed as follows:

1 year on 100,000 @ 8 %	8,000
2 years on 100,000 @ 6 %	12,000
3 years on 100,000 @ 6 %	18,000
Total interest cost	38,000
For net interest cost,	
add discount	2,800
Net interest cost	40,800

The net interest cost in percent is 40,800 divided by 600 accumulated bond years, or 6.80 percent.

This is the average annual cost to borrow, expressed as a percent per year, without any allowance for present value of the payments. No bond in the issue has a coupon rate of 6.80 percent, and none has a reoffering yield of 6.80 percent.

By computing the net interest cost of each issue, the issuer can select the bid with the lowest net interest cost and award the bonds to that bidder.

UNDERSTANDING TRUE INTEREST COST

The second common method of calculating interest cost is the true interest cost or Canadian interest cost. This interest cost is the present value, expressed as a nominal annual rate, compounded semiannually, which discounts the future cash flows of the issue to equal the bid amount for the issue. In financial analysis and engineering economy, this is called the internal rate of return and is a widely used technique in evaluating the desirability of undertaking a project.

Figure 9.2

TRUE INTEREST COST ANALYSIS

True interest cost (TIC) = 6.86
Present value of 1 due in one period
$$= 1/1.0343$$
$$= .9668375$$

YEAR	TOTAL PAYMENT	PRESENT VALUE FACTOR	PRESENT VALUE OF PAYMENT
.5	10,000	.9668375	9,668.37
1.0	110,000	.9347747	102,825.22
1.5	6,000	.9037752	5,422.65
2.0	106,000	.8738037	92,623.20
2.5	3,000	.8448262	2,534.48
3.0	103,000	.8168096	84,131.39
	338,000		297,205.31

Figure 9.1 states the true interest cost of the issue is 6.86 percent. This was computed by the computer program which figured the scale productions and net interest costs. Figure 9.2 shows the verification of this true interest cost amount. Each semiannual payment in the issue's flow of funds is shown, together with the present value factor for each payment and the present value of each payment. The sum of the present values of each future payment is indeed the amount bid for the issue.

True interest cost is computed by a mathematical technique called successive approximations. The computer selects a trial interest cost, and computes the present value of the future flow of funds. Based on the result, the computer changes the interest cost and recomputes the present value. It keeps on doing this until it gets an answer close enough for the purposes of the person using the program. The procedure could be also done by hand, and before computers were widely used it was computed by hand on the very rare occasions it was required.

The advent of computers has increased the percent of new issue that is awarded based on TIC rather than on NIC, although both methods are widely used. Since the mid-1960s, bond bidding scale calculations, including interest cost calculations, have been almost exclusively done on computers.

Many observers consider TIC a better measure than NIC because it allows for the time value of the payments, using present values. Many other observers consider either method a satisfactory way of selecting the best bid and awarding the bonds, especially if they are combined with suitable bidding restrictions on coupon selection.

If you are an investor, you won't need to compute either NIC or TIC, but you should understand what they mean and how they are used.

REPORTING COMPETITIVE SALES

Figure 9.3 shows a new issue for Aurora, Colorado, as reported in the Sealed Bids Invited Section of *The Bond Buyer.*

The notice states the essential information for a bid. The amount of the issue is $8,790,000. It sells on July 13, 1992 at 12:00 M. MDST. It is book entry. The maturity schedule is shown, the legal opinion is from Bowles & Lynch, and the financial advisor is Evensen Dodge, Inc. Further information on the issue could be obtained from Evensen Dodge, or from the City. Delivery date is about July 31, 1992; on or about this date, the City of Aurora will deliver the bonds and receive payment from the underwriter. The results of the last comparable sale are also shown. This will give an idea of the bidders, and reports their results at the last sale.

Figure 9.4 shows the results of the sale, as reported in the Results of Competitive Bond Sales on July 14, 1992. The bonds were won by a syndicate headed by Dain Bosworth, with Prudential Securities, Smith Barney and PaineWebber as the other managers, with an NIC of 4.8031 percent. The members of the syndicate are also listed. The coupons are reported, by year; they range from 2.70 percent in 1993 to 5.00 percent in 2000. These are ascending coupons. The reoffering yields are reported; they range from 2.70 percent in 1993 to 5.10 percent in 2000. The concessions are 1/8 on the 1993–1996 maturities, and 1/4 on the 1997-2000

Figure 9.3

COLORADO

Aurora, Colo., — $8,790,000 —
Sealed bids July 13, at noon MDST, for
purchase of 4-year avg. (book-entry) series 1992 park and street refunding unlimited tax bonds.
Dated July 1, 1992. Due Sept. 1:

1993	$ 430,000
1994	555,000
1995	1,295,000
1996	1,355,000
1997	1,430,000
1998	1,515,000
1999	1,615,000
2000	595,000

Paying Agent: To be designated. L.O.:
Bowles & Lynch, Denver. Delivery on or
about July 31, at The Depository Trust
Co., New York. Certified or cashier's
check for $87,900 payable to the City.
Financial Adviser: Evensen Dodge, Inc.,
Minneapolis.

Last Comparable Sale.

$25,510,000 — General obligation
water bonds, 1987 Series B, were sold
on Oct. 19, 1987, to a group headed by
Boettcher & Co., Inc., Prescott, Ball &
Turben, Inc., Smith Barney, Harris
Upham & Co., Inc., United Bank of Denver, N.A., NIC 8.8862%.

Reoffered at 7.20% in 1990 to 8.90%
in 1999. The bonds due in 1989, and
2000 to 2003 were not reoffered.

The Bond Buyer Index 9.17%.

Other bidders were:

Marine Midland Bank, N.A. and
Blunt, Ellis & Loewi, Inc. (Co-managers), no other members, NIC 8.8955%.

Morgan Stanley & Co., Inc., Bankers
Trust Co., New York, J.P. Morgan Securities, Inc., Bear, Stearns & Co., Inc.,
E.F. Hutton & Company Inc. (Co-managers) and NCNB National Bank of
North Carolina, Charlotte, NIC
8.98606%.

Merrill Lynch Capital Markets (alone),
NIC 9.01465%.

Donaldson, Lufkin & Jenrette Securities Corp. (alone), NIC 9.02035%.

Northern Trust Co., Chicago and associates, NIC 9.025166%.

PaineWebber Incorporated (alone),
NIC 9.063009%.

*A group headed by Citicorp Invest-
ment Bank, Goldman, Sachs & Co.,
Shearson Lehman Brothers Inc. and
First Boston Corp. in association with
Chase Manhattan Capital Markets, New
York and First Fidelity Bank, N.A., New
Jersey, NIC 9.0974%.

Prudential-Bache Capital Funding,
Dean Witter Reynolds Inc. and Manu-
facturers Hanover Trust Co. (Co-managers), no other members, NIC
9.103675%.

*Bid received late.

Source: The Bond Buyer. Reprinted here with permission.

209

Figure 9.4

COLORADO

Aurora, Colo., July 13 — $8,790,000 — Approximate — General obligation park and street (Book Entry) refunding bonds, Series 1992, dated July 1, 1992, due Sept. 1, 1993 to 2000. Non-callable.

Purchased by a syndicate headed by Dain Bosworth, Inc., Prudential Securities, Inc., Smith Barney, Harris Upham & Co., Inc., PaineWebber Incorporated, as 2.70s, 3.70s, 4.20s, 4.40s, 4.60s, 4¾s, 4.90s and 5s, at 99.1978, **NIC 4.8031%.**

L.O.: Becker Stowe Bowles & Lynch, P.C., Denver.

Reoffered at 2.70, 3.70, 4.20, 4.40, 4.60, 4.80, 5.00 and 5.10.

Concessions: ⅛ (93-96) and ¼ (97-2000).

Other members of the syndicate were: Colorado National Bank, Denver, Dougherty, Dawkins, Strand & Bigelow, Inc., Gabriele, Hueglin & Cashman Division of Tucker Anthony Incorporated, Piper, Jaffray Inc. and Northern Trust Securities, Inc.

Other bidders were:

Norwest Investment Services, Inc., First Interstate Bank of Denver, N.A., and Central Bank Denver, N.A. (Co-managers), no other members, 98.54, for 2¾s, 3½s, 4.10s, 4½s, 4¾s and 5s, **NIC 4.82%.**

Hutchinson, Shockey, Erley & Co., Rodam & Renshaw, Inc., A.H. Williams & Co., Inc. (Co-managers), Scott & Stringfellow Investment Corp. and American National Bank & Trust Co. of Chicago, 98.537, for 6s, 5.70s, 4.60s, 4¾s and 3½s, **NIC 4.835%.**

Harris Trust & Savings Bank, Chicago, Mellon Bank, N.A., Pittsburgh, J.C. Bradford & Co, Coughlin & Co., Inc., Crews & Associates, Inc., A. Webster Dougherty & Co., Inc., Isaak Bond Investments, Inc. and Mesirow Capital Markets, 98.5471, for 3s, 3.90s, 4¼s, 4½s, 4.70s and 4.80s, **NIC 4.8826%.**

George K. Baum & Co., First Chicago Capital Markets, Inc., FBS Investment Services, Inc., A.G. Edwards & Sons, Inc. (Co-managers), Southwest Securities Inc., Howe, Barnes Investments, Inc. and Affiliated Capital Markets, 98.8788, for 2.90s, 3.90s, 4¼s, 4½s, 4.70s, 4.90s and 5s, **NIC 4.96%.**

Merrill Lynch & Co. (alone), 98.868, for 3¾s, 4¼s, 4½s, 4.70s and 5s, **NIC 4.9932%.**

Kemper Securities Group, Inc., Clayton Brown & Associates, Inc. and Griffin, Kubik, Stephens & Thompson, Inc. (Co-managers), no other members, 100.00, for 7s, 5s, 4½s, 4¾s, 4.90s, 5.10s and 5¼s, **NIC 5.003%.**

Kirkpatrick, Pettis, Smith, Polian, Inc., **NIC 5.04%.**

Source: The Bond Buyer. Reprinted here with permission.

maturities. Note that the additional takedowns are not reported. This information is confidential to the underwriting syndicate. Seven other bids were received, with NICs ranging from 4.82 percent to 5.04 percent. The other bids and the bidding firms were reported.

REPORTING NEGOTIATED DEALS

Figure 9.5 shows a negotiated new issue for North Carolina Municipal Power Agency No. 1, as reported in *The Bond Buyer* on November 23, 1992.

This important new issue alone accounted for about 1/2 percent of the total new issue for 1992. It displays what an underwriter and an investment banker can do to structure a new issue to appeal to a wide variety of buyers. This issue has something for everybody.

If you want serial bonds, you have a choice of maturities from 1994 to 2011. If you want terms, you have a choice of maturities in 2015, 2017, 2018, and 2020.

If you want insured serials, you have a choice of four different insurance companies. If you want insured terms, you have a choice of two maturities, with two different insurance companies.

If you want zero-coupon bonds you have a choice of maturities from 2008 to 2012. If you want them insured, you can pick the 2011 or 2012 maturities; you are restricted to MBIA insurance in this case. If you want them uninsured, you have a choice of 2008, 2009, and 2010 maturities.

The capital appreciation bonds are not callable, but other bonds may have a call feature. The terms of 2015 and 2020 have a different call feature from the others, and the serials maturing in 2006 to 2011 are not callable.

The terms maturing in 2015, 2017, and 2020 were offered at dollar prices, rather than at a yield. The equivalent yield is shown in the report.

This issue has no concessions. This is common now with large deals. Dealers not in the account don't receive special price reductions.

Figure 9.5

NORTH CAROLINA

North Carolina Municipal Power Agency No. 1 (Raleigh), Nov. 20 — $1,222,555,000 — Catawba electric revenue (FGIC Insured 97 and 99-2000, FSA Insured 01 and 18, AMBAC Insured 06 and 08-09 and MBIA Insured 10-11 and 20/Book Entry) bonds, Series 1992, dated Dec. 1, 1992, due Jan. 1, 1994 to 2011, 2015, 2017, 2018 and 2020. First coupon July 1, 1993. Callable Jan. 1, 2003 at 102, declining to par Jan. 1, 2005. 2006 through 2011 non-callable and 2015 and 2020 callable Jan. 1, 2003 at par. Capital appreciation (MBIA Insured 2011-2012) bonds, dated Dec. 10, 1992, due Jan. 1, 2008 to 2012. Non-callable. Indexed CAP bonds, dated Dec. 10, 1992, due Jan. 1, 2012.

Purchased through negotiation by a syndicate headed by Goldman, Sachs & Co., First Boston Corp., Donaldson, Lufkin & Jenrette Securities Corp., J.P. Morgan Securities Inc., Alex. Brown & Sons, Incorporated, First Charlotte Co. A Division of J.C. Bradford & Co., Interstate/Johnson Lane Corp., J. Lee Peeler & Co., Inc., Legg Mason Wood Walker, Inc. and Wheat, First Securities, Inc., as follows:

$523,200,000 Serial, as 3½s, 4.10s, 4½s, 4.60s, 5.10s (98-99), 5.20s, 5½s, 5¾s, 5.90s, 6s (04-05), coupon rate not available (06-07), 6s (08-11).

$191,030,000 Term, due 2015, as 5¾s.

$135,495,000 Term, due 2017, as 6¼s.

$83,540,000 Term, due 2018, as 6.20s.

$123,990,000 Term, due 2020, as 5¾s.

$100,000,000 (Maturity Value), capital appreciation bonds, as bearing no interest.

$65,300,000 Indexed CAPS bonds, due 2012, as coupon rate not available.

L.O.: Hawkins, Delafield & Wood, New York.

Reofffered at 3.55, 4.10, 4.50, 4.65, 5.10, 5.15, 5.30, 5.50, 5.80, 5.95, 6.05, 6.10, not reoffered (06-07), 6.10, 6.15, 6.20 (10-11), 2015 at 92.00 to yield 6.433%, 2017 at 97.25 to yield 6.477%, 6.375, 2020 at 92.75 to yield 6.312%, CABs at 6.65, 6.70 (09-10) and 6.55 (11-12) and Indexed CAPs not reoffered.

Concessions: None.

Source: The Bond Buyer. Reprinted with permission.

UNDERSTANDING NEW ISSUE SPREADS

The spread of a new issue is the difference between what the underwriter pays for the issue and what he hopes to sell it for; it is his hoped-for gross operating profit. Out of the spread, the underwriter pays compensation to the sales representatives, other firm operating expenses, and expenses of the underwriting. Of course, he hopes also to have a net profit.

For example, suppose an underwriter has a new issue bond, which is still in syndicate and with a retail offering price of 100. In this case, the retail, or net, offering is 100. In the example of the new issue scale (Figure 9.1), the net offerings were 5.40 percent, 100, and 99 for the three maturities, respectively. The first maturity was offered at a yield of 5.40 percent to maturity, the second and third maturities were offered at dollar prices of 100 and 99 respectively; these dollar prices, like all bond dollar prices, are percent of par. The underwriter hopes to obtain these prices, and these are the prices at which he offers the bonds to his customers.

If the underwriter sells the bond to a bona fide municipal bond dealer who is not in the account, he frequently gives the dealer a concession; in our example, shown in Figure 9.6, the concession is one point, or $10.00 per $1,000 bond. In the case of the new issue scale, the concessions were 1/4, 3/8, and 1/2 for the three maturities, respectively.

The underwriter, who is an account member, in turn buys the bond from the syndicate account; he receives a further reduction, called the additional takedown. Note that even though the account member is a member of the syndicate, he must still actually do the transaction of buying the bond from the syndicate account; the syndicate is a separate business from the account member and has its own set of books. These are kept by the account manager. In our example, the additional takedown is an additional 1 point. Finally, in our example, the total spread is 2.5 points.

Figure 9.6

Price charged retail buyer (sale at the net)	100.000
Concession	1.000
Price charged dealers not in the account (sale at the concession)	99.000
Additional takedown	1.000
Price account member pays to take down the bonds (sale at the takedown)	98.000
Price paid to the issuer (bid price)	97.500

The full takedown equals the concession plus the additional takedown, or two points. If the underwriter sells the bond to a retail customer at 100, he makes a two-point operating profit on the sale.

The spread equals the net price minus the bid price, or 2.5 points.

In the case of negotiated new issues, the spread of a new issue is the underwriter's hoped-for gross operating profit margin on the new issue. Like all the other features of the issue, the spread is negotiated, as are each of its four components individually. These components are the average takedown, underwriting compensation, management fee, and expenses. Frequently, new negotiated deals, especially the large ones, don't have a concession.

The average takedown is the weighted average of all the takedown amounts of the different maturities of the issue; different maturities may, and frequently do, have different takedowns.

The underwriting compensation is the amount expected to be earned in underwriting the bonds; this is expressed in a per-bond amount, and is distributed to syndicate members according to their participation. This amount is a hoped-for amount; the amount actually distributed will be the member's share of the net syndicate profit.

The management fee is compensation for managing the issue and bringing it to market. It is distributed only among the managers, and not equally; the lead manager usually receives by far the largest amount. This is one reason why underwriters compete so vigorously for the position of lead manager in a new issue syndicate.

Expenses are those incurred by the syndicate for various syndicate activities. They include advertising, computer costs, legal expenses, and other miscellaneous items.

In the spring of 1994, a typical hoped for negotiated new issue spread might have been $10.50 per $1,000 bond, broken down as shown in Figure 9.7.

Figure 9.7

Average takedown	$ 7.50
Underwriting	.50
Management fee	1.50
Expenses	1.00
Total	$10.50

This is about in line with recent averages, but frequently spreads are much lower, sometimes as low as $7.00 per $1,000 of new issue. This is much lower than spreads in the 1980–1982 period, which might have been $30.00 per $1,000 bond, or sometimes even higher. As you can see, both negotiated and competitive new issue spreads have declined substantially since 1985. Present-day spreads show no sign of increasing much, and the industry is much less profitable than it was a few years ago.

UNDERSTANDING BIDDING RESTRICTIONS

Any new issue of municipal bonds put out for competitive bid must have some set of bidding restrictions, some of which are set by state law. For example, a common state law requires a minimum bid as a percent of par, sometimes 100 percent of par. These restrictions accomplish several purposes. They not only set the parameters to receive the bid, but they also allow the issuer to set restrictions that will maximize the salability of his bonds. The issuer's financial advisor should advise him on bidding restrictions.

Typical bidding restrictions specify the time and place of the bid, the size of the good-faith check (2 percent of the par amount of the issue is common), the nature of the institution on which it is drawn, and the payee, which is usually the issuer, and many other items. A bid form is provided. The bid form must be correctly filled out and signed, with coupon rates and the total bid amount in proper form. The interest cost calculation is provided for, although it is not usually considered part of the bid; this calculation is also done by the issuer or the issuer's financial advisor. They verify the interest costs of each bid to determine the lowest interest cost in order to award the bonds to the highest bidder (lowest interest cost). The bid must be submitted in a properly addressed envelope, and the envelope must be sealed. These, and similar restrictions, ensure that bids will be received in proper form, at the proper time, in the proper amounts.

Bidding restrictions help ensure that the forms of law have been complied with, that all the legal requirements have been met, and that the bonds have been legally issued. Bidding restrictions also help ensure that the issuer's financial objectives will be met. A certain amount of money must be raised, and the minimum bid requirement ensures that this amount will be available from the issue.

Coupon limitations ensure that the payments required by the issue are within the planned amounts; sometimes coupon limitations are set by state law. One possibility that has happened in the past is an extraordinarily high early coupon, combined with a very low long-term coupon; a famous case once gave a 50-percent coupon to the first several maturities of an issue. This required much larger than planned debt service payments in the early life of the issue.

It also gave very low coupons at the long end of the bond issue. This caused a problem if the issuer wanted to call the bonds. Many bond issues, such as the New York State bond issue shown in Figure 1.1, provide for call in inverse order of maturities. This means, for very low coupons, that the very low coupons would be the first ones called. This would discourage the issuer from calling the bonds at all and would obviate the purpose of the call option in the first place. For example, in the case of the New York State issue, the first bonds to be called would be bonds with a 2-percent coupon; the 3.40-percent bonds could only be called after the 2-percent bonds were called, or at the same time.

A common coupon limitation is the ascending coupon limitation. This limitation requires that no coupon be less than the coupon of the previous maturity. A level coupon issue is a special case of this, with all coupons the same. Another common coupon limitation is a limit on the difference between the highest coupon and the lowest coupon; for example, the highest coupon might be required to be no more than 2 percent higher than the lowest coupon. This limitation also would avoid the problem of very high and very low coupons.

HOW THE ALTERNATIVE MINIMUM TAX CAN AFFECT INVESTORS

During the 1980s, tax law changes provided for federal income taxation of certain municipal bonds under certain conditions. These bonds became subject to the alternative minimum tax (AMT). When the AMT taxation of municipal bonds was first introduced, bonds subject to AMT sold somewhat cheaper (higher yields) than bonds not so subject, but now there is little if any difference. Investors subject to the AMT bought bonds not subject to this tax, and investors who were not subject to AMT bought the bonds subject to AMT. They paid no income taxes on the interest anyway and possibly received some extra yield.

If you buy a bond which is subject to AMT, you should know about it. You salesperson should tell you, the official statement will tell you, and numerous reference publications will tell you whether your bonds are subject to AMT. If you are subject to the alternative minimum tax, you may not wish to buy AMT subject bonds. Whether you buy or not, you should know whether your bonds are subject to AMT.

HOW BANK-QUALIFIED BONDS WORK

Certain bonds are called "bank-qualified" bonds; this means that banks can deduct interest paid to carry the bonds. The bonds must be general obligation bonds, issued for a public purpose, and the issuer must plan to issue no more than $10,000,000 during the year. Bonds which otherwise meet these requirements, but are issued for both public and private purposes may still be bank qualified, depending on the portion of the issue devoted to private purposes. The official statement will state whether or not the bonds are bank qualified, in the opinion of counsel.

These bonds have developed a niche market among certain banks interested in buying them. Few retail investors have any special interest in these bonds. They may still, of course, be a suitable investment for a retail investor if they meet his or her objectives.

SELLING NEW ISSUES AND PRIORITY BUSINESS

Many sales from new issue accounts are "priority business," because they receive special treatment in buying bonds. All of this business is done with institutional customers. Institutional customers include mutual funds, unit investment trusts, banks, insurance companies, pension funds, and other major business and public customers. Pension funds rarely buy municipals, because they don't benefit from the tax exemption.

There are four types of priority business, of which two are important: group business and designated sales.

Group Business

In a "group net" sale, the underwriting account sells directly to the customer at the net price. A manager must actually bill the customer, deliver the bonds, and receive payment, on behalf of the group. In this case, the group receives the entire offering price, without any deduction for member takedown. Very occasionally, the customer buys the bonds from the group at the concession price; this is called a "group concession" sale. Group net sales are quite common; group concession sales are quite rare.

Designated Sales

In a "net designated" sale, the customer pays the net price, but designates certain account members to receive a special share of the sales profits. The customer designates the name of the firm and the amount of bonds; the firm receives the concession on their designation. For instance, if customer *A* buys $10,000,000 par amount of bonds, he or she might designate firms *B*, *C*, and *D* in the amounts of $4,000,000, $3,000,000, and $3,000,000 respectively. Firms *B*, *C*, and *D* will receive the concession on their respective designations. If the concession is 1/4 (one quarter of a point, or $2.50 per bond), *B* will receive $10,000, and *C* and *D* will each receive $7,500 as their designations. Bond buyers use designations to reward firms for various services for which they have been unable to compensate them for directly. These services might include bond research, portfolio appraisals, information services, and financial and other advisory services for which direct payment is impossible.

In a concession designated sale, the customer pays the concession price; the designees receive the additional takedown on their designations. Net designated sales frequently occur; concession designated sales are quite rare.

SWAPPING

Both institutional and individual investors frequently provide funds for new bonds by selling old bonds. This activity is called swapping. Swapping from the investor's point of view was discussed in Chapter 8. For the municipal underwriter and dealer, swapping also provides important advantages. It provides an additional source of profit, while also providing fresh inventory for sale to customers who may not be interested in the new issue, but might be interested in the bonds for which the new issue is swapped. The whole area of swapping, especially with institutional customers, offers a vast scope for creativity on the part of salespeople and underwriters.

THE NEW ISSUE SELLING PROCESS

Many computer programs exist to simplify and expedite the new issue sales process for individuals. Frequently, retail salespeople will be able to offer new issue bonds directly from computer systems to their customers, and confirm the sale immediately. This is possible because the new issue offering is frequently firm in price for a while and has a block of bonds to be offered. The offering may continue at the same price for a considerable period, while the computer keeps track of the number of unsold bonds, the amount of the sales, and the customers who bought the bonds.

Most municipal dealers have information bulletins on new issues, which are distributed to their salespeople and to their customers. You should ask your dealer for such information on bonds you are considering buying.

During the first part of the selling process, syndicate restrictions apply. These are contained in the agreement among underwriters, or syndicate letter. The most important restriction is that no sales take place under the takedown price without account approval. Approval is given by a vote of the account, with members voting according to their participation. Usually, bonds are sold under the takedown price when the issue is slow to sell, and a customer now bids to buy a large block of slow-moving bonds. The underwriter may also engage in market stabilization activities.

When all the bonds are sold, the manager may declare the bonds free to trade, and the syndicate restrictions no longer apply. The manager may apply this to all the bonds of the issue, or solely to selected maturities. The new bonds then seek their own level in the market. The underwriter hopes that this level will be slightly above the offering price; however, sometimes the market has fallen and the bonds trade below the offering price, or even below the takedown price. The bonds are still traded in the primary account.

When all the bonds are sold, or sooner if the manager thinks appropriate, the primary account is closed out. The bonds remaining, if any, are transferred to the secondary market accounts. Future trades are done in the secondary market account.

Sometimes investors who follow the market closely can purchase bonds after they have been declared free to trade and have fallen in the market place. Most individual investors are not in close enough touch with the market to do this and as a result don't find this available to them.

HOW A LEAD MANAGER MEETS HIS OR HER RESPONSIBILITIES

The lead manager has the responsibility of acting for the account in its relationships with the issuer, account members, regulatory authorities, some customers, and others. The lead manager must keep members informed of developments, notify the members of the amounts and maturities of unsold bonds (called "account balances"), and send them other notices as needed. Under the provisions of MSRB Rule G-17, Conduct of Municipal Securities Business, the lead manager is responsible for fair treatment of customers, account members, and the issuer. Actually, Rule G-17 applies to the entire range of municipal securities business conducted by the dealer or dealer bank, not just to new issue underwriting.

The lead manager must maintain syndicate records, according to the provisions of Rule G-8 (Books and Records to Be Made by Municipal Securities Brokers and Municipal Securities Dealers) and retain them according to the provisions of Rule G-9 (Preservation of Records). In general, syndicate records must be maintained for six years, unless the syndicate was unsuccessful in purchasing the bonds. The records must be reasonably available.

Note that Rules G-8 and G-9 apply to all municipal transactions, not just to municipal new issue.

If you are an investor, these rules don't concern you very much, unless something goes wrong. Then they become very important to you. You or your attorney should be able to obtain access to these records for up to six years after they were originally made, although you may have to visit an out-of-the-way warehouse to access them. The best policy is to make sure that everything is done correctly at the time you buy the bonds and as you go along, so far as you can determine from your vantage point as customer. In particular, study the official statement when you get it, and make sure that the bonds are as described to you.

The lead manager also makes allotments to account members of oversubscribed bonds. Bonds are said to be oversubscribed when account members place orders for more bonds than exist. When this happens, as it does fairly frequently, the lead manager has the responsibility of assigning bonds to account members; this is called "allocating" the bonds.

In doing the allocations, the lead manager keeps several factors in mind. One of the most important factors is how the member who is requesting the bonds has treated the manager in previous syndicate allocations that the requesting member has managed. Another important consideration is whether the bonds have been sold to a final customer. Sales to the final customer are said to be "going away" sales, and the bonds when thus sold are said to be "put away."

REGULATING THE NEW ISSUE PROCESS

Special regulations apply to the new issue of municipal bonds. The lead manager has the general responsibility of compliance with many of these, but some of them apply to all underwriters.

Four regulations apply solely or mainly to the new issue process. Three of these regulate the underwriting and sales process; the fourth concerns itself with an underwriting assessment.

The underwriting period, with a very few exceptions, starts when the underwriter purchases the new issue from the issuer, and ends when the issuer delivers the bonds to the underwriter and receives payment, although occasionally it may be longer.

How Underwritings Are Assessed by the MSRB (Rule A-13)

Most new issues have an underwriting assessment of $.03 per $1,000 of par value (as of October, 1994). A few short-term or variable-rate issues have an underwriting assessment of $.01 per $1,000 of par value (as of October, 1994). A very few, very small issues, very short-term issues, issues with very short put options or other redemption features, or issues with large denominations sold to a few knowledgeable investors may have no underwriting assessment. The lead manager has the responsibility of paying the assessment.

Regulating Sales of New Issue Municipal Securities During the Underwriting Period (Rule G-11)

All members of municipal new issue underwriting accounts have certain responsibilities to the account. Each member must disclose the capacity in which he is placing an order for bonds if the order is for his dealer account, for a related portfolio or a securities investment trust or for a related accumulation account sponsored by the member. Confirmations for the last three of these must be sent directly to the portfolio, investment trust, or accumulation account.

The member must disclose group orders he submits to the account. The lead manager must establish and disclose the priority provisions, and he must disclose the priority business and the itemized syndicate expenses.

Official Statements or Disclosure in Connection with New Issues (Rule G-32)

The underwriter must send out a copy of the final official statement, if it exists, to each buyer of a new issue during the underwriting period. If a final official statement does not exist, but a preliminary official statement does exist, the underwriter must send this to the bond buyer.

This rule applies to any dealer selling a new issue during the underwriting period, even if the dealer is not in the original underwriting syndicate. At one time, municipal bond dealers widely believed that if a dealer who sold new issue bonds during the underwriting period was not in the original account, that dealer was not required to send out the official statement to his customers. This view is not correct and was, in fact, the subject of an MSRB Interpretive Note at one time. Any customer who buys a new issue during the underwriting period must receive an official statement if one exists, whether or not the customer buys from a member of the original underwriting account.

If you buy municipal new issue, you should insist on receiving your official statement, especially since some mail rooms have been known to slip up in sending them out to bond buyers. This is the only document you will receive that outlines the terms of the issue and the bond contract.

How Calculations Are Done (Rule G-33)

This rule makes official the calculations and formulas presented in Chapter 7 of this book. The equation shown in the MSRB *Manual* for bond price calculation has been reproduced in that chapter.

HOW LEGAL WORK ON NEW ISSUES IS DONE

In the nineteenth century, municipal bonds did not have legal opinions attached to them. Investors relied on the integrity of the issuer and the underwriter. However, during the depression which started in 1893, some bonds defaulted. When the investors brought suit, they discovered that the bonds had not been legally issued in the first place and they could not recover their investment. This so discouraged investors that doubts were raised at the time whether municipal bonds could be sold at all. For example, how could an investor in Boston or New York be expected to buy a bond issued by Seattle or San Francisco if he or she could not even be sure that the bond was legally issued.

The answer was the legal opinion. Each new issue of municipal bonds carried with it an opinion by a highly competent and respected lawyer or law firm that the bonds had been legally issued and were valid and binding obligations of the issuer. The lawyer was paid by the issuer, but represented the investor. This worked, and ever since then new issues of municipal bonds have been issued with a legal opinion. The existence of the legal opinion made municipal bonds salable. Making sure that the bonds are legally issued is one reason for having bidding restrictions and enforcing them.

The legal opinion used to be a separate document, but starting in the 1960s issuers began to print it on the actual bond certificate, with resulting savings in paper and increased convenience. Bonds with separate legal opinions are now rare, although one of them is shown in Figure 1.1, the New York State bond.

The municipal bond legal opinion states that in the opinion of bond counsel:

1. The bonds have been legally issued; and

2. The bonds are exempt from federal income taxation, if they are, and exempt from state taxes, if they are so exempt.

There is also at least an implication that some due diligence has been exercised by the lawyers, that no major errors of commission or omission have been committed, and that full disclosure has been made to the prospective investors, so far as the lawyers can tell.

Of course, sometimes the lawyers make mistakes. Here are two examples.

Example 1: In June, 1926, the Nine Mile Halfway Drainage District in Macomb County, Michigan, issued $2,600,000 of bonds to build a sewage plant. The legal opinion was given by a municipal bond law firm which was both then and now well-known and highly respected. On May 1, 1932, the District defaulted and failed to make the required payment of interest and principal. The bondholders brought suit, but the judge ruled that although statutes allowed the construction of sewer plants by drainage districts, this particular plant placed too much emphasis on sewage and not enough emphasis on drainage, and was therefore outside the jurisdiction of the District. The bondholders brought suit to be reimbursed for the cost of the plant, which was upheld; $50,000 was allowed, and in 1949, after legal fees and other expenses, the bondholders collected $2.50 per $1,000 bond. The bonds were worth more as wallpaper; indeed, the author paid $10.00 for his specimen and $20.00 to have it framed, along with copies of *Bond Buyer* ads and announcements.

Example 2: In 1957, a group of public utility districts in the state of Washington joined together to form the Washington Public Power Supply System (WPPSS). The purpose of WPPSS was to assure the participants of future supplies of power. In due course, the WPPSS developed some nuclear power plants, and issued bonds to finance the construction of these plants. Some bonds, for power plants 1, 2, and 3, were guaranteed by a net billings arrangement with the Bonneville Power Authority. But financing for plants 4 and

5 were guaranteed by a "take or pay" contract with the individual public power district. Under this agreement, the individual public power districts promised to pay the costs of the financing, even if power was never actually delivered.

When WPPSS defaulted, the trustee for the bondholders brought suit to compel payment. After several appeals the Supreme Court of the State of Washington held that the individual public power districts did not have the power to enter into these agreements, and the bond contracts were not enforceable. The United States Supreme Court declined to consider the appeal.

In this case, the bonds were legally issued, but the collateral securing the bonds turned out not to be present.

Based on other lawsuits against almost everybody involved in bringing the issues to market, the bondholders did get some recovery, about 30 percent to 40 percent of their investment. They had to be content with this.

Institutional investors frequently concern themselves with the law firm providing the legal opinion. Individual investors rarely concern themselves with this and probably do not possess the resources to do an adequate investigation in any case. However, the individual investor should at least be able to find out the law firm providing the legal opinion and read over the opinion itself. This will be printed on the bond certificate, if it exists, and also in the official statement.

Very rarely, old bonds which would normally have the legal opinion on a separate document will be missing that document; these are called "illegals" and usually sell a little cheaper. If you own illegals, try to get a copy of the legal opinion; the trustee or issuer itself may be able to help you. The legal opinion will make your bonds more salable and more valuable. Default is not usually a concern with these issues.

UNDERSTANDING CLOSING AND SETTLEMENT OF NEW ISSUES

After the bonds have been sold, whether the sale was competitive or negotiated, a time period of about a month elapses before they are actually delivered to the buyer. During this period, the work of closing and settling the issue is done.

The legal work is finished, and the legal opinion is written and issued. The certificates must be printed and signed, if the issue is in registered form, or arrangements made with the depository if it is in book-entry form. If certificates exist, the legal opinion must be printed on the bonds. The bond insurance policy must also be printed on the bond if the bonds are insured. Plans for the closing meeting must be made. If the bonds are insured, the bond insurance firms must arrange for issuance of the insurance policy and receipt of the premium at closing.

A date is set for closing, and final calculations are prepared. The amount to be paid for the bonds has been previously set, but the amount of accrued interest must be calculated, and other fees and expenses finally determined. At this point, the account manager, account members, and bond buyers can be notified of the amounts owed, and can be sent final confirmations, which contain the final money figures.

UNDERSTANDING WHEN-ISSUED AND FINAL CONFIRMATIONS

When a bond trade takes place during the underwriting period, the buyer receives what is called a when-issued confirmation, rather than a regular confirmation. A when-issued confirmation states that a contract to make the trade exists and the terms of the trade. The trade will take place when, as, and if the bonds are issued, and will be cancelled only if the bonds are not issued. The when-issued confirmation cannot contain any money amounts, such as accrued interest, because these are not yet known.

You should understand that when you buy a bond during the underwriting period, and receive a when-issued confirmation, you have an obligation to buy the bonds if they are issued and an assurance that the bonds almost certainly will be issued. This is just as binding a trade as if it were a regular purchase of a security. You should make sure that you have the cash available when needed to pay for the bonds.

New issues are rarely cancelled; the few occasions on which this does happen are usually caused by either a new lawsuit, which prevents the lawyers from giving a clean legal opinion, discovery of incomplete disclosure of important facts (called "material information") in the official statement, or an important change in the status of the issuer.

During this period, and before you pay for the bonds, you should receive the final official statement for the issue, in compliance with MSRB Rule G-32. If no final official statement is being prepared, you should receive a notice to that effect, together with a copy of the preliminary official statement, if one exists. If no final official statement exists, there probably won't be a preliminary official statement either. The underwriter may instead send you a summary of the final official statement, but most underwriters simply send out the final official statement.

For almost all new issues, a final official statement is prepared. If you are buying an issue for which no final official statement is prepared, perhaps you should reconsider buying the bonds, if you can. It is extremely important to you that you receive information about the bonds you are buying.

Remember that you are entitled to receive a final official statement whether or not your dealer is a member of the original underwriting syndicate, and you should insist on receiving it. You should not pay for your bonds until you receive the final official statement.

When you receive your official statement, you should study it. You should make sure that the terms of the issue are as presented to you. You should especially study the call features, but you should also make sure that the other terms are as you understood them. These include the offering yield or price, coupon rate, physical form of the bonds, exemption from federal and state income taxes, whether they are subject to the alternative minimum tax, and other features.

Most retail investors don't read their official statements. They are wrong. Every investor should study every official statement he or she receives on his new issues.

You should keep the official statement in a safe place, but you do not need to put it in your safe deposit box because you can easily replace it at modest cost (about $10) from a Nationally Recognized Municipal Security Information Repository.

When the final money amounts and the delivery date of the bonds are known, the underwriter can send final confirmations to his or her customers.

At the closing, the issuer delivers the bonds to the account manager, who in turn pays for them. The bond insurance premium is also paid at this time, if the bonds are insured. The manager redelivers the bonds to the account members, who arrange delivery of the bonds to their customers. They also arrange the delivery of the final official statement to their customers.

Glossary

accreting a discount

The process by which a discount is accumulated as income during the life of the bond.

accrued interest

The amount of interest earned since the last interest payment date. It is added to the price in computing the total amount due to the seller.

accruing a discount

Same as accreting a discount.

accumulated bond years

In a new issue scale, the sum of the bond years for each maturity year, including the year of the accumulated bond years.

active sinker

A sinking fund which is calling or buying bonds.

additional takedown

An additional amount allowed to a syndicate member when he buys bonds from the syndicate for his own account or resale to a customer.

advance refunded

Bonds which have had arrangements made for payment by issuing new bonds. The proceeds of the new issue are either used to redeem the old issue or

231

advance refunded (*continued*)	placed into an escrow fund to pay interest on the old issue and redeem it either at maturity or an earlier call date.
agency	A public institution set up to accomplish a public purpose of some sort.
allotment	The bonds allocated to a syndicate member by the manager.
alternative minimum tax (*AMT*)	The federal income tax calculated by an alternative method when the taxpayer has sufficient amount of income otherwise untaxed or taxed at lower rates.
amortizing a premium	The process by which a premium paid for a bond is deducted from interest income during the life of the bond.
amount	The face value of a bond.
annuity certain	A series of payments, usually equal in size and equally spaced in time, which is guaranteed to be paid, as opposed to a life annuity which stops or is reduced when the recipient dies.
ascending coupon arrangement	An arrangement for coupons on a new issue in which each coupon is no lower than the coupon for the previous maturity.
authority	A public organization set up to accomplish a specified public purpose.
bank qualified bonds	Banks may deduct interest paid to carry (own) bank qualified bonds.

basis book	*See* bond basis book.
basis point	One one-hundredth of one percent.
bearer bond	A bond which has ownership indicated by a certificate which does not contain the owner's name and possession of which is presumed to indicate ownership.
bill—U.S. Treasury	A short term security, one year or less to maturity, issued by the United States Treasury, sold at a discount, which does not bear explicit interest. The interest is earned when the bill is sold at a profit or matures at face value.
bond	A security, usually with more than one year to final maturity date, with interest paid, usually semiannually, either by coupons attached to the bond or by interest paid directly to the owner.
bond—U.S. Treasury	A bond issued by the United States Treasury.
bond anticipation notes	Notes issued in anticipation of an issue of bonds. The notes will be repaid when the bonds are sold.
bond basis book	A book containing prices of bonds for a variety of coupons, yields, and times to maturity.
bond bidding scale	A display of the maturities, coupon rates, reoffering yields or prices, and other information on a new issue of municipal bonds.

bond insurance	Insurance that guarantees the payment of interest and principal due on a bond if the issuer does not pay.
bond swap	An exchange of bonds owned for other bonds, usually using separate buy and sell transactions.
bond years	A bond year is one bond ($1,000.00 face amount) for one year.
book entry	A system which records bond ownership in records kept in a central depository, rather than by individual certificates in the possession of the bond owner or his agent.
book value	The cost of the bond as adjusted for premium amortization or discount accrual.
bracket	The level of relative participation in a syndicate.
broker	A person who acts as an agent for another in executing an order to buy or sell.
call feature	The contractual provision that allows or requires the issuer to redeem the bond before maturity.
call premium	The amount over par which the issuer must pay to call the bond.
call price	The total amount the issuer must pay to call the bond. It equals par plus the call premium.
Canadian interest cost (CIC)	The same as true interest cost (TIC).

capital project	A municipal project to build or buy a capital improvement of some sort.
certificate of participation (COP)	A municipal security whose payments are made from revenues from a lease of property. The lease requires annual appropriations by the issuer.
certificated book entry	Book entry where the depository has certificates, either bearer or registered, and which are available to the bond owner upon request.
closed end	A mutual fund which does not sell additional shares of itself.
closing	The process in which the issuer is paid for his bonds and delivers the bonds to the underwriter.
competitive bid	An offering of bonds by an issuer who receives bids and selects the best bid.
compound interest	An arrangement by which interest paid on a loan earns interest itself.
concession	A small reduction in price offered to a bond dealer who is not a member of the syndicate account. More generally, a reduction in price to another dealer from the regular price charged a retail customer.
concession designated sale	A type of priority business. The customer buys the bond at the list price less the concession and designates certain account members, by name and amount, to receive the additional takedown on the sale.

confirmation	A notice from the broker or dealer to a customer stating the terms of a security transaction.
contra party	The other party in an interest rate swap, or any other transaction.
coupon	1) The small certificate which represents an interest payment on a bearer bond and is cut off (clipped) and presented for payment. 2) The rate of interest on the bond.
coupon instrument	A security which bears a stated interest rate whether or not it has an actual coupon.
CUSIP number	The unique number assigned to each security for identification purposes.
dated date	The day on which a bond starts to earn interest.
de-linked	The separation of a combined floater and inverse floater back into the two independent derivatives.
de minimus	A small or minimal amount, especially not enough to encourage the attention of the Internal Revenue Service.
dealer	A person who buys and sells (municipal bonds) for his own account and for sale to customers.
dealer bank	A bank which operates a separately identifiable section as a municipal bond dealer.

debt service	The combined interest and principal payable on a debt, possibly including other payments as well, which are required by the terms of the borrowing.
default	Failure of the issuer to make payments of interest and principal and perhaps other required payments as well.
defeasance	The provision for payment of a bond issue from sources other than the issuer.
delivery date	The date that a new issue is delivered to the underwriter for payment.
denomination	The face amount of a bond, or the allowable face amounts for an issue.
depository	An organization that holds securities (municipal bonds, in this book), maintains ownership records on its books for its members, and distributes to its members all payments from securities held by it for its members.
derivative	A security or other instrument which has its value related to (derived from) the value of some other security or other instrument. The best known derivatives are call and put options on common stocks.
designated sales	A kind of institutional priority business. The buyer buys at the net price and designates account

designated sales (continued)

members, by name and amount, to receive the concession on the sale.

detachable call option

A call feature which may be detached and sold separately by the bond owner.

detached call

A call feature that has been separately sold by the issuer as a separate security.

discount

The amount below par paid for a bond.

discount accretion

Same as discount accrual.

discount accrual

The periodic increase in book value of a bond to par.

discount bid

A bid of less than par for a new issue or for an individual bond.

discount paper

A security that is sold at less than par, with the discount considered interest, accrued during the life of the bond, and paid when the security matures.

discount price

A price of less than par.

disintermediation

The direct purchase of securities by investors rather than the investment through financial intermediaries.

dollar price

The price of a bond as a percent of par rather than as a yield basis.

escrow fund

A fund held by a trustee which is invested and produces an income and principal stream to make interest and principal payments on bonds.

escrowed	Escrowed bonds have a separate fund (an escrow fund) managed by a trustee who makes interest and principal payments from the fund. The issuer no longer makes interest and principal payments.
escrowed to maturity	Bonds which will have interest and principal paid as originally stated, including mandatory sinking fund payments, until the final maturity, with the payments are made by a trustee from an escrow fund.
extraordinary call feature	A call feature which allows or requires the issuer to call the bonds in the case of an unexpected event.
face amount	The par amount or final maturity amount of the bond.
final confirmation	A confirmation, sent out for a trade of a new issue of bonds, which shows the final money amounts due.
final official statement	The official statement for a new bond issue which is sent out after the terms of the new issue have been decided. The final official statement shows the final terms of the issue and other information.
financial advisor	A firm who advises issuers in the issuance of their bonds.
flat	Trading without accrued interest added to the price of the bond.

floater   A security whose interest rate fluctuates with the general interest rate level and is periodically reset, either by auction or by a relationship with a published interest rate.

forward   An agreement to make a trade at a future date, at a price and terms decided now.

full takedown   The total reduction from list price for a bond purchased (taken down) from the syndicate by an account member.

future   An agreement to make a trade at a future date, at a price and terms decided now, on an organized exchange with a standard contract and standard trading terms.

going away sale   A sale to the final customer.

gross production—total   The total amount of money received from the sale of a new issue of bonds, excluding accrued interest, if the issue is entirely sold at the list or offering prices.

gross production—unit   The gross production as above, expressed as a percent of par.

group business—sales   Sales by the syndicate as a group.

group concession sale   Priority business in which the customer buys the bonds from the account at the net less the concession.

group net sale   Priority business in which the customer buys the bonds from the account at the net offering price.

group order	An order to the syndicate account.
handshake	An informal arrangement in a negotiated new issue in which the issuer tells the underwriter that he or she has bought the bonds under the conditions now arranged. A handshake has no legal standing whatever.
hedging	An arrangement of trades meant to minimize the possibility of loss in the market.
high-low coupon arrangement	An arrangement for a new issue in which the earlier maturities have a higher coupon than the later maturities.
illegals	Bonds which do not have a legal opinion attached to them.
indenture	A statement of the contract between the issuer of bonds and the buyers of the bonds. Not all bonds have indentures.
institution	In the municipal bond business, a type of customer for bonds, which includes banks, trust departments of banks and other investment advisors, insurance companies, municipal investment trusts, municipal mutual funds, most large businesses, and frequently other municipal bond dealers.
institutional salesman	A salesperson who sells to banks, insurance companies,

institutional salesman (continued)

investment companies, businesses, security dealers and other firms, not generally to individuals.

interest cost

The cost of borrowing, usually expressed as an annual percentage rate.

interest rate swap

A deal between two parties in which each pays the other an amount of interest based on a theoretical "notional" amount of principal. One of the interest payments varies with the market, and the other is fixed. Interest rate swaps can continue for years. The principal is for calculation only; no such amount has actually changed hands between the parties.

inverse floater

A security whose interest payments fluctuate in an opposite direction to market interest rates.

investment banker

A person who works to bring negotiated new issues to market, soliciting business from issuers of bonds, working with underwriters to design the issue to meet market requirements and to market the issue.

investment grade

Securities with one of the highest four ratings are said to be of investment grade.

joint manager

A participant in a syndicate who may simply bear the title of manager, or who may sometimes lead the syndicate and may participate in the actual management of the syndicate.

lead manager	The manager in charge of running a new issue syndicate.
legal opinion	An opinion by a lawyer, usually specially trained in municipal bond law, that a new issue of bonds has been legally issued, is exempt from federal income taxes (if it is so exempt), state income taxes (if it is so exempt), and usually other statements as well.
letter of credit	An agreement by a prospective lender, usually a bank, that it will make a loan, provided certain conditions have been complied with.
level coupon arrangement	A coupon arrangement for a new issue with coupons the same for all the bonds.
life annuity	An annuity payable only during one (or more) lives.
linked	Combining a floater and an inverse floater, under the terms of the original issue agreement, to form again the original bond which was split up to make the floater and inverse floater in the first place.
load	A commission charged in the sale of mutual fund or municipal investment trust shares.
mandatory sinking fund redemption	A required redemption of bonds, usually at par, in amounts fixed by the indenture or other terms of the original issue agreement, to pay off all or part of the loan before final maturity.

market discount	The amount below face at which bonds trade.
market value	The price bonds are trading for in the marketplace.
maturity date	The date when the original principal amount becomes due and payable.
member	A partner or participant in a new issue syndicate.
money market funds	An open end mutual fund which invests in short term, high quality securities.
municipal investment trust	*See* unit investment trust.
Municipal Securities Rulemaking Board (MSRB)	An agency, authorized by Congress, which proposes rules for conduct in the municipal bond business, and otherwise participates in the regulation of the municipal business. The rules it proposes must be approved by the Securities and Exchange Commission.
mutual fund	An investment company which invests in securities and distributes income to its stockholders. Open-end mutual funds constantly sell and redeem their own shares; closed-end funds do not constantly sell their own shares.
national recognized municipal security information repository (NRMSIR)	An organization which maintains information on municipal securities, and has received recognition of its status; in 1994, this information consisted mostly of official statements on municipal bond issues.

negotiated new issue

A method of underwriting new issues in which the issuer selects the firms he or she wishes to underwrite the issue and works with them to do the underwriting.

net designated sale

Institutional or priority business in which the customer pays the net price but designates members of the account, by name and amount, to receive the concession on the designated amount of the sale.

net interest cost (NIC)

A method of computing the cost of borrowing on a new issue and awarding the bonds on competitive new issue. The total amount of interest paid over the life of the issue, plus the discount or minus the premium paid for the issue, is divided by the accumulated bond years for the issue.

new issue scale

The reoffering yields or prices of a new issue of bonds.

note

A short term instrument, usually three years or less from issue date to maturity date.

note—U.S. Treasury

A United States Treasury coupon security, with maturities up to ten years from the date of issue.

official statement (OS)

The municipal bond version of a corporate prospectus. An official statement for a new issue provides information about both the bonds and the issuer of the bonds.

open end	An open-end mutual fund constantly buys and sells its own shares.
optional redemption	A redemption in which the issuer has the choice of whether or not to redeem the bonds.
order period	A time, usually one hour, after the time of sale during which all orders received have equal priority in execution.
original issue discount	The amount below par at which a new issue of bonds is originally offered to the public, provided it meets the Internal Revenue Service requirement for treatment as interest.
oversubscribed	A case in which the syndicate has received orders for more bonds than exist.
par amount	The face amount of the bond, at which it will be redeemed at maturity.
participation	The share of a syndicate member in a syndicate, usually expressed in bonds.
paying agent	The agency which pays interest and principal when due on a bond.
placement	Refers to the type of customer or even the particular customers who buy a new issue of bonds.
pre-refunded	Same as advance refunded, although considered by some as a less accurate term.

preliminary official statement (POS)	An official statement issued before the actual sale of the bonds, and which therefore cannot contain the final coupons and offering prices, and frequently other information as well. The POS corresponds to the red herring prospectus for corporate securities.
premium	The amount over par paid for a bond or at which a bond is selling.
premium amortization	The periodic reduction of a price (or reduction of premium paid) down to par.
premium bid	A bid price which is greater than the par amount.
premium price	A price greater than par.
present value	The worth at the present time of a future payment or payments.
price	The amount, expressed as a percent of par amount, at which bonds are offered, bid for, or traded.
pricing	The act of setting the reoffering prices for a new issue.
primary market	The marketplace in which new issues are brought to market and traded.
priority business	Business which receives priority in execution from the syndicate.
priority provisions	The provisions in the syndicate letter or agreement among underwriters which establish which types of transactions will receive priority in execution.

pure book entry	A book entry system, with no provision for issuance of certificates to the bondowner.
put away	The bonds have been sold to the final customer.
put option	An option giving the owner of the bond the right to sell it back to the issuer at an agreed upon price, usually par.
rating	An opinion of the relative investment merit of a bond.
rating agency	A business which provides ratings on bonds.
re-offering yield	The yield at which a new issue bond is offered to the public.
refunded bonds	Bonds which have been redeemed by a new issue of bonds.
refunding bonds	Bonds which have been issued for the purpose of redeeming another issue of bonds.
registered bond	A bond which has the owner's name and address printed on it.
regulation	Governmental control, using a process of laws, rules, guidelines, inspections, supervision, and audit to achieve a desired (by the government) goal. In the municipal bond business, regulation is done by the Municipal Securities Rulemaking Board, the Securities and Exchange Commission, and a variety of security and bank regulatory agencies.

reinsurance	An arrangement by which an insurance company buys insurance from another insurance company to cover a risk which it (the first company) has insured.
retail	In Wall Street terms, retail business is business with individual customers.
retail broker	A broker who generally does business with individual customers.
revenue anticipation notes	Notes issued in expectation of receiving some revenues in the relatively near future, which will be used to pay off the notes.
rolled over	A process in which new securities are sold to repay maturing securities. The maturing securities are said to be "rolled over."
scientific method	*See* yield basis method.
secondary market	The marketplace in which municipal bonds which are already outstanding are traded.
serial bonds	A series of bonds with individual maturities, usually an annual series, which make up all or part of a bond issue.
sinking fund	A series of payments, required by the original bond contract, which repays part or all of a bond issue before maturity.
spread	The hoped-for gross profit margin on a new issue of bonds, or a block traded in the secondary market.

state and local government series (SLGS)	United States Treasury securities which are sold to municipal bond issuers, with terms designed so the issuer will avoid violating Internal Revenue Service arbitrage regulations.
step rate coupon bond	A bond with a coupon rate which increases periodically, until final maturity.
straight line method	A method of amortizing premium or accruing discount which amortizes or accrues an equal amount of premium or discount each year until maturity.
STRIPS (Separately TRaded Interest and Principal Securities)	A zero coupon United States Treasury security created by splitting up a regular bond into its separate interest and principal payments, and selling these separately. The new securities are separate securities, and each has its own CUSIP number.
structure (of a deal)	The characteristics of a new issue, including the maturity schedule, choice of serial bonds or term bonds with a sinking fund, use of zero coupon bonds and derivatives, the choice of coupon rates on the issue, the choice of call features, and other features of the new issue.
structuring a deal	The act of creating the structure of a deal.
successive approximations	A mathematical procedure which computes the desired value by adjusting the previously comput-

successive approximations (continued)	ed value and recomputing the desired value, continuing until the value obtained is within previously set limits of accuracy. Occasionally but wrongly called "trial and error."
syndicate	A short term partnership formed to underwrite a new issue of bonds. The syndicate is terminated when the bonds are sold or distributed to account members.
syndicate letter	The agreement of the partners in the syndicate.
take down	A reduction from the net offering price for an account member to purchase bond from the syndicate.
tax and revenue anticipation notes (TRANs)	Notes issued in anticipation of both taxes and revenues, which will be used to repay the notes when received.
tax anticipation notes (TANs)	Notes issued in anticipation of the receipt of taxes, which will be used to repay the notes when received.
tax-exempt commercial paper (TXCP)	Commercial paper which is offered by a tax-exempt issuer, short term, usually under 270 days from issue date to final maturity date.
tax-exempt money market fund	A money market fund which invests in short term high-grade tax-exempt securities, so that interest income received by the shareholders is exempt from federal income tax.

term bonds	Bonds which have a single final maturity date for all or a large part of the issue, usually with a mandatory sinking fund.
timing	In new issues, the setting of the time of the offering to obtain the best sale price for the issuer's bonds.
trader	A person who makes bids for and offers of municipal bonds to the firm's customers and to other firms.
transfer agent	A firm or agency which maintains ownership records for a security and issues new certificates to the new owners upon receipt of properly endorsed old certificates.
true interest cost (TIC)	The nominal annual rate, compounded semiannually, which discounts the flow of funds of an issue to the bid price for the issue. Also called Canadian Interest Cost (CIC). This is also called the internal rate of return for the issue.
trustee	A person or firm who represents the bond owners and acts for them if necessary.
underwriter—bond	A person who bids for or buys new issues of bonds and sets the reoffering prices for these issues.
underwriter—insurance	A person who examines new or outstanding bonds for possible insurance, and determines whether or not the bonds should

underwriter—insurance (continued)	be offered insurance and the amount of premium if insurance is offered.
underwriting period	The period from the time the bonds are sold to the underwriter until the bonds are delivered.
unit investment trust	A trust set up to own municipal bonds and distribute the income and principal pro rata to the trust owners. Trust shares are usually transferable, but the trust does not manage or trade the bonds it owns, although it may sell them if the supervisor of the trust thinks it desirable.
unlimited ad valorem taxes	Taxes levied on real estate without limit as to rate or amount.
U.S. Savings bonds	A zero coupon bond offered by the United States Treasury in small amounts, with the right of the owner to redeem the bond at any time after six months from issue.
variable rate bond, variable rate demand obligation (VDRO)	A bond with an interest rate which fluctuates according to the market and which the owner can redeem at predetermined set intervals.
volatility	The change in price of a bond for a given change in yield basis, or, more generally, the changeability of bond prices over a relatively short period of time.

when issued confirmation	A confirmation indicating that a trade in a new issue and the terms of the trade, with delivery to take place when, as and if the bonds are actually issued.
when issued trades	Trades in a new issue of bonds done before the bonds are actually delivered by the issuer to the underwriter for payment.
wire house	A large brokerage firm with many offices, usually nationwide or even worldwide.
yield	The interest rate earned, nominal annual rate compounded semi-annually, on an investment.
yield basis	Same as yield.
yield basis method	A method of amortizing premium or accruing (or accreting) discount using a price calculated using the yield at which the bond was originally purchased.
zero coupon	A bond which does not have explicit interest paid periodically (no coupons) but which does have a maturity. The bond sells at a discount and the earnings occur when the bond matures at par or is sold at a gain.

Index

A

Account balances, 221
Account. *See* municipal syndicate
Accumulated bond years, 204
Additional takedown, 205, 213
Administrative Rules, 149
Advance refunded, 45
   and bond swapping, 175
Agreement among underwriters, 199, 201
Allegheny County Industrial Development
   Authority bond, 4, 13-19, 135, 136
Allocations, 222
Allotments, 221
Alternative minimum tax, 217
Annuity certain, 100
   equation for, 101
Ascending coupon arrangement, 204
Ascending coupon limitation, 217
Aurora, CO, report of new issue sale on, 208
Average takedown, 214
Award of bonds, 200, 202

B

Bank-qualified bonds, 217
Bearer bond, 28-9
Bid form, 216
Bid, 205
Bidding restrictions, 215-217
Bloomberg Financial Markets, 178
Blue List, The, 171
Bond basis book, using, 126
Bond Buyer, 179
Bond Buyer, The, 183, 199, 208
Bond characteristics, change in, reason for
   swap 175
Bond contract, 1-4
   terms, 3
Bond dealer, acting as agent, 171
Bond insurance, 162-70, 192
   benefits, 163
   companies, 146, 168-9
   contract, 162
   improves bond salability, 165
   municipal investment trust, 167
   mutual fund, 167
   new issue, 167, 169

   payment if bonds are accelerated, 163
   place in market, 166
   portfolio insurance, 163
   providing homogeneity, 165
   rating of, 165
   regulation, 166
   reinsurance, 168
   salvage, 163
   secondary market, 167
Bond swaps, 145
   reasons for, 173
   with new issue, 219
Bond year, 204
Bond, life of, 2
Bond, is a loan, not ownership, 2
Bond, physical form, 27-32
Bonds with shorter term to maturity, as a
   response to bond market changes, 57
Bonds, purposes of, 134
Book entry form, 28, 31-32
   and volume increase 61
Book entry only, 31, 32
Bracket, 200
Brevard County, FL, COP vote, 65
Broker, 142
Brokers, municipal bond, 143
Buyer, 2

C

California Housing Finance Agency note, 4,
   19-25
Call feature, 34, 35-43
   bearer bonds, zero coupon, problem, 42
   escrowed bonds, question of whether
      defeased bonds can be called, 47
   extraordinary call, 35, 38-39
   extraordinary call, California Housing
      Finance Agency, 39
   extraordinary calls, concern, 42
   extraordinary calls, mortgage revenue
      bonds, 42
   long term revenue bonds, 42
   mandatory sinking fund, 35, 36-38
   official statement, 40
   optional redemption, 35
Call lottery, 40

Call notice, bearer bonds, 39
  book entry bonds, 40
  management, 40
  notice problem, 40
  registered bonds, 39
Call premium, 35
Canadian interest cost, 205, 206
Capital appreciation bonds, 211. *See also*
  Zero coupon bonds
Capital project, reason for financing, 195
Certificate form, 28
Certificate of participation (COP), 65-66
Certificated book entry, 31
Chemical Bank, as trustee, 3
Chicago Board of Trade, 179, 182, 183, 184
CIC. *See* Canadian interest cost
Closing date, 227
Closing, 202, 229
Committee for Uniform Securities Identifica-
  tion Procedure. *See* CUSIP number
Competitive bid, 197, 198-200
Competitive new issue, relative decrease in,
  189
Competitive sales, reports of, 208-211
Competitive, negotiated comparison, 198
Compound interest and annuity tables, use
  of, 101-115
Compound interest, 94-98
  equation for, 97
  need to state both rate and time period,
  94
Concession designated sale, 219
Concession, 200, 205, 211, 213
Contra party, 73
COP. *See* Certificate of participation
Coupon limitations, 216
Coupon payments, 2
Coupon, 2, 200
Covering the short, 184
CUSIP number, 77
  composition of, 77
  MSRB Rule G-34, 78
  Allegheny County Industrial Development
    Authority, example of, 78
CUSIP Service Bureau, 77

D

Dated date, 203
  same as delivery date for zero coupon
    bonds, 203
Dealer bank, 142

Dealer transactions, for most municipal
  bond transactions, 143
Dealer, 142
Default, 35, 47-48
  definitions of, 47
Defeasance, 34, 44
  reasons for, 45
Defeased bonds, call features, how handled,
  45
Definitional Rules, 149
Delinking floaters and inverse floaters, 71
Delivery date, 203, 229
  zero coupon bonds, 203
Delivery, 202
Depository Trust Company, 32
Depository, 31
Derivatives, municipal, 68-73
Detached call option, 72
  arbitrage restrictions, 72
Discount accretion. *See* discount accrual
Discount accrual, 118-120
  tax consequences, 123
Discount bid, 205
Discount paper, 83
Discount price, 116
Disintermediation, 58
  as a response to bond market changes 58
Duff & Phelps, 152, 157, 179

E

Educational financing authorities, 136
Escrow fund, 44
Escrowed, 46
  to maturity, 37, 46
Expenses, syndicate, 214, 215

F

Final confirmation, 227
Final money amounts, 227, 229
Final official statement, 223, 228
Financial advisor, 145, 196, 216
  investment bankers prefer not to act as, 145
  MSRB Rule G-23, 197
  and underwriting, 197
Financial Publishing Company, 127, 179
Fitch Investors Service, 152, 157, 180
Floaters, 69
  leveraged, 70
  rate determination, 69
Forward contract, 182
Free to trade, 220

Full takedown, 214
Future contract, 182

G

General obligation bonds, 134
    analysis of, 151
    relative decrease in, 189
General Rules, 149
Glossary of Municipal Securities Terms, 150
GO and revenue bonds, relative merits of 138
Going away sales, 222
Graham, Benjamin, 44, 79
Gross production, 204
Group concession sale, 218
Group net sale, 218

H

Handshake, 202
Health care authorities, 136
High-low coupon arrangement, 204
High-low coupon limitation, 217
Hospital authorities, 136
Houston, Texas, 134

I

Illegals, 226
Immobilized book entry, 31
Indenture, 3
    revision, reason for financing, 195
Industrial development authority, 135
Institutional sales, as part of bond depart-
    ment, 148
Insured money market funds, 60
Insured paper, 165
Interest rate swaps, 72
Interest rates, recent changes in, 49
    results of, 50
Interest, 2
Intermediaries, financial, 58
Internal rate of return, 206
Internal Revenue Service, and municipal
    mutual fund tax-exemption, 158
Inverse floaters, 69
    evaluation of, 71
    rate determination, 69
    volatility of, 71
Investment bankers, 144
Investment banking, as part of bond depart-
    ment, 147
Investor requirements, change in, reason for
    swap, 174

Investors, education of, 51-52
Issuer, 2
Issuers:
    authorities and governmental agencies,
        135
    governments, 134

J

J. J. Kenny Co., Inc., 180
Joint manager, 199, 201

K

Kansas Turnpike, escrowed bonds, call of, 47
Kentucky Turnpike, escrowed bonds, 46

L

Lead manager, 199, 201
Legal opinion, 224
Level coupon arrangement, 204
Leveraged floaters, volatility of, 71
Liaison personnel. *See* marketing personnel
Linking floaters and inverse floaters, 71

M

Management fee, 145, 214
Mandatory sinking fund, 201, 203
Market discount, 77
Markete stabilization activities, 220
Marketing personnel, 146
Marketing, as part of bond department, 147,
    148
Massachusetts Health and Educational
    Facilities Authority (Mass HEFA), 137
Material information, 228
Maturity date, 2
Maturity schedule, 199
Memphis-Shelby County Airport, 137
MOB spread. *See* Municipals over Bonds
    spread
Money market funds, 60
Moody's Investors Service, 152, 157, 180
MSRB. *See* Municipal Securities Rulemaking
    Board
MSRB Manual, 150
MSRB Reports, 150
Municipal Bond Index, 182, 183
Municipal bond industry trends, 186-91
    bond buyer changes, 188
    bond insurance, 191
    issuer changes, 186

Municipal bond industry trends, (*continued*)
   municipal bond complexity, increase in, 190
   municipal investment trusts, 192
   municipal mutual funds, 192
   municipal regulation, 191
   municipal regulation changes, 188
   Municipal Securities Rulemaking Board,
      reason for formation, 189
   New York City, default on notes, led to
      regulation, 188
   Securities Exchange Act of 1934 and
      municipal bond regulation, 189
Municipal bond price, calculation of, 115-7
   calculation of, MSRB Rule G-33, 123
   equation for, 124
   examples, 116
Municipal bond prices and yields, general
   rules for, 125-6
Municipal bonds, holdings of, 52
Municipal future, 182
Municipal future, puts and calls, trading, 184
Municipal investment trust, 139, 157-162
   comparison with municipal mutual
      funds, 161
   redemption of, 160
Municipal mutual funds, 139, 157-62
Municipal mutual funds, closed end, 139
Municipal mutual funds, open end, 139
Municipal Securities Rulemaking Board
   (MSRB), 149, 181
Municipal syndicate, 144, 199
Municipals over Bonds spread, 184
Munifacts, 171
Mutual funds:
   money market, 59
   tax free money market, 59

N

National Association of Securities Dealers
   (NASD), 149
Nationally Recognized Municipal Sec-urities
   Information Repositories, 178
Need for funds, reasons for financing, 194
Negotiated new issue, relative increase in, 189
Negotiated sale, reports of, 211
Negotiated underwriting, 197, 201-202
   comparison with competitive bid, 198
Net designated sale, 218
Net interest cost, 204, 205
   calculation of, 206
Net offering, 213

New Housing Authority (NHA) bonds, 137
New issue legal work, 224
New issue underwriting, as a source of deal-
   er offerings, 171
New issue volume, increase of, 55
New issue, closing and settlement, 226-7
New issue, investor purchase of, 194
New issue, reasons for, 194
New York City, financing current expenses
   a reason for default, 195
New York State bond, 2, 4-13, 134, 216, 224
New York State Dormitory Authority, 136
New York State, 199
New York Times, The, 199
NIC. *See* net interest cost
Nine Mile Halfway Drainage District, MI, 225
North Carolina Municipal Power Agency No.
   1, 195, 211-212
Notes, 64-65
   bond anticipation notes (BANs), 64
   revenue anticipation notes (RANs), 64
   tax and revenue anticipation notes
      (TRANs), 64
   tax anticipation notes (TANs), 64
Notional amount, 73
NRMSRS. *See* Nationally Recognized
   Municipal Securities Information
   Repositories

O

Official statement, 3, 138, 223
Order period, 200, 205
Organization, municipal bond department,
   147-48
Original issue discount, 76
   accrual of, 76
Oversubscribed, 221

P

Participation, 200, 220
Paying agent, 28
Paying current expenses, reason for financ-
   ing, 195
Placement, 201, 202
Port Authority of New York and New
   Jersey, 4, 134, 135, 199
Portfolio improvement, reason to swap, 177
Pre-refunded, 45
Preliminary official statement, 223, 228
Premium amortization, 120-23
   tax consequences, 123

Premium bid, 205
Premium price, 117
Present value, 98-100
    equation for, 99
Pricing, 201
Primary account, 220
Primary market, 144
Principal, 2
Priority business, 218
PSA. *See* Public Securities Association
Public Housing Authority (PHA) bonds, 137
Public Securities Association, 181
Purchases, banks, 141
Purchases, individual, 139
Purchases, property and casualty insurance
    companies, 141
Pure book entry,. *See* Book entry only
Put away (bonds), 222
Put bonds, as a response to bond market
    changes, 56
Put option, 34, 43-44
    as a valuable feature, 43
    United States Savings Bonds, 43

R

Rating agencies, 146, 152
Ratings:
    bond, 152-57
    chart, 153
    conditional, 156
    importance of, 156
    investment grade, 153
    not rated (NR), 156
    split ratings, 156
Records, retention of, 221
Rules G-8, G-9, 221
Refinance, reason for financing, 195
Refundings volume, increase of, 55
Registered form, 28, 29-31
Registered form, and volume increase, 61
Regulation:
    bank, 149
    bond insurance, 166
    dealer bank, 142
    distribution of official statements (Rule
        G-32), 223
    municipal bond, 149-50
    municipal securities not exempt from
        anti-fraud provisions of 1934 Act, 149
    sales during underwriting period (Rule
        G-11), 223

trends and concerns, 189
    underwriting assessment (Rule A-13), 222
    new issue process, 222
Reoffering price, 200
Reoffering yield, 200
Repricing a deal, 202
Research analysts, municipal, 146
Research, as part of bond department, 147, 148
Research, municipal, how done, 151-52
Reserves, adequacy of, 152
Responses to changes, contractual, 55
Retail broker, 146, 192
    methods of compensation for bond
        sales, 146
Retail business:
    how done, 170
    sources of offerings, 171
Retail buyers, 139
Retail offering price, 213
Revenue bond, 4, 134
    coverage of, 151
    debt service coverage, 151
    analysis of, 151
    relative increase in, 189
Risk, due to other factors, 54
Risk, increased bond risk due to increased
    volatility, 52-54
Rolled over, notes, 64

S

Sales representative, institutional, 145
Sales representatives, not allowed to bid for
    bonds, 144
Scale, new issue bidding, 202-205
Sealed Bids Invited Section, 199
SEC. *See* Securities and Exchange
    Commission
Secondary market purchases, as a source of
    dealer offerings, 171
Secondary market, 144, 220
Securities and Exchange Commission (SEC),
    149, 166
Securities Exchange Act of 1934 30
Security, as a guaranty for a COP, 65
Serial bonds, 203
Short sales, in when-issued trades, 185
    Internal Revenue Service concern with, 185
    municipal bonds, 184-6
Sinker. *See* Sinking fund
Sinking fund, 3, 36, 37
    Kentucky Turnpike, 37

Sinking fund, (*continued*)
    Port Authority of New York and New
        Jersey, 37
SLGS. *See* State and Local Government Series
South Carolina, State of, lawsuit, 28
Spread, 200, 201, 202
    new issue, 213-215
Standard & Poor's Corporation, 152, 157, 181
State and Local Government Series, 91-92
Structuring a deal, 201
Successive approximations, 207
Syndicate letter. *See* agreement among
    underwriters
Syndicate restrictions, 220
Syndicate. *See* Municipal syndicate

T

Takedown price, 220
Target funds, 60, 160
Tax swapping. *See* tax-loss swaps
Tax-exempt commercial paper (TXCP), 66
    as substitute for notes, 66
Tax-exemption, 29, 73-75
    alternative minimum tax (AMT), 74
    bonds with Commonwealth status, 74
    exemption from state income taxes, 74
    not protected by United States
        Constitution, 74
    not exempt from taxes other than
        income taxes, 75
Tax-loss swaps, 173
Term bonds, 203
TIC. *See* true interest cost
Time to maturity, change in, reason to swap,
    176
Timing, 201
Traders, 143
Trading, as part of bond department, 147
Transfer agent, 29, 30
Transfer regulation, SEC, 72-hour rule, 30
Transfers, 29
Treasury Direct, to purchase US Treasury
    securities, 61, 86, 87, 89
True interest cost, 205, 206
    calculation of, 207
    example, 207
Trust accounts, for individuals, 139
Trustee 3, 28, 30

U

Underwriters, bond, 144

Underwriting compensation, 214
Underwriting period, 222
Underwriting, as part of bond department, 147
Unit investment trusts. *See* municipal invest-
    ment trusts
United States public debt, 82
    marketable debt, 82
United States Savings Bonds, 90-91
    as zero coupon bonds, 2
    put feature, 56
United States Treasury bills, 82-86
    auction sales of, 85
    price calculation of, 84
    quotations of, 84, 85
United States Treasury bond future, 183
United States Treasury bonds, 88-89
    quotations for, 88
United States Treasury notes, 86-87
    quotations for, 87
United States Treasury securities:
    active markets, 80
    importance of, reasons, 79-81
    other securities trade off, 80-81
    used in hedging, 81
    widely held, 80
    yield levels, municipal yields compared
        to, 81
United States Treasury STRIPS, 89-90
Unlimited *ad valorem* taxes, 4, 134

V

Variable rate bonds (VRDO), 34, 44, 66-68
    as a response to bond market changes, 56
    contractual pattern of, 67
Variable Rate Demand Obligation (VRDO),.
    See Variable-rate bond
Volatility, recent increase in, 50-51
Volume, trading, 60

W

Wall Street Journal, 51, 81
Washington Public Power Supply System, 3,
    196, 225
    insured by AMBAC, 163
    ratings of, 157
When-issued confirmation, 227
Wire house, 147

Z

Zero coupon bonds, 2